# Tarot
## *for the*
# Magically
# Inclined

© Jen Davis

## About the Author

Jack Chanek is the author of several books on tarot and witchcraft. He is a High Priest of Gardnerian Wicca and has been reading tarot since he was eleven years old. Jack's work has appeared in *The Witches' Almanac*, *Studio Magicae*, and *Aries Witch*. His numerous television and podcast appearances include *Seeking Witchcraft*, *Oculus Alchemy*, and *The Witching Hour with Patti Negri*. He has taught workshops on tarot, Wicca, and Qabalah around the country. Jack holds a PhD in the history of philosophy and lives in Salt Lake City, Utah. Visit him at JackOf WandsTarot.wordpress.com.

# Tarot

*for the*

# Magically Inclined

Spells and Spirits to Stack
the Deck in Your Favor

## *Jack* CHANEK

LLEWELLYN
WOODBURY, MINNESOTA

FIRST EDITION
First Printing, 2025

Book design by Samantha Peterson
Cover design by Kevin R. Brown
Interior illustrations by Llewellyn Art Department
Tarot Original 1909 Deck © 2021 with art created by Pamela Colman Smith and Arthur Edward Waite. Used with permission of LoScarabeo.
Birth chart on page 84 was created using the Kepler Superb Astrology Program, with kind permission from Cosmic Patterns Software, Inc., the manufacturer of the Kepler program (www.astrosoftware.com, kepler@astrosoftware.com).

Llewellyn Publications is a registered trademark of Llewellyn Worldwide Ltd.

**Library of Congress Cataloging-in-Publication Data (Pending)**
ISBN: 978-0-7387-7801-3

Llewellyn Worldwide Ltd. does not participate in, endorse, or have any authority or responsibility concerning private business transactions between our authors and the public.

All mail addressed to the author is forwarded, but the publisher cannot, unless specifically instructed by the author, give out an address or phone number.

Any internet references contained in this work are current at publication time, but the publisher cannot guarantee that a specific location will continue to be maintained. Please refer to the publisher's website for links to authors' websites and other sources.

Llewellyn Publications
A Division of Llewellyn Worldwide Ltd.
2143 Wooddale Drive
Woodbury, MN 55125-2989
www.llewellyn.com

Printed in the United States of America

**Other Books by Jack Chanek**

*Qabalah for Wiccans*
*Queen of All Witcheries*
*Tarot for Real Life*

**Featured In**

*Aries Witch*

For Deborah,
the Hierophant to my Emperor.

# Contents

# List of Spreads

# Disclaimer

While best efforts have been used in preparing this book, neither the author nor the publisher shall be held liable or responsible to any person or entity with respect to any loss or damages caused, or alleged to have been caused, directly or indirectly, by the information contained herein. Every situation is different, and the advice and strategies contained in this book may not be suitable for you.

In the following pages you will find recommendations for the use of certain plants and incenses. Each body reacts differently to plants, scents, and other items, so results may vary person to person. If you are allergic to any of the plants or scents suggested in this book, please refrain from use.

Please note that the information in this book is not meant to diagnose, treat, prescribe, or substitute consultation with a licensed healthcare professional. This book is not intended to provide medical advice or to take the place of medical advice and treatment from your personal physician. Readers are advised to consult their doctors or other qualified healthcare professionals regarding the treatment of their medical problems. Neither the publisher nor the author take any responsibility for possible consequences of any person reading or following the information in this book.

# *introduction*
# The Hand That
# Turns the Wheel

I want you to think of a tarot card. Any card will do. When you hear the word *tarot*, what is the first image that comes to your mind?

Most people, when asked to think of a tarot card at random, will pick either Death or the Lovers. These are the two most famous cards in the deck; they have worked so deeply into the popular imagination that their imagery can be found on album covers and tattoos, even hanging in art galleries. If a character in a movie or TV show gets a tarot reading, you can bet good money that they'll turn up either or both of these cards. In the popular mind, they represent the things that all of us want to know about: sex and death, the mysteries of life, the unknowns that drive us to seek out tarot readings in the first place.

But when I think of tarot, I picture a different card altogether. The card that represents tarot to me is the Wheel of Fortune.

In tarot, the Wheel of Fortune represents the fickle and ever-changing nature of life. The Wheel turns, and as it turns it changes the lives of ordinary people, raising some up to new heights and bringing others crashing down. This is a card of pure, blind luck. It's unpredictable and uncontrollable. It may bring us the best days of our lives or the worst, but we simply do not know how the Wheel will affect us.

The Wheel of Fortune represents uncertainty about the future and all of the anxieties that come with it. Navigating life can be terrifying when we don't know what's coming our way. For many of us, that exact uncertainty is why we turn to tarot. We have questions, doubts, and anxieties; we seek out tarot readings to help provide us with answers, certainty, and security. Tarot is appealing because it shows us the turnings of the Wheel of Fortune, giving us a glimpse of what's coming our way so that we can prepare ourselves for fate's caprices. Fortune is mysterious, inscrutable, and terrifying, but tarot allows us to reclaim agency and control.

Tarot is an interpretive art rather than a predictive science, and tarot readers aren't omniscient. We get things wrong sometimes, and we can't pull the winning lottery numbers out of a deck of cards. Nonetheless, tarot gives us insight that we wouldn't otherwise have. It allows us to build a narrative through which to make sense of ourselves and the world around us, to see the major themes in our lives, and to forecast where we're going based on where we are now. It's a wonderful tool to understand the turning of the Wheel.

But what if we could use it to do more than just understand? What if we could use it to turn the Wheel of Fortune in our favor?

Tarot is commonly used for prediction or introspection; readers use it to receive and interpret information about the world in a way that's fundamentally passive. But that's not its only use. It's been a tool of divination since at least the eighteenth century, and in that time it has also been used for much more. Readers have associated the seventy-eight cards of a tarot deck with a magical worldview, connecting them to the four elements, the planets and the signs of the Zodiac, and the process of initiation and alchemical transformation. All of this has turned tarot into a magical tool in its own right, one that can be used for meditation, personal growth, and directing future events.

Where divination is passive, magic is active. Magic is about exerting an influence on ourselves or on the world. Around the globe, practitioners from various traditions use magical techniques to attract lovers, improve their finances, process traumas, and much more. People use magic not just to observe the Wheel of Fortune's turning, but to *change* it.

Even among tarot readers who don't practice magic, you'll find a common refrain: Tarot offers a glimpse of what the future may be, but that future is not immutable. Tarot reading doesn't consign you to an inevitable fate; rather, it shows you what's coming your way and equips you to change course if you need to. With tarot, the line between seeing fate and changing fate has always been blurred.

This book is about the intersection of tarot and magic—how magic can inform a tarot reading, and how tarot can be used for magical purposes. I'll start with a brief introduction to tarot, covering the structure of a deck and the basics of how to perform a reading. Then, I'll provide a similar introduction to the basics of magic, walking through what magic is, what it can and can't accomplish, and the fundamentals of how to use it. Together, these chapters will provide you with all the basic knowledge you need in order to use the rest of the book.

The remainder of part I of the book will explore magical perspectives on the tarot deck to show how it fits into a larger magical worldview. Over history, lots of different esoteric correspondences have been overlaid onto the structure of the deck, incorporating tarot into a variety of magical systems. I'll walk you through some of the most important and widespread correspondences, blending tarot with the four elements, the signs of the Zodiac, the seven classical planets of astrology, and the Qabalistic Tree of Life.

Magical correspondences in tarot are somewhat flexible, and you'll find variation in how different practitioners map these occult concepts to their tarot decks. For my purposes here, though, I'll focus primarily on the correspondences used by a nineteenth-century secret society called the Hermetic Order of the Golden Dawn. The Golden Dawn was an incredibly influential organization, running from 1887 to 1903 and leaving an indelible mark on modern magic and modern tarot. Today, many magical groups still practice using the Order's original rituals and organizational structure. The members of the Golden Dawn tried to connect all of Western occultism in a single unified system of magic—and tarot was one of the key tools they used to produce the symbols and structures of that system. To this day, the divinatory meanings you'll find listed in most tarot books derive from the magical system of the Golden Dawn, as does classic tarot imagery familiar from decks like the iconic Rider-Waite-Smith tarot. In learning how to view tarot through a magical lens, the Golden Dawn is an excellent place to start.

That does not mean, however, that all of the magic taught in this book will be rehashing the rituals of the Golden Dawn. Quite the contrary, in fact. The Golden Dawn's magical correspondences are a fantastic point of entry to viewing tarot in a magical way—but once you've adopted that magical worldview, the ways you can use tarot in magic are innumerable. In part II of the book, things will get experimental. Taking the foundational knowledge you gained in part I, I'll share how to incorporate tarot as a magical tool in your rituals and spells, and I'll do so without adhering to any one system of magic.

Occultism is a big, wide world, and there are lots of different ways to do magic. Some people use magic only for meditation, introspection, and the development of their higher selves. Others use it for concrete, practical results like attracting a lover or finding a job. Some prefer elaborate ceremony with specific robes and tools crafted for each occasion; others lean toward simplicity. In this book, I'll walk through a little bit of everything so that no matter what your approach to magic is, you can learn how to bring tarot into it.

The magical techniques I share here are my own, based on my personal practice. They're the result of experiments I've performed and innovations I've made over my years as a reader and magician. This is important to keep in mind as you work your way through the book: The magic I share in part II is what has worked for me, but I'm only one person. Your magical practice won't look exactly the same as mine, and as you read this book and try the techniques I offer, you may find yourself wanting to adjust them, expand on them, or try something altogether new. That's a good thing!

This book is not meant to be the be-all and end-all of tarot and magic; it is, rather, the reflection of one practitioner's experience, which you can take as a jumping-off point for your own magic. If you try the approaches given here and like them, please use them freely, but don't feel constrained to do everything exactly as I say. Magic is always at its best when it's living and dynamic. Don't be afraid to experiment, to get your hands dirty, and to try new things even if they're not mentioned in the text. In doing so, you'll discover far more about the magic of tarot than any book could ever teach you.

Before you dive into reading the book, there is one logistical matter that needs to be taken care of: You're going to need a tarot deck. For a book about tarot reading and tarot magic, having a deck on hand is essential. In fact, I'd recommend having two decks if you can. You'll want one deck to use for your readings, but some of the exercises and magical techniques in this book involve using the cards themselves as magical tools, talismans, or ingredients in spellcasting. This means removing cards from the deck and potentially altering them in ways that make them unusable for ordinary reading. So, if you want to have an intact deck to use for divination, it's a good idea to keep a spare on hand for magical use.

If you don't want or can't afford a second deck, that's not a problem; if a spell or ritual calls for the use of a particular card, you can always print out an image of the card on ordinary paper and use that instead. If you're artistically inclined, you can draw or paint the image of a card and use that for magical purposes, rather than relying on a deck with someone else's artwork. Really, as long as you have access to tarot imagery in a way that lets you use it for both reading and magic, you're good to go.

I've been reading tarot since I was a child, and it's through tarot that I first began to practice magic. My earliest experiments with spellcasting involved using the symbolic language of tarot to express the changes I wanted to see in the world around me, and many of the techniques you'll find in this book are ones I've been using my entire adult life. The language of tarot is one of symbolism, imagery, dreams, and imagination—the same as the language of magic. As such, tarot is already deeply magical. The powers of magic gain expression when we give them voice through reading tarot, and the archetypal images of tarot are made real when we draw them into the world through magic. Tarot and magic have always been connected; this book will teach you to notice that connection and apply it.

Let's start turning the Wheel of Fortune together.

*part one*
# A Magical Worldview

# chapter one
# A Quick and Dirty Guide to Tarot Reading

This book is, first and foremost, about tarot, so it's important to start with tarot fundamentals. What is a tarot deck? How does a reading work? Can just anyone read tarot?

Depending on your level of experience, you may already know the answers to these questions. If you're a seasoned tarot reader, you may have picked up this book looking specifically for information about the connection between tarot and magic. If that's the case and you don't want a refresher on tarot fundamentals, you're more than welcome to skip ahead to chapter 2, where I start talking about magic. If you're new to tarot, however, or if you want to make sure that my perspective on tarot is not totally alien to your own, this chapter will cover all the basics and make sure we're on the same page.

Part of tarot reading is personal and intuitive, and it varies from one person to the next; that's the kind of thing you can't learn from a book but have to explore through trial and error. Conversely, part of tarot is about having a shared symbolic language through which we can interpret the world around us. Tarot has a structure and an internal logic that help to guide us as readers; if you put the same cards in front of two different readers, they'll have their own interpretive takes, but they'll nonetheless pull similar themes to the fore of their readings. I could tell any tarot reader in the world "I did a career reading for someone and drew the Eight of Swords and the Four of Pentacles," and they would have a sense that my client was feeling trapped in their career but unwilling to forego financial security. This shared language allows readers to situate themselves in an established framework, to communicate with each other, and to learn from each other. These commonalities—the core that makes tarot what it is—are the subject of this chapter.

## How to Perform a Reading

You can read tarot for yourself or for someone else; either way, the process is fundamentally the same. First, the person receiving the reading (called the *querent*) asks a question. Then, the reader randomly draws a number of cards, identifies those cards' themes, and fits them to the question that's been asked. If you ask a question about your new lover and draw cards that are associated with deceit and betrayal, that gives you a very different answer than if you ask the same question and pull cards associated with nurturing and empathy.

The challenging part is knowing how to identify the themes in the cards. Some of this is a matter of consensus, and there is broad agreement among tarot readers about the principal meanings of the cards, although each individual reader will have their own spin on those meanings; the appendix to this book includes a set of basic keywords for all of the cards in the deck. Nevertheless, even if you have a list of keywords on hand, there's still an intuitive element to tarot reading. You have to figure out how to bridge the gap between the abstract meaning of the cards and the particular details of the question you've asked. Ultimately, the only way to learn how to do that is by practice.

If you've never done a tarot reading before, it can be a scary prospect to dive in and start reading the cards, but that's the best way to learn. With that in mind, let's do a reading together right now. Get your tarot deck, think of a question you'd like the answer to, and shuffle the cards. Then, pull one card at random from the deck. This card is the answer to your question.

Don't look up the "official" meaning of this card just yet. Before you look at what anyone else has to say about the card, take a moment to examine the card closely. What is happening in the image? Are there any people or animals on it? If so, what are they doing? What other details stick out to you? Think about the overall impression that this card gives you. If you had to describe the card with just one word, what word would you use?

This is a lot of information to sift through, but if you can parse all of it, you've found the answer to your question. For example, a peaceful, idyllic scene of children playing in a courtyard may speak to you about nostalgia, innocence, and youth; a tempestuous image of a lightning-blasted tower may make you think of turmoil and catastrophe. From the visual language of the card, you can extract a thematic core. Then, all that remains is for you to apply that thematic core to your situation.

Sometimes, this is easier said than done. If you ask "Where should I go on vacation?" and you draw a card that makes you think of youth, you may be left scratching your head. Surely the reading isn't suggesting you should spend a week's vacation working in a kindergarten. But maybe the card is an invitation for you to explore places from your own childhood, favorite summer vacation spots that you haven't revisited in a long time. Likewise, if you ask "What should I cook for dinner?" and pull a card that looks like catastrophe, the answer to your question probably isn't "You should cook something terrible." Instead, it might be an indication that cooking isn't a good idea tonight; maybe you should consider eating out instead.

After you've spent some time examining a card and figuring out what you think it means and how it relates to your question, go ahead and flip to the appendix at the back of this book to see what I've said about the card. Think of this not as checking whether your reading was right or wrong, but as adding an extra layer of information. You may have seen something in the card that I don't see, and that's okay! The card meanings given in this book aren't automatically better or more authoritative than the ones you find for yourself, but they can serve as an invitation for you to consider your readings from another perspective, potentially shedding some light on things you wouldn't otherwise have noticed. Learning how to match cards to your questions takes time. It's not easy at first, but the more you practice it, the better you'll get.

Sometimes, you want a more complex and nuanced answer to a question—the kind of answer that you can't get out of just one card. Once you feel comfortable with one-card readings, try pulling two or three cards at a time. Do the same basic process of examining a card and asking yourself what's happening in its visual landscape, but now look at multiple cards together. What themes does each card appear to represent on its own? When those themes are brought together, what story do they tell and what is the overall takeaway from them?

The meaning of a card can be significantly influenced by the cards that surround it. Let's suppose you draw a card that shows several people locked in some kind of tussle. If you place this card alongside the catastrophic image of a collapsing tower, it would make sense to think of the tussle as something awful and harmful. But if you place the same card next to an idyllic image of childhood innocence, all of a sudden it's transformed into the kind of play fighting that siblings do, without the dangerous or aggressive undertones it previously had.

Reading cards in combination can be a difficult and frustrating process at first. That's normal, the same way that learning any other new skill is hard. Don't be discouraged if reading tarot doesn't come easily to you right away. Just like riding a bike or playing the piano, it's something that anyone can learn how to do, but it takes a lot of practice, and you will struggle with it when you first start out. Stick with it, practice as much as possible, and—if you're so inclined—take notes of your readings so that you can revisit them later on and see how much you've learned.

## The Structure of a Deck

A tarot deck is typically composed of seventy-eight cards, although some decks might have an extra card or two added into the mix. Each of these seventy-eight cards has a particular set of themes or ideas that are associated with it. These themes aren't haphazardly assigned; they are, rather, the product of the deck's internal structure. The seventy-eight cards of a tarot deck are divided into a number of smaller groups, each of which is associated with a particular range of themes. Looking at these smaller groups and the ways in which they overlap, we can begin to get a sense of individual card meanings and how they fit into a larger whole.

## *Major and Minor Arcana*

The first division of the deck is between the so-called *Major Arcana* (Latin for "greater mysteries") and the *Minor Arcana* ("lesser mysteries"). The Major Arcana are a set of twenty-two trump cards that are more or less separate from the rest of the deck. These are the cards most people picture when they think of tarot: the ones with titles like Death or the Lovers. As befits their name, the Major Arcana represent the big, universal themes of human life, the moments of significant transformation that we all go through. Their themes capture things like fate, initiation, suffering, renewal, and completion. By contrast, the Minor Arcana represent smaller, more everyday themes—not an archetype like fate, but something quotidian like jealousy, friendship, or hard work.

Each of the Major Arcana is assigned a number in sequence from zero to twenty-one. Individual decks might have some variation in the names of these cards and the order in which they're given, depending on the preferences of the deck creator. That said, there's a fairly standard order you'll find in most commercially available tarot decks:[1]

0. The Fool

I. The Magician

II. The High Priestess

III. The Empress

IV. The Emperor

V. The Hierophant

VI. The Lovers

VII. The Chariot

VIII. Strength

IX. The Hermit

X. Wheel of Fortune

XI. Justice

XII. The Hanged Man

XIII. Death

---

1. One of the most common variations is for cards 8 and 11—Strength and Justice—to be swapped so that Justice is number 8 in the sequence and Strength is number 11.

XIV. Temperance

XV. The Devil

XVI. The Tower

XVII. The Star

XVIII. The Moon

XIX. The Sun

XX. Judgement

XXI. The World

Both the Major and Minor Arcana represent important themes in human life, and they'll both show up in tarot reading, but these themes are on different scales. The Minor Arcana reflect the situations we encounter in our day-to-day lives, whereas the Major Arcana are bigger and more dramatic. They mark the places where the road forks before us and our lives are permanently changed.

### The Four Suits

Setting aside the twenty-two Major Arcana, there are fifty-six Minor Arcana remaining in the deck. These are divided into four suits of fourteen cards each. As with the Major Arcana, you'll find a little bit of variation in how these suits are named from one deck to another, but the most common names for the suits are *Pentacles*, *Swords*, *Cups*, and *Wands*. Each of these suits, in turn, is associated with a particular range of themes.

- Pentacles are material. They're associated with health, work, money, the home, and security.
- Swords are rational. They're connected to thinking, writing, speaking, analysis, and intellect.
- Cups are emotional. They're linked to intuition, feeling, relationships, family, and spirituality.
- Wands are appetitive. They deal with themes of passion, sexuality, anger, desire, and willpower.

These themes affect the meanings of individual cards in each suit; for example, the Ace of Cups deals with an overflowing of emotion, whereas the Ace of Pentacles typically represents a material investment. But beyond individual card meanings, they also affect the balance of a reading as a whole. If you draw multiple cards in a reading, the balance of the suits tells you something about the situation at hand. A preponderance of Swords tells you that you might be overthinking things, too many Wands might indicate that you need to let your temper cool off, and so on. The suits of the Minor Arcana can help you draw connections between cards in a reading, knitting together individual cards to form a single, cohesive answer to your question.

### The Pips

Each suit of the Minor Arcana is further subdivided into a set of ten numbered cards (often called the *pips*) and four face cards (called the *court cards*). The pips are numbered Ace through Ten, like the number cards in a poker deck. Each number in tarot carries its own range of thematic meanings; there is something that all of the Aces have in common, that all of the Twos have in common, and so on up through the Tens. Each tarot reader develops their own sense of the numerological meanings of the pip cards, and no two readers see the numbers exactly the same way. My own understanding of the pip cards is as follows:

- Aces are beginnings and potential.
- Twos are duality and reciprocity.
- Threes are dynamism and change.
- Fours are stability and foundation.
- Fives are hardship and strife.
- Sixes are equilibrium and reevaluation.
- Sevens are perspective and intention.
- Eights are freedom and motion.
- Nines are fulfillment and culmination.
- Tens are consequences and endings.

These meanings combine with the meanings of the suits to help indicate the significance of individual cards. For example, the Two of Cups is about duality and reciprocity in the context of emotions and relationships; consequently, this card typically represents partnership, such as a romance or a strong friendship. The Six of Swords is equilibrium and reevaluation in the context of thought and rationality; it represents scientific inquiry, inquisitiveness, and changing your mind. Individual card meanings aren't just a combination of number plus suit—there is often additional nuance to them above and beyond the correspondences listed here. Nonetheless, the significance of a card's number and suit always bring to bear on its meaning.

Moreover, as with the other categories we've explored, you can look at numbers not just with individual cards, but in the balance of your reading as a whole. If you draw all the Threes in a reading, that tells you that something in your querent's situation is changing rapidly. If your reading is heavy on Sevens, that might be an invitation for your querent to introspect and evaluate their own perspectives. Looking at these structural elements can help you gain a sense of a tarot reading as a larger, interconnected unity, rather than just stringing together a series of isolated card interpretations.

### The Court Cards

Each suit of the Minor Arcana has fourteen cards, but the pips only run from Ace through Ten. The remaining four cards are face cards, known in tarot as the *court cards*. These cards are typically titled the Page, Knight, Queen, and King. The court cards represent people and personalities—and as such, they can be some of the most difficult cards in the deck to understand, because people are messy and complicated. As a starting point for understanding these cards, think about the four roles they represent and the functions they fulfill in the context of a medieval court:

- Pages are obeisant. They carry messages or act at someone else's behest.
- Knights are engaged. They intervene directly and take action to accomplish their goals.
- Queens are persuasive. They win other people over to their point of view.
- Kings are powerful. They wield explicit authority and command others.

The court cards often represent people who are involved in the situation you're reading about, including the querent's friends, foes, or even the querent themself. Thus, a King might represent someone's boss, whereas a Knight would be a colleague or competitor. These roles combine with the four suits to give more specific personality profiles: The Queen of Swords persuades people by appealing to reason, whereas the Queen of Pentacles makes people feel safe and secure.

If a reading doesn't include many court cards, then the querent is able to act independently in their situation. If, on the other hand, your reading is cluttered with the courts, this indicates that the querent's situation is one that involves a lot of other people, for good or for ill. These people might be working to the querent's benefit or detriment, but either way, their influence should not be ignored.

## Reading with Spreads

If you're performing a reading with multiple cards, it can be unclear how to organize all the information you receive. If you're trying to decide between two romantic prospects and you draw the Queen of Cups and the Queen of Wands, how do you know which card represents which person? If you're doing a reading about your career trajectory and you pull the Eight of Pentacles, does that show where you're heading or where you've already been?

In order to help provide some structure to their work, many tarot readers like to employ formalized card layouts known as *spreads*. A tarot spread is a fixed number of cards arranged in a particular way; each position in the spread is assigned a particular area of inquiry answered by the card placed there. In this way, you can take a fairly complicated question and break it down into smaller, more manageable pieces. Rather than trying to answer the whole question all at once, you identify its component parts, answer each of those, and then bring your smaller answers together to provide a holistic answer to the question as a whole.

Not all tarot readers use spreads. Some readers feel like spreads are too rigid, because they box in the meanings of the cards and force you to interpret each card a certain way; these readers prefer a free flow where they can intuitively identify how the cards relate to each of the myriad components of the question at hand. Whether you use spreads or not is largely a matter of personal preference; I myself go both ways depending on the circumstances and my mood. For beginners, I do recommend starting out by reading with spreads, because the additional structure can help you make sense of what might otherwise be an overwhelming amount of information. You can always stop using the technique if you end up disliking it, but as with most things, I think there's value in giving it a fair shot.

### Past/Present/Future Spread

The most common spread you'll encounter is a simple three-card reading, with the cards arranged in a horizontal line. These cards are interpreted in chronological order: The leftmost card is the past, the central card is the present, and the rightmost card is the future. Reading the cards in this way gives you a sense of progression and development. Rather than just giving you a snapshot answer of what your situation looks like in the present moment, this spread shows you where you've been and where you're heading if you stay on your current path.

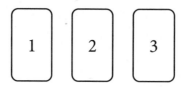

1. The past

2. The present

3. The future

Already, this spread gives you a great deal more context than a one-card reading, and potentially more than an unstructured three-card reading as well. It shows you how your situation is changing over time, how your present circumstances result from the past, and what the likely outcome is going to be.

Consider this example. If you ask "Does he love me?" and you draw only one card, in which you see stagnation and boredom, you might think the answer is no. But now suppose that you draw three cards: In the center is the card of stagnation, but on the left is a card of infatuation, and on the right is a card of new beginnings. Here, we get a more robust and nuanced answer to the question: In the past, he loved you deeply, but things are stagnating right now. All hope is not lost, though, if you can find a way to rekindle the spark of passion going forward.

### Crossroads Spread

A slightly more complex spread adapts this same chronological structure and adds a vertical element to it. Place a card in the center of your reading. Then, place a second card on top of it, rotating this card 90 degrees so that it's horizontal. The two cards together form an equal-armed cross. Place cards to the left and right of this central cross, and then place two more cards: one below it and one above. The result should look something like a crossroads.

1. The present

2. The problem

3. The past

4. The future

5. The root cause

6. Advice

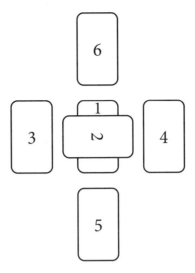

This spread gives you the same basic chronological structure that the three-card Past/Present/Future spread does. However, it adds a layer of depth: Instead of just showing you *what* happens across time, it shows you *why*. The horizontal axis of the spread is chronological, but the vertical axis is analytical. It shows you the problem at hand, the hidden root cause of that problem, and overall advice on how best to deal with the problem. This spread shows you the intersection of *what* and *why* in a way that doesn't just describe your situation; it equips you to act on it and—if need be—to change it for the better.

### Celtic Cross Spread

The third spread we'll discuss here (and the last one for this chapter) is one of the most famous spreads in tarot. It's known as the Celtic Cross. If you've ever seen a tarot reading on TV or in a movie, it's likely that this was the spread being used; likewise, if your tarot deck came with a companion book that describes how to read with spreads, there's a good chance this is included among them. There are a number of minor variations on the Celtic Cross spread, but the following is the one I use.

Deal out six cards exactly as you did in the Crossroads spread. Then deal four more cards to the right of them, in a vertical line starting from the bottom.

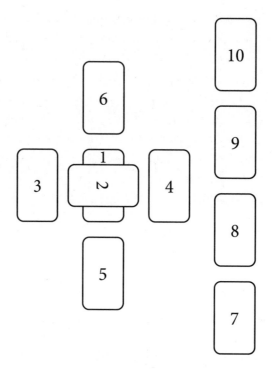

1. The present

2. The problem

3. The past

4. The future

5. The root cause

6. Advice

7. Self-perception

8. External influences

9. Hopes and fears

10. The long-term outcome

The first six cards are interpreted the same as in the Crossroads spread. The final four cards give further insight into the influences at play. At the bottom of the line, there's a card representing the querent's self-image and self-perception. The next card up represents other people or external influences affecting the querent's situation. Above that is a card for the querent's hopes or fears, which are often two sides of the same coin. And finally, at the very top of the stack, there is a card forecasting the long-term outcome of the situation, looking even further afield than the Future card in position 4.

The Celtic Cross is a bit of a difficult spread to work with. I find that for most questions, I don't actually need all the information the Celtic Cross provides; I'm often better off with the narrower scope of something like the Past/Present/Future or Crossroads spreads. But if you really want to get an in-depth understanding of an issue—and particularly if you want psychological insight into how the querent is perceiving and reacting to the problem they face—the Celtic Cross is a useful spread to have in your back pocket.

### Targeted Spreads

You'll have the opportunity to explore more spreads over the course of the book, but these three are a good set to get you started. There are countless tarot spreads available, and new ones are always being created. Some spreads, like the three I've shared here, are all-purpose: They're designed to give you useful information about any question you ask. Other spreads are designed for more specific use.

Depending on the question you're asking, you may want to use a spread that's tailored to give you specific insights. Decision-making spreads, for example, are usually structured in two parts: one looking at option A and one looking at option B. Readings about romance and relationships will typically use spreads that have cards devoted to each of the partners involved. The information you need in a reading often depends on the question being asked, so it makes sense to use a spread that's sensitive to a particular question rather than a catch-all.

Additionally, some spreads are designed with a particular theme in mind. This theme might be visual—there are spreads shaped like hearts, smiley faces, Christmas trees, and more—or it might be more abstract. In my time as a tarot reader, I've used spreads taking inspiration from the months of the year, the archetype of the Hero's Journey, occult concepts, and even famous nursery rhymes. Just about any means of organizing information can be turned into a spread, and sometimes you'll find that a particular organizational structure is exactly what you need for a given reading.

You can also come up with your own spreads. This is intimidating at first, but it's an easy skill to pick up. If you're faced with a question and can't find a spread that you feel adequately answers it, think about what information you really want out of your reading. What do you need to know in order to answer your question? How can you break that down into its component parts? Write those parts in a list, then design a spread assigning one card to each of the parts you've identified. Voilà! Your very own custom-made tarot spread.

## Reading with Reversals

Depending on how you shuffle and lay out your cards, you may find that you deal some cards upside-down. These are known as *reversals*. Some tarot readers ignore reversals, simply flipping each card to an upright orientation as they draw it. However, other readers like to interpret an additional layer of meaning with reversed cards.

There are a variety of ways that people choose to interpret reversals. Reversals don't feature heavily in the magic I'll be discussing in this book, so I won't go into too much depth here, but I've provided a brief survey of a few principal approaches you might find.

### Weakened Meaning

Some readers see a reversed card as being weaker than it would be if it were upright; it still carries the same basic energy, but it's somehow moderated or tempered. So, if the Nine of Cups represents exuberant joy when it's upright, you might interpret the reversed Nine of Cups as still signifying happiness, but maybe not the same level of exultant bliss. In a similar vein to this, reversals might represent obstacles or delays; the energy of the card is present, but something is getting in its way and slowing it down.

### Opposite Meaning

A second approach is to think of a reversed card as the mirror image of its upright meaning. If an upright card means charity, its reversal might mean selfishness; if the upright card means stagnation, the reversal might mean growth. This approach is less suited to the more dramatic, extreme cards in the deck; it's very hard to look at an image of chaotic destruction and say "This would normally mean catastrophe, but since the card is upside-down, the blood and flames actually represent everything working out perfectly."

Nonetheless, some cards have twin meanings that can be two sides of the same coin, and in those instances, reversals can help you discern between two distinct but related themes. There's a deep connection between giving and taking, between indecision and action—and these contradictory things often show up as meanings for the same card. In tricky cases, a reversal can point you to one of these surprising and seemingly contradictory themes.

### Negative Meaning

A third approach to reversals is to interpret every card as a negative, harmful, or bad version of its upright self. If the Ten of Wands represents hard work, its reversal is toil without reward; if the Hierophant represents authority and tradition, its reversal is dogmatism and zealotry. Personally, I don't care for this approach to reversals, because I think it skews readings and makes them too negative. After all, not every card in the deck is cheerful even when they're upright. Interpreting every reversed card negatively adds seventy-eight more bad omens into the mix, and it means a sizable majority of readings would come out negative. To me, at least, that doesn't seem like an accurate reflection of reality, and I think it puts the reader at a disadvantage when trying to give a faithful reading.

That's not to say that reversals *never* mean something negative—I've certainly come across readings where they did. However, I'm leery of casting my net too wide, and I think it's a misstep to start thinking that every reversal must simply be a worse version of the upright card.

### Intuition and Reversals

Reading with reversals—like all tarot reading—ultimately relies a great deal on your intuition. If you choose to include reversals in your readings, you have to determine on a case-by-case basis what each reversal means. The approaches shared here are useful guidelines to help you make that determination, but there is no formula that can cleanly convert an upright card meaning into a reversed one. You have to trust your gut and look at the context of the reading in order to find the interpretation that best fits with the question you've asked and the other cards you've drawn.

One general rule that I find helpful is to think of a reversed card as saying "Yes, but..." The original meaning of the card is still present somehow—a reversal isn't completely disconnected from the upright card—but there's a caveat. The reversal indicates that you want to take a closer look at what the card is doing, because not everything is as it seems. If you draw the Eight of Cups reversed, you can say, "This card normally deals with themes of disengagement or abandonment, *but* that's not the whole story in this case." Your job as the reader, then, is to figure out the "but."

## Interactions Between Cards

When you lay out multiple cards for a reading, regardless of whether you're using a designated spread or something more freeform, it's important not to fall into the trap of looking at each card in isolation and neglecting the larger reading. The cards are working together to tell a cohesive story, and each part of that story contributes to the larger whole. It's good and useful to look at each card's individual meaning, but you also want to take a step back and look at the big picture. Try not to miss the forest for the trees.

One of the best ways to do this is to look at the visual connections between the cards in your reading. Imagine these cards not as a set of unrelated images stacked side by side, but as parts of a single, cohesive painting. What does that painting look like? What's happening in it? Who are the characters depicted?

Take a particular look at the people depicted in your deck. Is anyone facing toward another card? Consider their body language and what it looks like they're doing. Are they speaking? Reaching out a hand to help? Charging into battle? Now, think about what they're facing toward. If they're going to battle, what are they battling against? If they're offering help, who is the recipient?

This visual dynamic can tell you a great deal about how the energies of different cards interact. When the Knight of Swords charges away from the dreamy Moon and toward the practical Seven of Pentacles, he's on a mission to stop fantasizing and start getting things done. If he's going in the other direction, however, his task is completely reversed; now, he has decided to stop holding himself back and allow himself to dream bigger. Together, the cards tell a visual story that would be lost if you just looked at each one by itself.

When you evaluate your reading as a whole, rather than just as a series of disconnected parts, make sure that you also look for shared symbols across the cards. Are there any cards that share particular images? What do those images make you think of? These repeated motifs can indicate obscure connections and can help you pay attention to themes that might not otherwise be obvious. If you see a butterfly on several cards in your reading, for example, you might start to think about transformation and rebirth as a core theme for the reading. Then, you can see which cards contribute to the theme of transformation by identifying which ones feature the butterfly imagery.

## Learn by Doing

This chapter has offered a *very* quick rundown of the fundamental skills involved in reading tarot. There is a great deal more to discuss, but space is limited, and this book isn't just about how to read tarot—it's about how to use tarot for magic. Hopefully, this is enough to give you at least a basic grasp of the skills involved in tarot reading so that you can continue to develop those skills as you explore the magical themes and techniques presented in the rest of this book.

The most important advice I have for learning how to read tarot is that you have to practice. Tarot is a skill like any other; you'll only get good at it through lots and lots of practice. Just like learning to play the piano, you'll be clunky and mechanical at first, but the more time you put in, the better you'll get at it. Try to perform a tarot reading every day, even if it's just on a small, simple question. This is like running scales on the piano: It keeps you engaged, gives you an opportunity to apply the skills you've learned so far, and lets you push yourself a little bit more each time. Eventually, you'll find that you're comfortable with the fundamental skills, so much so that you don't have to consciously think about the basic steps of tarot interpretation. From there, you can push yourself further, learning more advanced techniques. You'll be performing complex readings—or playing elaborate sonatas—sooner than you know.

## chapter two
# What Is Magic?

*Magic* is a notoriously difficult word to define. Around the world, people have developed methods to change themselves and the world around them, and many of these methods are the sort of thing we might call magic. But what counts as magic and what doesn't? This will largely depend on who you ask.

The famous occultist Aleister Crowley defined magic (or rather, *magick*, as you'll sometimes see the word spelled) as "the Science and Art of causing Change to occur in conformity with Will."[2] This is probably the best-known definition of magic that you'll encounter in occult spaces, but personally, I don't think it's a very good one. Every day, we cause lots of things to change through acts of our will, but we aren't generally inclined to think of those changes as magical. Admittedly, the word *will* has a somewhat idiosyncratic meaning for Crowley; it doesn't mean willpower in the conventional sense, but rather something like a higher purpose or a true calling. Even so, I'm not satisfied with Crowley's definition of magic. If my true calling is to be a great musician, writing a symphony is causing change to occur in conformity with will, but when I talk about magic, Beethoven's Fifth isn't what I have in mind.

The anthropologist James Frazer had an altogether different take on magic. He suggested that magic is a failed attempt at science—that it's a way people try to control the world around

---

2. Crowley, *Magick*, 126.

them because they don't understand the actual causal mechanisms governing the universe. Frazer wrote that "magic is a spurious system of natural law as well as a fallacious guide of conduct; it is a false science as well as an abortive art."[3] This definition excludes the example of the musician, but it still doesn't sit right with me. It strikes me as too easy and too simple to say that everyone practicing magic is simply doing bad science. If I cast a spell to try to enhance my artistic creativity, I'm fully aware that what I'm trying to do isn't accomplished by ordinary causal mechanisms. I know the difference between Newton's laws of motion and whatever it is that I'm trying to do as a magician. I don't pretend to claim that all magical practitioners have a deep understanding of science—most people in the world don't—but I think that, by and large, people are capable of distinguishing between the kind of direct causation we interrogate in the natural sciences and the more symbolic, abstract, mysterious connection that magic tries to build.

Both Crowley and Frazer agree that magic is an act of change: Magic seeks to make something different than the way it was before. Moreover, magic is a *directed* change. It's not just a change that happens by accident, but rather it's done consciously and deliberately.

That's a good starting point. Now we just have to narrow our parameters.

What strikes me as unique about magic is not the purpose of the desired change (e.g., whether or not it's in accordance with true will), but rather the manner in which that change is achieved. If I try to attract clients for my business by contacting an advertising agency, that's not magic. If, on the other hand, I anoint my doorframe with a consecrated oil every morning in order to draw in potential customers, I'm doing something magical. Magic is distinguished from other acts of directed change not by its ends, but by its means.

Generally speaking, the types of action we consider magical tend to fall into two main categories. On one hand, there is magic that relies on symbolic enactment of a desired goal. Say I want to attract love into my life, so I paint a picture of a heart and sleep with that picture under my pillow; the heart represents love, and by keeping it close to me, I symbolically bring love to myself. This kind of magical action is known as *sympathetic magic*. On the other hand, there is magic that relies on the intervention of an outside power. Say I want to sell my home, so I bury a statue of Saint Joseph upside-down on the property; this communicates (rather forcefully) that I want Joseph's help with the sale. In this kind of magic, the magician persuades someone or something—a planetary intelligence, elemental power, angel, demon, ghost, saint, fairy, deity, or some other type of spirit—to intercede on their behalf. There's not a single widely used name

---

3. Frazer, *The Golden Bough*, 26.

for the types of magic that fall under this umbrella, but for the purpose of this book, I'll call this *intercessional magic*.

These aren't neat categories, and the boundaries between these two types of magic are blurry. Lots of magical actions involve both sympathetic and intercessional elements. While keeping a painted heart under my pillow to attract love, I might ask the goddess Venus to bless my spell; while appealing to Saint Joseph to sell my home, I bury his statue on *my* property as a way of symbolizing exactly which home needs to be sold. The distinction between sympathetic and intercessional magic is a useful tool to help us understand the wide variation in practices that can count as magical, but occultists are unbothered by theoretical divisions between this or that type of magic. They do what works. As both James Frazer and Aleister Crowley noted, magic is an art, and as such it resists rigid taxonomy.

Nonetheless, you'd be hard-pressed to find any magical practice that doesn't include either sympathetic or intercessional elements. Likewise, if you're doing something that relies on sympathy or spiritual intercession, there's a very good chance that someone somewhere would consider it magic.

All of that considered, here's the definition of magic that I'll use for the purpose of this book:

*Magic is the practice of causing directed change through either sympathetic or intercessional means.*

This is an imperfect definition, of course. For one thing, it seems like all prayer would count as magic according to this definition, because prayer is an attempt to persuade a deity or other powerful spirit to intercede on someone's behalf. Lots of people would resist lumping prayer and magic together in this way. The problem, however, is that the distinction between prayer and magic is often kind of arbitrary, and it depends on who you're asking. As one scholar has noted, "For many people magic is other people's religion," and what looks like prayer from the inside often looks like magic from the outside.[4]

There are surely exceptions to the definition I've provided, because there will always be exceptions when trying to define something as protean as magic. Ultimately, whether something counts as magic largely depends on whether the people doing it think of it that way. This definition isn't meant to be the be-all and end-all of what magic is, but it's close enough to give you a sense of the general shape of the thing.

---

4. DuBois, *Out of Athens*, 60.

Now, let's dive into some more specific topics to give more depth and nuance to the sketch of magic we have so far.

## Similarity and Contagion

Sympathetic magic operates according to symbolic thinking. Its basic principle is known as the *law of sympathy*: whatever is *like* a thing actually *is* that thing (for magical purposes, at least). If you want to cause some change in the world, you create a symbolic representation of the thing you want to affect—something that is like your target in a relevant way. Then, you use that representation to act out the change you want to see. The idea is that by changing the representation, you'll change the thing itself, because symbolically the two are one and the same.

When you first encounter this concept, it can sound somewhat silly. Adult humans know the difference between representation and reality. When we see an actor performing in a film, we understand that they are a person playing a part. We understand that Hannibal Lecter isn't a real person; he's a character played by the actor Anthony Hopkins. Here is representation, there is reality, and the two are distinct.

But sometimes, representation and reality can collapse into each other. René Magritte's famous painting *The Treachery of Images* depicts a large wooden pipe; written beneath it in careful script is the caption "This is not a pipe." And indeed, who would ever think that it was? It is very clearly a painting of a pipe, but not a pipe itself. If someone tried to stuff tobacco into *The Treachery of Images* and smoke it, they would be unceremoniously escorted away by the security guards in the Los Angeles County Museum of Art.

Magritte's painting and caption aren't trying to correct an error in judgment on the part of the viewer. He's not saying, "Ah, I see you may have mistaken this for an actual pipe, but in fact it's just a painting!" Rather, he's calling attention to the close relationship between a thing and a representation of that same thing—a relationship that often goes unremarked and unquestioned. Just as intuitively as we understand that a painting is not a pipe, we also understand that in some sense it *is*. If you pointed out *The Treachery of Images* and asked me, "What's that painting over there?" it would make perfect sense for me to reply, "It's a pipe." Although we know how to mark a distinction between reality and representation, we often allow that distinction to collapse when we're interacting with the world around us. This is not a pipe, except that it is.

Sympathetic magic is about deliberately collapsing that distinction. I create a symbolic representation of the thing I want to affect, and even though I know it's just a symbol, I decide to treat it as if it weren't. I decide that by acting on the representation, I am also acting on the reality; whatever I do to my symbol will also effect a change in the thing itself. I take *The Treachery of Images*, cross out the word *not*, and proudly declare, "This is a pipe." And then I stuff it with tobacco and light it up as the security guards haul me off the museum grounds.

This sounds irrational. That's because it kind of is. Sympathetic magic relies on a different way of seeing the world, one that works through symbolism and image. It's a poet's way of engaging with the world, not an engineer's. Nevertheless, it's something we all understand on some gut level. Sympathetic magic is quite easy, really, because it speaks to a deep part of us: one that understands the world through symbol and art, and one that recognizes "This is not a pipe" as a lie.

## *The Law of Similarity*

Sympathetic magic relies on creating a symbolic representation of something and then acting on it. The next question is obvious: How do we create that representation? In conversations about sympathetic magic, people usually identify two primary ways of establishing a sympathetic link. These are known as *similarity* and *contact*.[5]

Similarity is just what it sounds like; it's establishing a connection based on close resemblance to the thing you're trying to affect. One of my favorite spells is a simple rain spell that involves going outside and pouring water on the ground. There's slightly more to it than that, but that's the main activity. The spell doesn't have a lot of bells and whistles, but its symbolic meaning is clear: I want water to come from the sky and fall upon the earth. The water I pour resembles the water in the clouds, and the effect resembles the rainstorm I want to produce. It's simple, clear, and effective.

There are countless ways to establish sympathy through similarity. You can represent a person through a photograph or a doll dressed as them. I once did healing magic for a cat using a small, cat-shaped plastic toy. I've used chocolate coins to represent money in prosperity magic, a heart-shaped seashell to heal someone with cardiac issues, and a map of my neighborhood to do protective magic for my home. There is no set way to do this kind of magic, as long as you can find a symbolic resemblance.

You can also go further afield than direct visual representation. A colored candle with someone's name carved into it can be a powerful representation; it is similar to them not because it looks like them, but because it bears their name. In one memorable instance, I had a colleague who was spreading vicious gossip in the workplace and causing trouble for everyone else. He

---

5. Frazer, *The Golden Bough*, 28.

reminded me of a croaking toad. So, I got a plush, toad-shaped dog toy with a squeaker in it, and I removed the squeaker, thereby silencing the toad's voice. I've also planted seeds to represent projects I wanted to sprout, lit candles to illuminate things I wanted others to know about, and used magnets to draw things together or string to bind them. The similarity in your magic can be as abstract as you need it to be.

As a general rule, the closer your resemblance is, the better your magic will be. A photograph of someone is a better representation than a stick figure drawing of them, and it will work better for the purposes of a spell. Likewise, someone's full legal name identifies them better than their first name alone. As you're developing sympathetic representations, get creative and think outside of the box, but always come back to the question of similarity. How well does your magic really identify the target of your spell?

## The Law of Contact

After similarity, the second main way of establishing a sympathetic representation is through contact (also referred to as *contagion*). If you can get your hands on something that has been in close contact with your target, then your magic becomes symbolically close as well. This is where a lot of old-school witchcraft comes in: Classic spells often call for a drop of blood, a lock of hair, dust from someone's footprint, or other bodily fluids. You can use an item of someone's clothing or a favorite piece of jewelry to represent them magically, or a copy of someone's resume to help them find a job. All of these items have magical potency because they come from a particular person; they've been in contact with that person and, therefore, are directly linked.

Contact doesn't just apply to people, though. When I was applying to graduate school, I bought a teddy bear from the university bookstore of my top-choice school. Because the teddy bear came from a particular school, it established a magical link between me and that university. The last time I was looking for new housemates, I collected stones from the yard around my house—one stone for each vacant room. The stones came from the home I was trying to fill; because of that, the symbolic effect of the spell wasn't just "I need people to live with," but rather "I need people to live with *here*."

The distinction between similarity and contagion is sometimes blurry. Someone's signature, for example, is similar to them because it bears their name, but it also derives power from having been written by them directly—a form of magical contact. Often, a spell will involve both forms of sympathy, in different measures and in different ways. The most important thing is that you establish a strong representation of the thing you're trying to affect so that when you act on that representation (e.g., by planting your seeds or lighting your candle), you are symbolically acting on the thing itself.

## Spirit Relationships

Intercessional magic relies on the aid of incorporeal spirits to accomplish a goal. Typically, practitioners work to cultivate lasting relationships with these magical spirits; a spirit is a person (albeit not a living human person), and as such it deserves to be treated with dignity and respect. It would be wildly inappropriate to show up to a stranger's house and say "I need your help with my dating life"—and if you did so, you'd likely have a door slammed in your face. You'd only ask someone for romantic advice if they were a trusted friend, a professional dating coach, or connected to you in another way that made the request appropriate. Similarly, asking spirits for magical assistance is often a matter of cultivating a relationship with them, getting to know them, and giving them a reason to help you. Otherwise, you're showing up on a stranger's doorstep with an unprompted request. Setting aside how rude it is, an approach like that is unlikely to get you the results you're looking for.

Magical relationships, like relationships between humans, are variegated. There is no right way for a relationship between a magician and a spirit to look. Furthermore, the number and type of magical spirits attested to worldwide is so vast as to be practically limitless. Because of this, it's difficult to talk in general terms about how to cultivate magical relationships. What we can do, however, is draw a parallel between magical relationships and interpersonal human ones, thinking about what the latter might teach us about the former.

### Relationships of Transaction

In many relationships, the two people involved are equals: Each of them has something to offer the other, and they engage in a fair trade so that they both get what they want. This type of relationship is found between two colleagues or between a vendor and a client. It's a quid pro quo: You help me, and I help you in return.

Transactional relationships are likewise found in the magical world. In these relationships, a spirit helps a magician and receives an offering of some sort in return. These offerings depend on the individual spirit and the service being rendered, but they might include a glass of wine or a plate of food, incense, recited poetry, or a particular service (donating to a meaningful charity, picking up trash from the beach, and so on). These are professional working relationships where a spirit helps you achieve what you want, and in return you offer them something that they want. These relationships can be one-off interactions, or they can last for an extended period of time, building up a strong professional relationship with a particular spirit over the course of many requests and many offerings.

## Relationships of Authority

Sometimes, we have relationships where we expect other people to help us because we are in some position of authority over them. When a boss tells an employee to perform a certain task, it's understood that the task will get done—not because the two people are close friends, but because there is a hierarchy in place and the employee is expected to follow certain instructions. The same can be true with magical relationships. If you occupy a position of respect in the eyes of a spirit, that spirit will help you with magical tasks, even if you don't have a close personal connection to them.

There are a variety of techniques to establish this position of authority. Some involve extended ritual purification, including such things as sexual abstinence, fasting or a vegetarian diet, and ritual bathing. Other techniques involve appealing to someone else to grant you their authority; if you're conjuring a fairy, you might first petition a more powerful fairy to give you authority over them. In all cases, the point is to set you up as someone worth listening to so that a spirit will do what you ask, even if they don't already know you.

Just as with professional hierarchies, there are limits to how far this authority goes. My boss can ask me to perform tasks within my job description, but she can't ask me to run personal errands for her. Similarly, a magician working from a place of authority still has boundaries that must be respected. Authority is only respected insofar as it's used responsibly, and a magician who pushes too far is likely to lose the good will of the spirits they work with.

## Relationships of Affection

Not every relationship is professional. Sometimes people help us simply because they like us and care about us, whether they're family members or friends. Likewise, you may find that some spirits are inclined to help you not because of what they get out of the equation, but simply because they want what's best for you. In these relationships, there's not a strict tit-for-tat expectation of reciprocity. That said, you still want to show some care for the spirits you're working with, thank them for their help, and potentially leave offerings for them when you feel it's appropriate to do so. Just as in an ordinary human friendship, you don't want to take someone's affection for granted. Don't be the sort of person who always has demands but never stops to say "thank you" or do things for other people.

## *Relationships of Supplication*

Finally, there are relationships where we're not particularly close to someone and we don't exactly have anything to offer them, but they're in a position to help us and we ask them for that help anyway. In these cases, we're usually relying on someone's beneficence and good will, like when charities ask for donations, a college student applies for a scholarship, or an unhoused person asks for help buying dinner. In these cases, we do our best to convince the other party that they should help us—charities will try to convince you that they support a good cause, and the scholarship applicant will demonstrate academic excellence—but we understand that the choice of whether to help us is ultimately theirs. We can ask, but that doesn't guarantee the answer will be "yes."

Magicians will sometimes have similar interactions when they try to persuade a spirit to help them rather than commanding, negotiating, or appealing to a privileged personal connection. In these cases, humility is key; the magician is asking, not demanding. Magical rites of supplication will usually include a detailed invocation of the spirit in question (with lots of praise and description of how wonderful the spirit is) followed by a justification that explains why the magician deserves the spirit's help and why the task at hand is worth accomplishing.

## The Card Catalogue of the Universe

All magic draws on a feeling of interconnection and interdependence. We live in a world where no one and nothing is completely isolated. We are all in relationship with each other and with the world around us. As humans, we're social creatures, and we meet our emotional and physical needs by helping each other and supporting each other as members of a community. As living beings, we are part of a cycle of life much larger than ourselves: we sow and harvest crops, raise and slaughter livestock, take warmth from the sun and water from the rain. Each of us is only part of a much larger whole, and the same is true of everything else around us.

Magic relies on the feeling that we are all connected not only to other people, but to the whole of the universe. The operating principle of magic is that we can effect change through indirect action; this indirect action, in turn, is only possible if things are connected to each other. We've already explored some of the ways in which things can be linked, but magicians draw on a wide array of magical connections. Many of these connections are obscure, indirect, and not obvious at first glance. A and C might not seem like they have anything to do with each other, but if A is connected to B and B is connected to C, then there is a link between A and C that can be used for magical purposes, even if that link isn't immediately apparent. In this way, magic opens up endless possibilities for connecting one thing to another, so long as we can find what they have in common.

This way of linking things together—not through direct resemblance, but through some common intermediary point—is often referred to in magic as using *correspondences*. Magical correspondences act almost like a card catalogue of information about the universe: You can take one thing, look at its correspondences, and learn a great deal of magical information about it based on the other connections it has. If I want to do a love spell and I know that the planet Venus is associated with love, I can look up other things associated with Venus and compile a list of minerals, crystals, herbs, incenses, and other components that I can potentially use to put together my spell.

These correspondences can come from a variety of places. They're a shared vocabulary that magicians can use to work their magic, but that vocabulary is shaped by geography, history, science, and culture. Like all symbols, magical correspondences can vary across contexts, meaning different things to different people and at different times and places. Because of this, there is no complete nor correct set of correspondences to use in magic, but there are a few basic principles that can help guide us in understanding where correspondences come from.

### Physical Observation

Sometimes, magical correspondences are as simple as looking at a thing and observing its physical properties, then thinking about how those properties might relate symbolically to the rest of the world. In many ways, this is like establishing a link for sympathetic magic; the process is just a bit more abstract and wide-ranging. For example, sunrise is symbolically a time of rebirth and renewal. If you're conjuring a spirit to help you get a fresh start in life, you might decide to face east for the conjuration, because that's where the sun rises. You could further understand the magical correspondences of the direction east by thinking about other things associated with new beginnings: youth, springtime, the waxing moon, and so on. From a simple physical observation, you derive a whole world of correspondences, a sense of the symbolic interconnectedness of the universe that can be used in magic.

Medieval magicians used physical observations of this kind to try to uncover the magical and medicinal properties of various features of the natural world. They believed in something known as the *doctrine of signatures*: the idea that in creating the world, God had put "signatures" on its natural features in order to indicate what they could be used for.[6] Different items

---

6. Graves, *The Language of Plants*, 3.

with similar signatures would correspond to the same sorts of things, and in this way magicians built up a network of correspondences. Thus, bitter and poisonous plants corresponded to Saturn, the malefic planet named after a god who ate his own children, while pale and watery plants corresponded to the moon, the ruler of the tides.

These correspondences were thought to indicate medical as well as magical uses for things in the natural world. As our understanding of science has grown more systematic, the doctrine of signatures has fallen out of favor in medicine and been replaced with a more sophisticated understanding of the chemical properties of different medicines. Nonetheless, physical observations of this kind remain extremely useful for magic. They allow us to build out a complete magical universe so that nothing we do is in isolation. Every act, object, direction, or time of day has a potential magical significance.

## *Occult Tradition*

All symbols occupy a particular cultural context, and magical symbols are no different. Sometimes, there's an element of "because I said so" to magical correspondences. Over time, a group of magical practitioners develops a set of symbols and correspondences that work well for them, and these symbols become entrenched as magical tradition. There's nothing inherent about these correspondences that requires them to be the way they are, but they become useful if you're working in the tradition that they belong to. Practitioners in the past have done the work of building up an understanding of the magically interconnected universe, and by using the correspondences that they've developed, you save yourself the trouble of having to reinvent the wheel.

Each magical tradition has its own set of correspondences developed over time. It's worth noting that these traditions diverge from each other and often contradict each other. Western alchemy is built on the four elements of earth, air, water, and fire; esoteric Taoism, on the other hand, has five elements, the *wu xing* of wood, fire, earth, metal, and water.[7] Some practitioners find these differences confusing and frustrating—how are we supposed to know which set of correspondences is the *right* one? The point, however, is that there is no right set of correspondences. There are just different traditions, each with their own way of looking at the world.

I like to think of traditional correspondences as ways of modeling reality. Lots of different models can exist. Some are complex, some are simple, and sometimes they overlap in contradictory ways so that it's not useful to try to use two different models concurrently. Even so, each

---

7. Wen, *The Tao of Craft*, 16.

model is a valuable way of looking at the magical world and gaining information about it, so long as we understand that each model offers its own perspective and doesn't have to align with what other models tell us.

Generally speaking, if you're working with a kind of magic that comes from a particular tradition, you're best served to use the magical correspondences from that tradition. In the case of tarot (the subject of this book), a lot of tarot as we know it today was developed in the context of nineteenth- and early twentieth-century British esoteric orders. These orders developed a robust set of magical correspondences that work well with tarot, so that's largely what we'll be sticking to for the purposes of this book. Keep in mind, though, that the correspondences I discuss here are only one tradition, and there are lots of other valuable ways of modeling the magical universe.

### Personal Connections

Finally, not all magical correspondences have to be shared with other people. Sometimes we develop personal insights into magical connections. These insights aren't derived from any objective observation about the world, nor are they given by occult tradition, but if they have a deep significance to us, we can still use them in our magic—although someone else who didn't share our perspective would likely not find them useful in the same way.

Magic draws on symbolism and abstract connection, and sometimes symbols have a personal rather than a social significance. Culturally, roses represent love and beauty, but if I have a severe allergy to roses and they always leave me itchy-eyed and runny-nosed, beauty probably won't be the first thing I think of when I see a rose. Instead, roses might have a personal significance of discomfort and illness. Because of that connection, I might use roses in my magic in a different way than other people would.

Magic is always and inevitably a personal undertaking. There's value in tradition and following in the footsteps of people who have gone before, but that doesn't mean you can't step off the trail and do some exploring of your own. You can complement more established correspondences with a personal, intuitive understanding of the interconnected universe that surrounds you, drawing on your perspective as an individual to make your magic uniquely yours.

## High Magic and Low Magic

Practitioners of magic sometimes talk about a difference between high and low magic. This can mean a couple of different things depending on context. On one hand, it can refer to how elaborate or simple a magical working is; "high" magic involves a great deal of ceremony, precise timing, and tools made to exacting specifications, while "low" magic is more informal and flexible. On the other hand, the high/low magic distinction can refer to different types of goals that people accomplish through magic. "High" magic in this sense usually refers to magical work aimed at spiritual growth, self-improvement, and connection with the divine or the practitioner's own higher self. "Low" magic, on the other hand, refers to magic aimed at concrete, practical results like getting a job or attracting a lover.

### Ceremonial and Folk Magic

Another term that's often used for high magic—in the sense of complicated, elaborate ritual—is *ceremonial magic*. The idea, of course, is that this kind of magic tends to involve a great deal of ceremony. There's a lot of setup involved in this genre of magical work. Usually, ceremonial magic needs to be performed according to precise timing—on a particular day and hour, during a given season or moon phase, or when certain astrological conditions are met. Sometimes, it needs to be conducted in a specific geographic location or a sacred space set up according to predetermined specifications. The tools used for this magic often have to be made with hard-to-find materials, specially consecrated, and used only for specialized magical purposes. The magical operations themselves are often long and drawn out, involving repeated conjurations and invocations, lots of props and costuming, and a good deal of high theatrics.

This can sound exhausting, maybe even somewhat silly, but there is a point to it. All of the persnickety details of ceremonial magic serve to make that magic *special*. They set magical work apart from the ordinary world, establishing a space distinct from the mundane. In ceremonial magic, there's a sharp line dividing the sacred from the profane—and when we step across that line, we find ourselves in a position to do magical, miraculous things that seem out of reach in our everyday lives.

By contrast, some magic is simple and down to earth, without the bells and whistles that characterize ceremonial magic. This magic is sometimes known as *folk magic*. It includes simple charms, prayers, and spells that anyone might perform, without the need for special equipment, timing, or ritual. If you've lost your car keys and need to rush out the door to your doctor's appointment, you don't exactly have time to construct an elaborate temple space and wait until the planetary conjunction of Mercury and Jupiter—you need to find your keys *now*. So, you might utter a simple incantation of "Tony, Tony, look around! Something's lost and must be found!" to get Saint Anthony to aid you. Folk magic tends to be straightforward, uncomplicated, and to the point. It's usually directed at goals that need to be accomplished right away.

As with all of the distinctions I've drawn so far, the line between ceremonial and folk magic is often blurry and indistinct. Some magical practices, like the Goetic conjurations given in Solomonic grimoires, are elaborate and clearly ceremonial; others, like picking up a penny off the street for good luck, are so simple that they almost seem like they shouldn't count as magic at all. But between the two extremes, you'll find a wide range of traditions and operations that defy rigid categorization. Some people have special tools they use, while others use whatever's at hand; some will only do magic on the full moon, while others do it whenever they feel it needs to be done. Nonetheless, when we're trying to get our heads around the diversity of magical practices that exist in the world, the ceremonial/folk spectrum is one helpful way of thinking about what magic can look like.

### Theurgy and Thaumaturgy

The second thing people sometimes mean when they talk about "high" versus "low" magic is a distinction between different magical goals. Goals for meditation, personal improvement, or communion with the divine are sometimes classed as high magic or *theurgy*. Material, practical goals are conversely classed as low magic or *thaumaturgy*.[8] These two approaches to magic use a lot of the same techniques, whether sympathetic or intercessional, but they orient in different directions. Theurgy is oriented inward; it tries to produce changes within the magician. If you're doing magic to help work through your traumas, heal old wounds, find forgiveness, achieve union with the divine, or communicate with your own higher self, you're doing theurgy in this sense. Thaumaturgy, on the other hand, is oriented outward; it tries to produce changes in the world.

Aligning these two types of magical goal with "high" or "low" magic may seem a bit strange. What's higher about internal change as opposed to external change? The distinction here carries a bit of a value judgment with it: By calling theurgy "high" magic, we may implicitly be condoning it as better or more pure than the "low" magic of thaumaturgy. Indeed, that value judgment is exactly why the terms have historically been used that way. Some magicians, especially in the late nineteenth century, felt that magic should only really be used for self-improvement, and that there was something vulgar about magic used for practical ends. Because of this, they identified internal magic as more elevated than external magic, and the terminology stuck.

---

8. Bonewits, *Real Magic*, xv. In other contexts, the word *theurgy* is used to refer to a specific philosophical and magical movement from antiquity rather than high magic in general.

You'll still find some practitioners who feel this way, but personally, I think that magic is magic, regardless of what you use it for. Magic for self-improvement is entirely legitimate; so is magic for practical ends. I don't think either is inherently better than the other, and you'll find that magical techniques can be applied equally well toward both types of goal.

## Science (Or, What Magic Isn't)

In any discussion of magic, there's an important question that begs answering: What can magic actually do? We can establish all the sympathetic connections we want, call the names of every spirit we know, and perform elaborate ceremonies timed to the minute, but what can we actually hope to accomplish by doing all that? And perhaps just as importantly, what *can't* we hope to accomplish?

Magic doesn't do the impossible. You'll never find a spell that can turn your enemies into toads, make a broomstick fly, or travel back in time. Nothing can overturn the deterministic natural laws that govern the universe—so if you want to learn how to fly, you're better off getting a pilot's license than greasing up a broomstick with poisonous herbs.

Nonetheless, magical practitioners do think that magic can accomplish *something*; that something just takes place within the limits set by science. Embracing magic doesn't—and shouldn't— mean rejecting science. We still know that matter is made up of atoms, that bacteria can cause disease, and that an object at rest remains at rest unless acted on by some outside force. Magic isn't meant to replace these or any other observations that have been made by scientists over centuries of careful experimentation. Rather, magic is another way for us to act within the world that science has described.

At bottom, science is a method of discovering truths about the world through observation and experimentation. These truths, in turn, can be used to explain, predict, and control our surroundings. Considering how much science has done to advance human society and improve our lives, many of us are accustomed to using the words "truth" and "science" interchangeably. We think something is only real if it's scientific, and if someone is making outlandish claims that can't be backed up scientifically, we are—rightly!—skeptical. If someone tells me they can cure cancer with chamomile tea, I'm going to want to see some peer-reviewed research before I believe them.

Because of this, it's often tempting to try to legitimize magic by wrapping it up in scientific language. People will sometimes invoke quantum physics, string theory, or other complex and obscure theories as ways of trying to give a scientific veneer to their magical practice, putting forward the idea that magic is really just science that isn't yet properly understood.

Personally, I don't agree with that. I understand the appeal of blurring the line between science and magic, because it lends authority and legitimacy to the things we do as magicians—but I think that doing so is ultimately a disservice to both science and magic. On the scientific end of things, attempts to apply scientific theories to magic usually result in gross misrepresentations of the science involved. Quantum mechanics and string theory are complicated scientific topics, and there's a great deal of technical work involved in understanding them. When we talk about these theories without having done that technical work, we inevitably end up with an oversimplified and inaccurate understanding of what the science actually says. I have a friend who is both a witch and a physicist, and he is insistent on keeping scientific terminology out of conversations about magic. In his words, "I won't talk about quantum physics with anyone who can't do the math."

On the magical end of things, trying to explain spells with scientific jargon loses something at the heart of what magic is. Magic is poetic, symbolic, abstract, and beautiful. To my mind, magic is an art, not a science; a spell is a song we sing to the universe in the hopes that the universe will hear it and be moved by its beauty. If we break that down into scientific terms, the beauty is lost and we're left with something cold and dead, like if we reduced a great symphony to a series of overlapping sound waves. The point of magic is in the humanity of it, and that's something we lose when we try to adopt an overly clinical and scientific perspective.

My view is that magic is no more scientific than poetry, music, or painting. Importantly, though, it doesn't have to be scientific to be real or legitimate. Poetry, music, and painting can all change the world, and the same is true for magic. They just change the world in a different way than science and technology do.

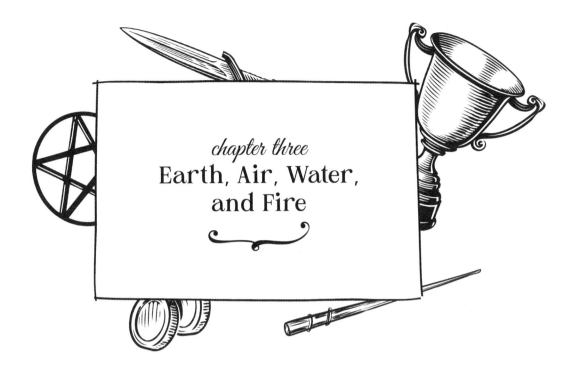

## chapter three
# Earth, Air, Water, and Fire

Now that we're situated with a shared understanding of both tarot and magic, we can begin to see how the two come together. My goal is to establish tarot as part of our magical universe: How does the tarot deck fit in with everything else we do as magicians, and how can magic inform our understanding of tarot's internal structure? The best starting point is a conversation about the elements.

The four elements of earth, air, water, and fire are the building blocks of much of Western occultism. They date back to classical Greek philosophy, and although their roots are pre-Socratic, they're best known from the works of Aristotle, who proposed that all matter was defined by two basic qualities: temperature and moisture. Matter could be hot or cold, and it could be wet or dry; the different combinations of temperature and moisture provided the four basic states of matter, which he called the elements. According to Aristotle, "The elementary qualities are four.…For Fire is hot and dry, whereas Air is hot and moist (Air being a sort of aqueous vapour); and Water is cold and moist, while Earth is cold and dry."[9] These four elements were the foundation of Aristotle's theory of physics, and they remained a staple of European philosophy and natural science well into the sixteenth century.

---

9. Aristotle, *On Generation and Corruption.*

As magical practitioners, we're less interested in the elements as a theory of physics; after all, we have our own periodic table of the elements, which provides a much more sophisticated and informative explanation of what makes up the world. Nonetheless, the four elements are still symbolic building blocks that help us build our magical universe, and we can choose to view magic—and tarot—as being built up from these four key components, just as Aristotle imagined the physical world was.

To do this, we need to reach for a deeper understanding of what these elements symbolize. For Aristotle's theory of physics, it was enough to say that earth was defined as being cold and dry, but for magic, that really doesn't tell us much. What does earth (or air, water, or fire) represent? What does it correspond to? And how does that appear in the tarot deck?

## Earth

Earth is the most solid of the four elements, and in many ways the most real. Wherever we go in our day-to-day lives, we are walking upon the earth. It supports us and stabilizes us; it's the foundation upon which we build our homes. We dig into the earth to plant seeds, and earth nourishes those seeds and allows them to grow, providing us with sustenance. Symbolically, then, the element of earth represents everything material in our lives. This includes physical objects and possessions, as well as our own bodies, health, and nutrition. Thinking beyond that, earth is connected to money, which provides us with security and stability for our lives and without which we couldn't have our earthly possessions. Earth is practical, reliable, persistent, and dependable.

## Air

Where earth represents material concerns, air is ephemeral. The wind is capricious, here one minute and gone the next, changing directions at a moment's notice. There's a great deal of freedom associated with air, and we often see birds in flight as symbols of liberation, but with that freedom comes a sense of inconstancy: Because air can go anywhere, it can't be relied upon to stay in one place. Sometimes, air can be cruel and callous, just as the wind cuts us to the bone, but it can equally be a gentle breath of fresh air. This fleeting, wide-ranging quality means that air is associated with thoughts and fantasies. Inspiration, creativity, and playfulness belong to air, as does communication: I cannot speak to someone without my breath.

## Water

Still waters run deep, and water is the most mysterious of the four elements. In the human body, water is the tears we weep when we are overwhelmed by grief or joy, and it is the blood that our heart pumps through our veins. Because of this, elemental water is associated with the heart, with feeling and emotion. Water is compassionate, empathetic, and sensitive. Just as we use water to wash ourselves clean physically, elemental water is symbolically connected to cleansing and healing of all kinds. The unsounded depths of the ocean represent the great unknown, and water is connected to the mysteries of death, divination, and the unconscious mind. Water is receptive and ever-changing; it follows the path of least resistance, always going with the flow.

## Fire

Finally, fire is forceful and dynamic. Its power is one of both creation and destruction. We need it to cook, to keep us warm in the winter, and to make new things in a forge or crucible. But when fire gets out of control, it becomes a blaze that destroys everything in its path. Fire is heat, and that heat is symbolically connected to passion and sexuality—as well as to destructive impulses like anger and violence. Fire's endless capacity to consume means that it is associated with all of our appetites, but also with a sense of determination, willpower, and firmness of purpose. Sometimes, that can be zealotry; other times, it is devotion. Finally, fire has a hypnotic, beautiful, appealing quality to it, and elemental fire represents charisma, beauty, and seduction.

## The Elements and the Suits

The four elements are everywhere in tarot, but nowhere are they more obvious than in the four suits of the Minor Arcana. Take a quick glance back at the descriptions of the four suits given in chapter 1. The four minor suits of the tarot deck correspond to four basic areas of human experience: Pentacles are material, Swords are intellectual, Cups are emotional, and Wands are appetitive. These categories correspond neatly—and not by accident—to the elements of earth, air, water, and fire.

The Minor Arcana aren't just suits in a deck of cards. They're a set of magical tools that encompass the four elements, and by extension the whole of the universe. Every area of our lives falls under the domain of one of the four elements—and therefore, under the domain of the suit and tool connected with that element. If I'm worried about my finances, my problems are governed by earthy Pentacles; if, on the contrary, I'm struggling to feel like my emotional needs are being met in a friendship, that challenge belongs to the watery Cups. Viewing things through this elemental lens gives me the tools (literally and figuratively) to better understand my world and to change it.

Take a look at the Magician card, number I of the Major Arcana. The Magician is poised to perform his miracles, with one hand pointing to the heavens above and one directed down at the earth below. His table is set with the tools of his craft, and if you look carefully, you'll notice that these are the same as the elemental tools represented in the suits of your tarot deck. With his pentacle of earth, his sword of air, his cup of water, and his wand of fire, there is nothing the Magician can't do.

Understanding this elemental perspective helps us see the balance of a reading—and when a reading is off balance, it helps us see how equilibrium can be restored. In chapter 1, we looked at the distribution of the suits in a tarot reading and what that can mean: An overabundance of Swords can mean that the querent is overthinking things; on the contrary, too many Cups can mean they're being too emotional and not acting rationally. This alone is a good starting point for assessing the condition of a reading, but with the help of the four elements, we can take it even further. The elements show how each suit can help to redress imbalances caused by too much or too little of the others.

THE MAGICIAN.

|  | HOT | COLD |
|---|---|---|
| WET | Air | Water |
| DRY | Fire | Earth |

Remember Aristotle's two basic qualities: temperature and moisture. These provide a blueprint for how the elements interact and balance each other out. Air is hot and wet; its opposite is earth, which is cold and dry. Fire is hot and dry; its opposite is water, which is cold and wet. This means that if you have too much fire in your life, you balance it by bringing in more water. If you have too much air, you bring in more earth.

The same applies to tarot readings. If you have a reading that consists entirely of cards in the suit of Wands, it's overwhelmed by fire. Your querent is hotheaded and overly concerned with their own desires. Too much elemental fire causes problems if it's not rounded out by other elemental qualities, so your querent needs to counterbalance fire with its opposite and bring in the empathetic, emotional, receptive energy of the suit of Cups. With a reading like this, you would tell your querent that they should try listening more to the people around them, making decisions from a place of deep feeling rather than impulsive wanting.

Elemental balance isn't just a matter of opposites. If you perform a reading and see cards from the suits of Pentacles, Cups, and Wands—but no Swords—your querent can improve their situation by bringing in that missing elemental energy of air, taking the time to think about their situation and adopt an analytical perspective.

Those examples are clear-cut, where there's obviously too much or too little of one particular suit, but what about more complicated cases? The truth is that you can look at the elemental balance of a reading no matter what cards turn up in the spread. The basic rule is that you want to have as much air as you have earth and as much fire as you have water. No matter how many cards are in your reading, looking at balancing those two pairs of opposites will show you what course of action needs to be taken to restore equilibrium.

Try this as an exercise: Ask a question and perform a reading for yourself with the Crossroads spread from chapter 1. Now, on a separate piece of paper, note down the number of cards you have in each suit.

For example, let's say we did a six-card reading and drew the cards on the previous page. We have one card from the suit of Swords, one from the suit of Cups, no Wands, and two Pentacles. Right away, it's obvious that this reading isn't elementally balanced. The imbalance is subtler than if we only had one suit, but there are no Wands here and too many Pentacles. The reading shows too much earth and water, so what needs to be done is to add more air and fire. A reading like this would call for you to be more communicative and direct in order to bring those missing elements into your life.

Sometimes, of course, an elemental imbalance is exactly what you want to see in a reading. If you're doing a reading about your financial prospects, an abundance of Pentacles is a good thing; if your subject is love, you'll be delighted to see lots of Cups. There are cases where the particular subject matter of a reading falls under a specific elemental domain, in which case you would expect (or at least hope) to see cards primarily connected to that element. With general readings, however, the goal is usually going to be balance: Looking at the scope of a querent's life as a whole, you want to see the elements evening each other out without any one element dominating over the others, because all four elements are important areas of human life.

## Four Elements Spread

This is a simple spread designed to give you advice on a given problem from the point of view of earth, air, water, and fire. It's useful when you want to ensure that you are considering a situation from all angles and not letting one perspective dominate others.

1. Earth: What it would be practical to do

2. Air: What you think you should do

3. Water: What you feel like you should do

4. Fire: What you want to do

5. What you ought to do, all things considered

## Making Your Own Elemental Tools

The suits of the Minor Arcana represent the elements, but they are also depictions of specific magical tools: items that can be ritually used to draw on the power of the elements in any magical work that you do. In a pinch, you can use the cards themselves to stand in for those tools; if you're doing work that calls for a pentacle and you don't have one on hand, you can pull the Ace of Pentacles out of your tarot deck and use that instead. It's a convenient substitution, and one I've used many times to great effect. Still, it *is* a substitution. As you do magic, and particularly magic involving tarot, you may well find that you want an actual set of elemental tools rather than the depictions of them in your deck.

If you're an experienced magical practitioner, you may already have some or all of these tools on hand. Swords are common in Solomonic evocations, cups are used to make offerings in many forms of ancestor veneration, and so on. The idea of uniting these four tools as the basis of elemental magic comes largely from the Hermetic Order of the Golden Dawn, which is responsible for much of the overlap between tarot and magic today. This same idea later became popular in Wicca and other forms of modern witchcraft, and many Wiccan traditions and practitioners today use four elemental tools inspired by the suits of the tarot deck.

Even if you already have some or all of these tools, I would gently encourage you to acquire a set specifically for use in your tarot-related magic. We're exploring a particular approach to magic here, and even where it bears resemblance to other types of magic you already practice, you may find value in having a ritual setup and a set of tools devoted entirely to the magical work you're doing with tarot. For myself, I've found that doing this has let me explore tarot in greater depth and take my tarot work in directions that I hadn't previously explored with my other magic.

### The Earth Pentacle

The pentacle is a flat disk with magical symbols decorated on it, visually reminiscent of a plate or a shield. In the magical system of the Hermetic Order of the Golden Dawn, the pentacle is painted with a six-pointed star and decorated with Qabalistic colors denoting the sphere of Malkuth (see chapter 6). This is one viable way to design the elemental tool of earth, especially if you're working in the context of the Golden Dawn's larger system of Qabalistic occultism, but it's not really tarot-specific enough for my tastes. If I'm using an earth pentacle for tarot-related magic, I generally want it to look like the pentacles I see in my tarot deck.

In tarot, this tool is often depicted as a large golden disk marked with a five-pointed star inscribed inside of a circle—but most of us can't afford a piece of gold that size, and probably wouldn't want to spend money on it even if we could afford it. Nonetheless, I like the idea of a circle containing a five-pointed star. This is what will show up if you type "pentacle" into a Google image search, and it's immediately recognizable as belonging to the suit of Pentacles.

Because the pentacle is a tool of elemental earth, I like for my pentacle to be made out of an earthy material. Gold is fine if you can afford it and have a flair for the dramatic, but cheaper options include ceramic, wood, or stone. Never underestimate the magical value of a flat rock you picked up off the ground! If you want to stick with something metallic, brass and copper are much cheaper than gold, but they still bear a striking visual resemblance to the pentacles you'll see depicted in your tarot deck.

Depending on what your pentacle is made from, you may want to paint or decorate it with earthy colors. There are a handful of options here. If you want to stick with the Golden Dawn's Qabalistic correspondences, the classic colors are citrine, olive, russet, and black. A more intuitive approach would be to decorate your pentacle with the colors of soil, foliage, and bedrock: greens, browns, grays, and blacks.

## *The Air Blade*

I'm not going to suggest you buy a sword. If you have a sword or have easy access to one and you want to use it for magic, great! Go for it. But it is in no way necessary for elemental magic, and the reality is that most of us don't live the sort of lives where we can easily waltz down to the local convenience store and pick up a claymore. The suit of Swords in tarot is associated with air because swords are cutting and incisive, requiring careful handling and strategic direction—much like our thoughts and our words. To replicate this symbolism, you can use just about any blade.

I've had a variety of tools to represent the suit of Swords over my years practicing tarot magic. They include a paring knife, an oyster knife, a letter opener, a blunted prop dagger, and a real dagger. All of them have worked well for me, and to date I've never had a real sword. For our purposes here, I recommend that you go out and find a blade of some kind that you can safely keep in your home and use for magical purposes. The details of that blade are entirely up to you. It can be sharp or dull, large or small, ornately decorated or a simple kitchen knife.

Blades are made out of lots of different materials, and some people—especially those made uncomfortable by sharp knives—prefer to have a symbolic blade carved out of wood or stone as opposed to a real metal knife. Personally, this isn't to my taste. I find it magically significant for the elemental tool of air to be made out of an alloy like steel, because producing steel requires the airy qualities of human ingenuity and creativity. However, that's my preference in magic, and your feelings on the matter may well be different. If you fall in love with a non-metal blade and want to use it as your air tool, go right ahead.

Some magical traditions, including some strands of Wicca, use the four tools of tarot but swap around their elemental correspondences. The most common switch is that many people associate the blade with fire and the wand with air. If you're familiar with alternate elemental correspondences from previous magical experience, you may be tempted to switch things around for your tarot work as well. You're a grown-up, and I can't stop you from doing that if you choose to, but I would discourage that choice. Remember, we're trying to work tarot-based magic here, so we should be using tarot-based elemental correspondences. If you're using a tarot deck that has different elemental attributions than the ones given here, you may want to design your tools around that deck. Otherwise, I would strongly encourage you to stick with the traditional elemental correspondences of the tarot suits, at least for the purposes of the work you do with this book.

As with the pentacle, you might choose to decorate your blade with elemental colors. In Golden Dawn magic, the handle of the air dagger is painted yellow, with various magical words and symbols marked on it in blue. Another option would be to use the colors you see in the sky: blue, white, purple, and gray.

### The Water Cup

Tarot decks often depict the suit of Cups with enormous gold or silver chalices, but once again, that's impractical for most people living in the modern world. Theoretically, just about any drinking vessel could serve as your elemental cup; the purpose of the cup is to hold water or another beverage, to serve as a receptacle and a container. A *World's Best Grandma* coffee mug does that job just as well as a spectacular jewel-encrusted chalice.

Still, I have a preference—partly magical, partly aesthetic—for my cup to at least vaguely resemble the cups I see in my tarot deck. Generally speaking, I like my water cup to be goblet-shaped and have a stem. That is purely a matter of preference, and if you want to use a coffee mug instead, there is absolutely no reason not to. Personally, I've found that it's easier for me to make a magical connection with this tool if it looks a certain way. The water cup is sometimes compared to the legend of the Holy Grail; it's a sacred, life-giving vessel, and drinking from it bestows magical blessings and power.[10] Because of this connection, I want to be able to imagine that when I drink out of my cup, an armor-clad knight looks on in approval and tells me, "You chose…wisely."

The cup can be made out of any material as long as it's water-resistant and impermeable. Silver or other silver-colored metals tend to be popular, as do ceramic and wood. Personally, I have a soft spot for glass; I think the translucent nature of glass lends itself well to the symbolism of elemental water. My first water cup was a cheap wineglass I picked up from the dollar store, and although I've had fancier ones since, I don't think any of them have been better or more effective.

Depending on the material you choose for your cup, do take a minute to make sure it's food-safe. The cup is unlike other magical tools in that you actually drink from it, so you want to make sure you don't unintentionally poison yourself. Pewter is beautiful, but it can leach toxic chemi-

---

10. Crowley, *Magick*, 167.

cals into your beverage, especially if you pour something acidic like wine into it. Be smart, and don't let aesthetics supersede safety concerns.

Commercially available cups—especially ones marketed to witches and Pagans—often come pre-decorated, but you always have the option of personalizing your cup. As I mentioned, I'm a sucker for a see-through wineglass, but blue is an obvious color choice for the elemental tool of water (and is the Golden Dawn standard). Other watery colors include turquoise, green, and silver. If you like, you can decorate your cup with waves, sea creatures, or anything else that feels particularly watery to you.

### The Fire Wand

Finally, we come to the fire wand. In tarot, this is often depicted simply as a branch of wood, varying in length from a short stick to a quarterstaff. Practically speaking, a shorter wand is easier to use for diverse magical purposes; you certainly can have a five-foot wand if you want to, but it'll be inconvenient for working in smaller spaces, and it won't travel well if you want to bring it with you to do magic outside of your home. The length of your wand is a matter of personal preference. For myself, I find that the best wand length is the distance from the crook of my elbow to the tip of my middle finger. This distance is roughly equivalent to an ancient unit of measurement known as a *cubit*, and it's given as the recommended length of a wand in some texts of Solomonic magic, so there's precedent for it. Plus, it's a convenient and workable size.

When I think about wands in connection with fire, the image that immediately comes to mind is that of a torch. The wand carries the power of elemental fire because it can be lit to provide illumination and warmth. It is made of combustible materials, and it holds within itself the potential for the chemical reaction that produces fire. In the Golden Dawn's system of magic, this symbolism is made even more explicit by carving the wand's tip into the shape of a flame. Because of this connection, I like for my wand to be made out of wood so that it could, in principle, be set on fire. Some practitioners prefer wands made out of crystals or other materials, and there's no problem with that if it's your preference—but make sure that the material you choose for the wand helps to somehow connect it back to the symbolism of elemental fire.

If you decide on a wooden wand, there's the question of what kind of tree your wand should come from. This is a matter of both convenience and personal preference. If you like, you can choose wood from a tree that's associated with fire. Ash trees, for example, are particularly valued for firewood, because ash has a dense wood grain and a thin layer of bark. Other trees, like the giant sequoia, are pyrophytic, meaning that they have evolutionarily adapted to withstand wildfires. Either of these may be a valuable wood to choose for your wand. However, there's also the simple matter of what's available to you: If you live somewhere that giant sequoia trees grow, it's very easy to pick a fallen branch off the ground and turn it into a wand. If you live somewhere without giant sequoias, you'll likely have to choose something else when making your magical tools.

Your wand can be as plain or as decorated as you'd like it to be. I tend to favor simple wands that look like plain sticks with the bark sanded off. However, if you prefer, you can decorate your wand by burning or carving designs into it, attaching crystals or beads, painting it, or decorating it. Golden Dawn wands are red and yellow, but fire is also associated with orange, gold, and other warm tones.

## The Elemental Court Cards

The fourfold division of suits in the Minor Arcana is the clearest place we see the presence of the four elements in a tarot deck. However, it is not the only place. The elements are also crucially significant to our understanding of another fourfold division in the deck: the court cards. In addition to numbered cards running from the Ace through the Ten, each suit of the Minor Arcana has four face cards named after the members of a medieval court: a Page, a Knight, a Queen, and a King.

Each set of court cards has a primary elemental energy determined by its suit. All of the court cards in the suit of Pentacles are earthy personalities concerned with material needs, whereas all of the court cards in the suit of Wands are fiery people driven by desire and will-power. Even so, there are lots of different ways to be earthy or fiery. While there are similarities between the court cards, each has its own distinct personality determined by its element and rank. Pages are pragmatic and dedicated, Knights are quick and free-spirited, Queens are receptive and changeable, and Kings are forceful and domineering.

By now, you probably recognize the elemental keywords I'm using to describe each card's qualities. Pages are earth, Knights are air, Queens are water, and Kings are fire. Thus, while each card has a primary elemental energy given to it by its suit, it also has a secondary elemental energy given by its rank. Together, the two help us understand the card's overall personality.

### Pages

Pages are the bottom of the hierarchy, and as such, they're the ones who have to take care of all the menial tasks that no one else wants to do. They're associated with earth because they do the grunt work of the court cards. They're charged with being practical and implementing the plans given to them by their superiors. Often associated with youth or new beginnings, Pages are the sort of personality that provides the fertile soil in which something new can grow (an idea, a business venture, and so on). Each of them applies this earthy attitude to bring manifestation to the things associated with their respective suits. Some decks depict the Pages as young women and others depict them as young men, but their gender is much less important than the personalities they represent. For the purposes of this book, I'll refer to the Pages as women.

- The Page of Pentacles is the earthiest of the earthy. Cautious, measured, and slow to act, this is someone who likes to invest in new projects because she sees the potential for growth.
- The Page of Swords brings earthy practicality to the airy ideas of the Swords. She's an inventor and an innovator, the kind of person who can take abstract ideas and make something concrete out of them.
- The Page of Cups combines the earth's grounded nature with watery empathy. This is a sensitive listener who pays attention to the needs of others and feels deeply for them.
- Finally, the Page of Wands uses her earthy nature to manifest fiery passion. An imaginative artist, she brings a spark of joy to the creation of new things.

## Knights

Knights are free-roaming wanderers, the only members of the tarot court typically depicted on horseback. Like the wind, they are never in one place for long, always questing forward to find something new. While they have lots of thoughts and dreams, they often lack maturity and the ability to put their plans into action. Still, these airy personalities are unrivaled in their idealism, enthusiasm, and freedom of spirit. They provide a breath of inspiration to their respective elements and suits, bringing in much-needed ideas and perspectives.

- The Knight of Pentacles tempers his airy nature with earthy realism. He is a dedicated workhorse, and if he is given a task, he will set his mind to it and not stop until it's done.
- The Knight of Swords is air upon air. He's full of thoughts and plans, but his head is stuck in the clouds. He can be absent-minded and bad at follow-through.
- The Knight of Cups brings airy idealism to the emotional Cups. He's a true romantic, a knight in shining armor who wants to live in a beautiful world of chivalry and gallantry.

- The Knight of Wands combines air's restlessness with fire's drive. He's a rebel and an adventurer, always looking for the next thrill and not afraid to get into a fight.

## Queens

Queens exercise authority in the court, but it's an indirect authority. As a woman, a Queen doesn't have the liberty of saying what she wants outright; instead, she has to come across as tactful, diplomatic, and understanding. Because of this, the Queens embody a receptive, reflective, adaptive nature characteristic of elemental water. They have a deep insight into other people—but that doesn't mean that they don't have their own inner lives. As with the sea, the Queens have an apparent stillness and placidity that conceals a surprising depth.

- The Queen of Pentacles combines water's nurturing nature with the fecundity of earth. She sets herself to the cultivation of her environment, delighting in making things thrive.
- The Queen of Swords uses watery intuition to direct her airy intellect. She is insightful and precise, a manager who weighs every detail and assesses people and situations scrupulously.
- The Queen of Cups is water at its most changeable. A chameleon who can adapt to any situation, she has an uncanny understanding of other people and knows how to be understood in turn.
- The Queen of Wands is watery depth met with fiery charisma. Charming and suave, she is a natural leader who draws loyalty and trust from those around her.

## Kings

What the King wants, he gets. Kings in tarot are powerful figures, people in positions of authority who are driven, commanding, and intense. They are connected to elemental fire through willpower, strength, and passion. They also have fiery appetites; because no one ever tells the King no, he is accustomed to having his own way, and Kings can become demanding and self-centered if they go unchecked. Nonetheless, Kings burn bright. They are the center of attention wherever they go, and while the intensity of their fiery personalities can be overwhelming at times, their dynamism is unmatched.

- The King of Pentacles has a fiery appetite for earthy material pleasures. He is prone to decadence and luxury, a sybarite who loves the finer things in life.

- The King of Swords brings fiery dominance to airy intellectual pursuits. A ruthless strategist, he calculates what resources are at his disposal and how to use them to achieve his ends.
- The King of Cups meets fire's authority with the gentleness of water. He is a counselor and a guide, someone who compassionately helps others find their way.
- The King of Wands is fire at its most forceful. He is energetic and powerful, the expert who knows exactly how good he is at what he does.

## The Elements in the Major Arcana

Finally, we can also find the four elements in the Major Arcana. The majors have their own unique symbolism, largely set apart from the suits of the Minor Arcana. Where the minors express the elemental themes we encounter in day-to-day life, the majors are designed with universal symbolism in mind. They're meant to transcend the everyday. Because of this, the Major Arcana cards don't correspond to the four elements the way that the minor suits do. However, they are not completely set apart. There are still some points of contact between the greater and lesser mysteries; because of this, there are four cards in the Major Arcana that are traditionally associated with the elements. These cards each have their own complex symbolism that's not restricted to their elemental correspondences, but they do connect to the fourfold division of the elements as well.

### Earth: The World

Which card could best represent elemental earth? It is, well, the World. It's the earth we stand on, the totality of our planet and our known material existence. Everything we can see, touch, and taste is encompassed by this card. Beyond its elemental significance, the World is a card of completion and fulfillment, representing the "happily ever after" achieved at the end of a successful quest. This meaning is enhanced by its elemental connection, as earth signifies abundance, prosperity, wealth, and fruitfulness.

### Air: The Fool

Air can go anywhere and do anything, much like the free-roaming Fool. The Fool has their head in the clouds, dreaming of the possibilities of things to come. However, they can be absentminded; if they neglect to pay attention to the path in front of them, they may end up inadvertently walking off a cliff. This combination of freedom, dreamy idealism, and impracticality is characteristic of elemental air. More broadly, the Fool represents unactualized potential: They *could* do everything, but they haven't actually done anything yet. The Fool is newness incarnate—much like a breath of fresh air.

## Water: The Hanged Man

At first glance, the Hanged Man may seem like a surprising card to connect to elemental water; in many decks, there isn't any water shown in the image of this card. But the Hanged Man is a card of introspection, reflection, and depth—all of which are characteristic of water. Confronted with suffering, the Hanged Man chooses to turn inward and make peace with his surroundings, going with the flow rather than fighting against the ties that bind him. In his adaptability, his search for emotional stillness, and his choice to follow the path of least resistance, the Hanged Man embodies the qualities of water. In this way, the elemental correspondence adds further depth to a card often associated with suffering, showing the wisdom waiting beneath the surface.

## Fire: Judgement

Judgement is a vibrant card of awakening and transformation, both of which are characteristic of elemental fire. Nothing goes through fire unchanged; wood burns and turns into smoke and charcoal, water boils and becomes steam, and even metal melts and is reforged. Fire is the element of transmutation and becoming, and nowhere in tarot are those features more apparent than in Judgement. This card depicts the dead coming back to life, awakened to a new existence where their old selves are left behind. It represents a sudden, radical act of transformation, and its connection to fire helps reinforce that symbolism even further.

chapter four
# The Zodiac

Astrology is one of the oldest and most pervasive systems in Western esotericism. Most people are familiar with sun sign astrology—the kind that you read about in your local newspaper's horoscope section—but may not know how intricate and sophisticated astrology can be. Astrologers use their craft not only to describe people's personalities, but also to predict events, to answer divinatory questions, to plan their activities, and even to change the world magically. Although the popular imagination tends to associate astrology with oversimplified platitudes like "I'm an Aries so I'm competitive," astrology as a discipline has an extraordinary amount of depth, complexity, and specificity.

Astrology is the art of tracking and interpreting the motions of particular celestial bodies. It relies on a familiar magical principle: the idea that everything is connected to everything else. The motions of the heavens are interrelated with events here on Earth. We may not see a direct, causal connection between them, but understanding the former can help us gain insight into the latter. This is similar to how tarot reading works, and it's unsurprising that tarot and astrology overlap with each other.

To understand the connections between astrology and tarot, first we have to understand the twelve signs of the Zodiac. These are the signs familiar from horoscope columns: Aries, Taurus, Gemini, and so on. Most people think of the Zodiac as a calendar of sorts, which divides the 365 days of the year into twelve roughly equal portions. Thus, the time between March 21 and April 19 is the "month" of Aries, between April 20 and May 20 is Taurus, and so on. Understood this way, the Zodiac carves up the months of the year in a way that's similar to—but slightly offset from—the Gregorian calendar. In reality, however, the Zodiac isn't a way of measuring time at all. Instead, it's a way of measuring space.

There's a lot of complicated geometry involved here, but here's the simple version: The Zodiac is an imaginary circle drawn around planet Earth. The twelve signs divide that circle into twelve equal segments. From the point of view of Earth, various celestial bodies appear to pass through these segments as they move across the sky. Over the course of a year, the sun appears to move through one sign of the Zodiac every month—hence, the common conception of the Zodiac as a sort of calendar—but other celestial bodies move at different speeds. In this way, the Zodiac lets us track the motion of objects through the sky relative to each other, to Earth, and to the fixed position of stars in outer space.

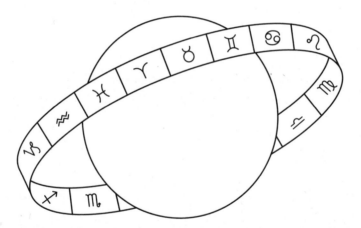

Each sign of the Zodiac is associated with a few key themes. These are familiar from the personality profiles you might read in your horoscope, but they have application beyond describing people's personalities, and they also align with the meanings of the tarot cards they correspond to. Before jumping into those correspondences, let's get a basic handle on what the twelve signs are and the different energies they represent.

## ♈ *Aries*

Aries is associated with new beginnings and raw power. Filled with a lust for life, this sign connects to direct action, competition, and drive. On the more negative side, Aries can also exemplify selfishness and aggression. The symbol of this sign is the ram.

## ♉ *Taurus*

The symbol of Taurus is the bull: steady, determined, and reliable. This sign is associated with patience, hard work, and resilience, as well as sensual comforts and material pleasures. Negatively, Taurus can sometimes represent stubbornness, dogma, and an unwillingness to embrace change.

## ♊ *Gemini*

Gemini—symbolized by a set of twins—is a sign of duality and changeability. Often associated with quickness, intelligence, and curiosity, Gemini has a dual nature and represents the reality that there are two sides to every situation. On the negative side, it can be connected with gossip or indecisiveness.

## ♋ *Cancer*

Cancer's symbol is the crab: hard on the outside, soft on the inside. This sign is associated with deep feelings, protectiveness, and nurturing. It represents both the challenges and the rewards of being emotionally vulnerable. It can also be associated with feeling too much and taking everything to heart.

## ♌ *Leo*

Leo is the lion, fierce and regal. It's a sign associated with charm, charisma, and being in the spotlight. Leo represents leadership and loyalty, but the other side of that coin is vanity and selfishness, and those are some of the negative things this sign can also represent.

## ♍ *Virgo*

Virgo is the sign of diligence, dedication, and attentiveness. It's connected to logic, problem-solving, and careful, systematic reasoning. Virgo is the sign most associated with meticulous work—but negatively, it can represent pedantry and condescension. The symbol of this sign is a young maiden.

### ♎ *Libra*

Libra is symbolized by a set of scales, and the key to this sign is a quest for equality, seeking justice, and moderating conflicts. It's further associated with the principles of balance that guide art and aesthetics. Negatively, it can represent equivocation and people-pleasing.

### ♏ *Scorpio*

Scorpio is never what it seems. It's a sign of hidden depth and complexity, associated with determination, intensity, and guardedness. Its symbol is the venomous scorpion, and it is intimately connected to the cycle of death and rebirth. Its mysterious nature can manifest negatively as manipulation or dishonesty.

### ♐ *Sagittarius*

Sagittarius is an adventurous sign associated with idealism, philosophy, and altruism. It also represents adventure and the need for freedom. Sagittarius is the most honest and direct of the signs, but it can also be too blunt or naive. Its symbol is a centaur holding a bow.

### ♑ *Capricorn*

Capricorn—the goat—is a reliable, down-to-earth sign. Connected with relentless practicality, professionalism, and realism, Capricorn represents seeing things as they are and choosing to face hard truths rather than running away from them. Negatively, it can be associated with pessimism or emotional indifference.

### ♒ *Aquarius*

Aquarius is associated with innovation, revolution, and invention. This is the sign of imagining a better world and refusing to be constrained by others' expectations. Negatively, its uniqueness and creativity can turn into rebelliousness and unpredictability. It is symbolized by a person holding jugs of water.

### ♓ *Pisces*

Pisces is a dreamy, imaginative, romantic sign and is symbolized by a pair of fish. Just like the boundless ocean, Pisces feels everything. Associated with empathy and artistic inspiration, Pisces is a sign of compassion and benevolence. Negatively, Pisces can represent poor boundaries and being easily overwhelmed.

# The Zodiac in the Major Arcana

Just as each of the four elements corresponds to a card in the Major Arcana, the twelve signs of the Zodiac appear in the majors as well. These astrological correspondences help us to understand the majors in a new light, and this can prove useful when they turn up in a reading. Here are the twelve zodiacal cards of the Major Arcana, with a brief overview of how each zodiacal correspondence affects the meaning of its given card.

### ♈ Aries: The Emperor

The Emperor is the ruler of the Major Arcana—brash, willful, and strong. He carries with him the forcefulness of Aries, but also its impetuousness. As someone who is used to getting his way, the Emperor doesn't always react well to obstacles, and his personality can become domineering.

### ♉ Taurus: The Hierophant

The Hierophant is a card of conservatism, tradition, and established wisdom. He is defined by Taurus's patient, careful dedication to tasks, as well as its stubborn unwillingness to embrace change. The Hierophant's wisdom is that it's often best to slow down and do things the right way.

### ♊ Gemini: The Lovers

The duality of Gemini is present in the two bodies of the Lovers. This card is sometimes associated with making a choice, letting Gemini's characteristic indecisiveness shine through. Its astrological connection emphasizes the importance of careful thought when we start to romanticize things as the Lovers tend to do.

### ♋ Cancer: The Chariot

The Chariot's driver wears armor to protect himself, much like the shell of a crab. The Chariot's motion and constant striving conceal a deep vulnerability: Is the Chariot driving toward something or running away? Cancer asks us to consider the emotional depths of the action we see in the Chariot.

### ♌ Leo: Strength

The maiden in the Strength card has the kind of easy grace and confidence associated with Leo. Her strength is not brute force, but Leo's exemplary character; she guides the lion to do her bidding not by commanding it, but by being the sort of person it wants to obey.

### ♍ *Virgo: The Hermit*

Virgo is the sign that does everything itself because it doesn't trust others to get the job done. Similarly, the Hermit isolates himself, seeking wisdom from within rather than drawing on community. Virgo's logical mind parallels the Hermit's quest for wisdom, but often at the cost of loneliness.

### ♎ *Libra: Justice*

Even-tempered and equanimous Libra finds expression in Justice, the card most concerned with equality and balance. Justice aims to treat everyone impartially, balancing truth on Libra's scales, but like Libra, it has to be careful to remember that what looks fair and what's really fair aren't always the same.

### ♏ *Scorpio: Death*

Death corresponds to Scorpio, the sign of death and rebirth. This is a frightening card for many, but just as with Scorpio, it contains hidden depths. The difficulty of releasing the past and allowing things to end is a core theme of Scorpio that manifests in the Death card.

### ♐ *Sagittarius: Temperance*

Temperance is a card of transmutation and becoming. It aligns with Sagittarius's idealism and its constant striving to remake itself as something newer and better. This card often depicts an angel, representing the higher self and the philosophical aspirations characteristic of Sagittarius.

### ♑ *Capricorn: The Devil*

The Devil points to materialism, addiction, and bondage. Here, we see Capricorn's pragmatism on full display: We have to confront unpleasant material realities directly rather than pretending they're not there. Capricorn tells us that the Devil has to be dealt with head-on.

### ♒ *Aquarius: The Star*

Much like Aquarius, the Star envisages a better world. She looks to the heavens above for inspiration about how to improve the world below. This card of healing and hope exemplifies Aquarius's refusal to settle for less than how things ought to be.

⊂ *Pisces: The Moon*

The Moon is the card of dreams and illusions. It corresponds to dreamy Pisces, which is guided by intuition and feeling rather than anything quantifiable that can be scrutinized in the cold light of day. Like Pisces, the Moon has to be wary not to let feelings surpass reality.

## Predicting Timing

One of my favorite uses for the Major Arcana's zodiacal correspondences is to predict when events are going to happen. This technique draws on the popular idea of the Zodiac as a calendar, with each sign corresponding to a period of roughly one month. Think about an event that you expect to happen sometime in the coming year, but you don't know exactly when. Now, set aside all of the deck except for the twelve zodiacal cards of the Major Arcana. Shuffle these twelve cards and draw one. This card tells you the month in which you can expect the event to happen.

The sun's apparent passage through the sky is slightly different from one year to the next, so the exact date ranges may vary by a day or two on either side, but the time periods associated with each card are roughly as follows:

- **The Emperor:** March 21–April 19
- **The Hierophant:** April 20–May 20
- **The Lovers:** May 21–June 21
- **The Chariot:** June 22–July 22
- **Strength:** July 23–August 22
- **The Hermit:** August 23–September 22
- **Justice:** September 23–October 23
- **Death:** October 24–November 21
- **Temperance:** November 22–December 21
- **The Devil:** December 22–January 19
- **The Star:** January 20–February 18
- **The Moon:** February 19–March 20

There are a variety of techniques for predicting timing with tarot, and each is suited to some contexts better than others. This technique works best with something that could genuinely happen at any time over the course of a year. If you're working with an event that has a much narrower or broader expected time frame—anything from a span of weeks to years—this will probably not be the most helpful way to figure out when that thing is going to happen.

Predicting timing is notoriously difficult with tarot; the future is often uncertain and liable to change, so it's hard to guarantee exactly when something will happen. However, in my own practice, I've had a good success rate using this technique to nail down a time frame within the span of a given year.

## Triplicity, Modality, and the Minor Arcana

The signs of the Zodiac don't exist in isolation. They're part of a cohesive, unified system, and each sign connects to the others in ways that add depth and meaning to its symbolism. Astrologers use a number of techniques to connect the signs to each other, but two of those techniques in particular will be important for us to understand tarot through an astrological lens. Those techniques are known as *triplicity* and *modality*.

Triplicity is a way of dividing the twelve signs of the Zodiac into four elemental groups. There are three signs given to each element, hence the name *triplicity*. Starting with Aries and working through to Pisces, the signs follow a fixed elemental order so that the four elements are equally distributed around the wheel of the Zodiac.

- Aries, Leo, and Sagittarius are fire signs.
- Taurus, Virgo, and Capricorn are earth signs.
- Gemini, Libra, and Aquarius are air signs.
- Cancer, Scorpio, and Pisces are water signs.

This helps us connect the signs to each other. Passionate Aries, charismatic Leo, and adventurous Sagittarius all have fiery qualities to them. Determined Taurus, meticulous Virgo, and realistic Capricorn share something earthy. Inquisitive Gemini, diplomatic Libra, and imaginative Aquarius are united by a common element of air. And finally, sensitive Cancer, mysterious Scorpio, and empathetic Pisces are manifestations of elemental water. In this way, we can see how some signs are alike and others are radically different; Libra and Aquarius have much more in common than Sagittarius and Cancer do. These connections will be particularly helpful to us once we start exploring the zodiacal correspondences of the tarot.

The second key technique for drawing connections between the signs is modality. This divides the Zodiac into four segments, each of which has a beginning, a middle, and an end.

The signs at the beginning of each segment are called *cardinal* and are associated with newness and initiative. The signs in the middle are called *fixed* and have connotations of solidity and stability. Finally, the signs at the end are called *mutable* and are associated with change and transformation.

- Aries, Cancer, Libra, and Capricorn are cardinal signs.
- Taurus, Leo, Scorpio, and Aquarius are fixed signs.
- Gemini, Virgo, Sagittarius, and Pisces are mutable signs.

Again, this shows us similarities and differences between certain signs. The cardinal signs all symbolize beginnings and things in their early stages—whether that's the youthful exuberance of Aries or Cancer's delicate emotional nurturing. The fixed signs all show things that are set and reliable, from Taurus's stubbornness to Aquarius's world-changing determination. The mutable signs all show things in evolution: Sagittarius constantly aspires to better itself, and Pisces is always changing in response to the people around it. Because of their shared modality, signs like Leo and Scorpio have something in common that Capricorn and Gemini do not.

|         | CARDINAL     | FIXED        | MUTABLE         |
|---------|--------------|--------------|-----------------|
| EARTH   | ♑ Capricorn  | ♉ Taurus     | ♍ Virgo         |
| AIR     | ♎ Libra      | ♒ Aquarius   | ♊ Gemini        |
| WATER   | ♋ Cancer     | ♏ Scorpio    | ♓ Pisces        |
| FIRE    | ♈ Aries      | ♌ Leo        | ♐ Sagittarius   |

Each sign is a unique combination of triplicity and modality. There is exactly one cardinal fire sign, one fixed earth sign, and so on. These qualities serve to unite the Zodiac signs—drawing connections between them so that we can find the things they have in common—and to differentiate them, marking each sign as unique.

Triplicity and modality are essential to understanding how the Zodiac shows up in the Minor Arcana. Through their elemental correspondences, the four minor suits correspond to the earth, air, water, and fire signs. Through their numbers, individual cards correspond to sections of the cardinal, fixed, and mutable signs. The Two, Three, and Four of each suit correspond to the cardinal signs; the Five, Six, and Seven correspond to the fixed signs; and the

Eight, Nine, and Ten correspond to the mutable signs. This creates links between three cards and one Zodiac sign:

- ♈ **Aries (Cardinal Fire):** Two, Three, and Four of Wands
- ♉ **Taurus (Fixed Earth):** Five, Six, and Seven of Pentacles
- ♊ **Gemini (Mutable Air):** Eight, Nine, and Ten of Swords
- ♋ **Cancer (Cardinal Water):** Two, Three, and Four of Cups
- ♌ **Leo (Fixed Fire):** Five, Six, and Seven of Wands
- ♍ **Virgo (Mutable Earth):** Eight, Nine, and Ten of Pentacles
- ♎ **Libra (Cardinal Air):** Two, Three, and Four of Swords
- ♏ **Scorpio (Fixed Water):** Five, Six, and Seven of Cups
- ♐ **Sagittarius (Mutable Fire):** Eight, Nine, and Ten of Wands
- ♑ **Capricorn (Cardinal Earth):** Two, Three, and Four of Pentacles
- ♒ **Aquarius (Fixed Air):** Five, Six, and Seven of Swords
- ♓ **Pisces (Mutable Water):** Eight, Nine, and Ten of Cups

That's not all, though. Each card corresponds to specific degrees of its given sign. Remember that the Zodiac is an imaginary circle drawn in space around planet Earth. One full rotation of this circle is 360 degrees, and it's divided up into twelve equal signs, each of which occupies a 30° slice of space. Those 30 degrees can be further divided into 10° segments known as *decans*. Each card corresponds to a particular decan: the first, middle, or last ten degrees of its sign.

|  | 0°–9° | 10°–19° | 20°–29° |
|---|---|---|---|
| ♈ ARIES | Two of Wands | Three of Wands | Four of Wands |
| ♉ TAURUS | Five of Pentacles | Six of Pentacles | Seven of Pentacles |
| ♊ GEMINI | Eight of Swords | Nine of Swords | Ten of Swords |
| ♋ CANCER | Two of Cups | Three of Cups | Four of Cups |
| ♌ LEO | Five of Wands | Six of Wands | Seven of Wands |
| ♍ VIRGO | Eight of Pentacles | Nine of Pentacles | Ten of Pentacles |

| | 0°–9° | 10°–19° | 20°–29° |
|---|---|---|---|
| ♎ LIBRA | Two of Swords | Three of Swords | Four of Swords |
| ♏ SCORPIO | Five of Cups | Six of Cups | Seven of Cups |
| ♐ SAGITTARIUS | Eight of Wands | Nine of Wands | Ten of Wands |
| ♑ CAPRICORN | Two of Pentacles | Three of Pentacles | Four of Pentacles |
| ♒ AQUARIUS | Five of Swords | Six of Swords | Seven of Swords |
| ♓ PISCES | Eight of Cups | Nine of Cups | Ten of Cups |

In this way, the Minor Arcana become a map of the whole Zodiac—and, by extension, of the heavens surrounding our planet. The tarot deck isn't just a tool for divination: It's a symbolic microcosm of the known universe. Working magically with the tarot deck allows us to bring the stars themselves down to Earth in order to learn from them and to benefit from their wisdom.

Now, that's all very poetic, but what does it mean in concrete terms? For one thing, you can use the zodiacal correspondences of the Minor Arcana for predictions involving timing, much like the technique described previously with the Major Arcana. Using the Minor Arcana this way will narrow your predictive range to a period of about ten days as opposed to a month—although, again, exact timing is notoriously difficult to predict with tarot. You may have to experiment with this method to see how well it works for you.

Zodiacal correspondences can also help us identify the predominant energy in a reading, which can help with interpretation. Consider the Crossroads spread on the previous page. The past, the problem, and the root source are all Sagittarius cards; together, they indicate that the querent's current problems are in part caused by overcommitment that stems from Sagittarius's need to do as much as possible. The advice and future cards, on the other hand, are Capricorn: They tell the querent to take a step back, realistically assess their situation, and move forward with a pragmatic understanding of their own limitations. In this way, zodiacal correspondences can help you see the major themes of a reading even before interpreting each card individually.

## Zodiac Spread

This is a tarot spread designed to use the symbolism of the twelve signs of the Zodiac in order to help you identify problem areas in your life. This spread is useful for introspective work, as it shows both your strengths and your weaknesses—it can open you up to the changes you need to make in your life.

1. Aries: What is your power?

2. Taurus: What are you committed to do?

3. Gemini: What are you curious about?

4. Cancer: What makes you vulnerable?

5. Leo: What example do you set for others?

6. Virgo: What do you pay attention to?

7. Libra: What are you bringing into balance?

8. Scorpio: What about you is not as it seems?

9. Sagittarius: What is your philosophy?

10. Capricorn: What is your reality?

11. Aquarius: What are you changing?

12. Pisces: What are your dreams?

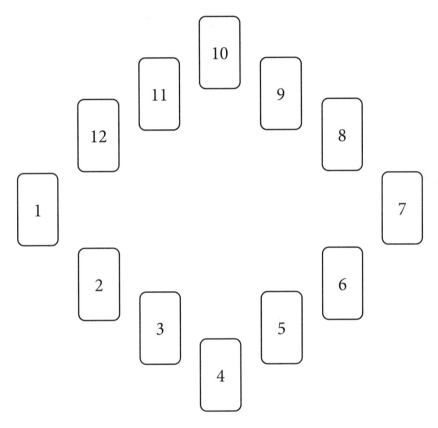

You can interpret this spread as a standalone twelve-card spread, but I'd encourage you to apply the zodiacal correspondences you've learned here. For each card position, look at the sign that is "officially" assigned to that position as well as the sign corresponding to the card you've drawn, if there is one. Are they the same? Are they different? What does that tell you about your reading? For example, if your first card—the Aries position—is the Three of Cups, that tells you that the seat of your power is found in sensitive Cancer. This is a very different message than if you had drawn a card associated with Leo or Aquarius instead.

# The Zodiacal Court Cards

Finally, we come to the court cards. Zodiacal correspondences are possibly most important with the court cards, because these cards typically represent people and personalities; the signs of the Zodiac are a helpful way of picking those personalities out and identifying the people involved in any particular situation. If you see a court card in your reading that signifies the influence of a third party, its zodiacal connections can help you identify the person in question. The astrological correspondences may indicate broad personality traits, or they may specifically represent a person with a particular sun sign.

The court cards are notoriously complex and may represent people based on various factors including age, occupation, personality, social status, and gender; keep in mind that zodiacal correspondences are one tool you can use to interpret these cards, but they should never be used at the expense of all the others. If you draw the Queen of Pentacles and think it represents your boss, but her sun sign doesn't align with the Queen's astrological correspondence, don't let the zodiacal mismatch prevent you from interpreting the card in the way that makes sense to you. Tarot is always an interpretive art, and correspondences like these are meant to facilitate and guide your intuition—not to supplant it. Use these correspondences when they're helpful, but don't feel beholden to them when they're not.

As with the numbered cards of the Minor Arcana, the court cards have zodiacal correspondences based on triplicity and modality. Thus, the Wands represent the fire signs, Pentacles are the earth signs, Swords are the air signs, and Cups are the water signs. The Queens are cardinal, the Knights are fixed, and the Kings are mutable. The Pages are set apart and have no astrological correspondences, much like the Aces. This arrangement gives the following set of zodiacal correspondences to the court cards.

### ♈ Aries: Queen of Wands

The passionate, dynamic Queen of Wands has the energy and drive of Aries. She fully engages with everything she does and wins others over with her enthusiasm, but she has to be careful not to let that enthusiasm fizzle out if her eye is drawn by something new.

### ♉ Taurus: Knight of Pentacles

No card embodies the persistence and work ethic of Taurus better than the patient Knight of Pentacles. Although his devotion can become bullheadedness, there is no one more willing to roll up their sleeves and get to work; the Knight embodies Taurus's quiet sense of commitment.

### ♊ *Gemini: King of Swords*

The King of Swords is intellectual, analytical, and strategic; like Gemini, he looks at problems from every angle, trying to understand the pros and cons of every situation. This strategic mindset makes him a successful problem-solver, but it can sometimes appear as a coldness toward others' emotional needs.

### ♋ *Cancer: Queen of Cups*

The Queen of Cups corresponds to sensitive, gentle Cancer. With a deep insight into what people feel, even when they don't say it out loud, the Queen understands things that few others do. This sensitivity cuts both ways, however, and she can be easily hurt by those she trusts.

### ♌ *Leo: Knight of Wands*

The Knight of Wands possesses Leo's bright, easy charm. The most outgoing of the Knights, he chooses his own path rather than being led by others—but this can also lead to rebelliousness and an insistence on always being the one in charge.

### ♍ *Virgo: King of Pentacles*

The King of Pentacles makes the most out of everything in his life, keeping his checkbook balanced and his coffers full. He is endowed with Virgo's exhaustive attention to detail but can also be persnickety at times. He gets upset if things aren't exactly the way he likes them.

### ♎ *Libra: Queen of Swords*

The Queen of Swords is a champion of equality for herself and for those around her. She gives freely but expects just as much from others, a quality characteristic of Libra. Although she is always fair, her sense of fairness can clash with her desire to be well-thought-of.

### ♏ *Scorpio: Knight of Cups*

The Knight of Cups is a true Prince Charming who is easy to love but contains hidden complexities. People project a fantasy onto the Knight, much as they do with Scorpio, and it can be hard for the individual to live up to the image in someone else's head.

### ♐ *Sagittarius: King of Wands*

The King of Wands has the nobility, honesty, and higher aspirations of Sagittarius. These lofty goals sometimes get the better of him, and he can get holier-than-thou if left unchecked, but he truly means well and aspires to make himself and others the best they can possibly be.

### ♑ *Capricorn: Queen of Pentacles*

The Queen of Pentacles is a caretaker defined by Capricorn's pragmatism. She cares about what people need, but she doesn't hesitate to ignore what they want. She is trustworthy and reliable, but she often gives advice that people don't want to take even when they know they should.

### ♒ *Aquarius: Knight of Swords*

The Knight of Swords possesses Aquarius's love of abstractions. No one is better at dreaming up plans for things that have never been tried before. However, the Knight's head can sometimes get lost in the clouds, and he needs others to bring him back down to earth.

### ♓ *Pisces: King of Cups*

The King of Cups is a confidant who feels his friends' problems as if they were his own. Blessed with Pisces's boundless empathy, he is sincere and caring, but he struggles to maintain boundaries and to hold on to a part of himself that is not given over to anyone else.

*chapter five*
# The Planets

Now that we understand the Zodiac and its connection to tarot, we can turn our attention to the other building block of astrology: the planets. In contemporary astronomy, a planet is defined as a large body that occupies a fixed elliptical orbit around a star; in our own solar system, there are eight planets ranging from Mercury to Neptune (and excluding the beleaguered Pluto). Originally, however, the word *planet* had a slightly different meaning. It derives from the Greek *planēt-*, meaning "wanderer."[11] In contrast with the fixed stars that make up the Zodiac, planets were originally understood to be the wandering stars: the heavenly bodies that appear to move across the sky in a consistent and predictable path. This is the definition that is still used by astrologers today.

Because of this difference in definitions, the planets in astrology are not exactly the same as the ones you know from astronomy. There is overlap, to be sure, but the astrological definition of a planet also includes the sun and the moon, neither of which would be considered a planet by contemporary astronomers. Classical astrology, which predates the invention of the telescope and the discovery of our solar system's outer reaches, only counts the planets that can be seen with the naked eye, so outer planets like Uranus and Neptune are left off the list. And

---

11. *Merriam-Webster Dictionary*, "planet," accessed January 2, 2025, https://www.merriam-webster.com /dictionary/planet.

finally, Earth itself doesn't count as a planet in astrology, because when we look up at the sky, Earth is below us—it's not one of the celestial bodies we see in the heavens above.

As a result, there are seven planets in classical astrology: the sun, the moon, Mercury, Venus, Mars, Jupiter, and Saturn. These are the seven wandering stars that can be seen with the naked eye. Many contemporary astrologers have incorporated Uranus, Neptune, and Pluto into their work as well, along with smaller celestial bodies like asteroids and comets, but those bodies can only be seen with the aid of a telescope, and their use in astrology is a modern innovation. For the purposes of this book, I'm going to stick with the classical seven planets.

The seven classical planets are essential to astrology, but we also find them in tarot. The planets help to structure and organize the tarot deck, much like the four elements and the signs of the Zodiac. Each of the planets is associated with particular themes, topics, and areas of life. In an astrological reading, those themes are shown by the planets' positions relative to each other and to Earth. In tarot, we can identify the same themes in the cards. Tarot is structured according to a set of planetary correspondences, which—just like the elemental correspondences—add depth and nuance to the meanings of the cards. Seeing tarot through a planetary lens provides you with a new set of tools for interpreting readings as well as a better grasp of how the deck fits together as a whole.

## The Planets

Before we can talk about the specifics of planetary correspondences within the tarot deck, we need to have a better understanding of the planets themselves. It's useful to think of astrology as a storytelling medium where the planets are the characters and the signs are the environment. The planets are the ones acting, interacting, and reacting; the signs are their background and the circumstances they're reacting to.

The symbolism of the planets connects with observable astronomical facts about them, but also with history and mythology. For example, five of the planets are named after deities in the Roman pantheon, and by identifying those deities, we get much clearer insight into what these planets are all about.

One useful tool for doing this is the doctrine of *rulership* and *exaltation*. Although each of the planets moves through all twelve signs of the Zodiac at its own speed, there are certain signs where each planet is considered more or less comfortable. These signs can tell us a great deal about a planet, and they can help us identify its core themes and imagery.

Every planet has one or two signs of rulership; these are the signs of the Zodiac with themes most closely aligned with the planet, and they're where the planet is considered most at home.

Additionally, every planet has a sign of exaltation: This is not its home, but rather a beloved vacation spot where the planet can really shine. Conversely, each planet also has signs of *detriment* and *fall*, where it is uncomfortable and out of its element.

By identifying these key components, we can get a clear understanding of the unique themes of each of the seven classical planets.

## ☉ *The Sun*

The sun is the brightest and most visible planet in the sky. It is of central importance to human life, providing us with light and warmth, nourishing crops, and guiding the change of the seasons. As such, it corresponds astrologically to topics of the greatest importance: daytime, the known world, conviction, illumination, power, logic, absolute truth, and the self. The sun is responsible for maintaining harmony and balance; without it, our whole solar system would fall apart.

Psychologically, the sun represents the ego, a person's core consciousness. This is why in popular astrology, people ask "What's your sign?" when referring to the sign of the Zodiac that the sun was in at the time of birth. The sun is representative of our most basic self, the foundation upon which the rest of our psychological complexities are built.

The sun's sign of rulership is Leo, and the sun embodies Leo's confidence and exuberance. The sun's exaltation is Aries, which contributes energy and raw power. The sun's signs of detriment and fall are Aquarius and Libra, respectively; this planet is uncomfortable with Aquarius's off-kilter energy and Libra's uncertainty and equivocation.

## ☽ *The Moon*

Whereas the sun is the conscious, rational self, the moon represents the unconscious, emotional self. Intuition, dreams, psychism, and emotion are all the providence of the moon. It rules over divination, magic, nighttime, the physical body, changeability, and mystery. The moon waxes and wanes in a perpetual monthly cycle and is therefore associated with all cyclical things. The ebb and flow of the tides is caused by the moon's gravity, establishing a symbolic connection between the moon and the mysterious depths of the sea. The moon is also commonly associated with motherhood, menstruation, and reproduction.

Psychologically, the moon is the unconscious mind. Of all the planets, the moon appears to move the fastest as it progresses through the Zodiac; it is highly changeable, just as our moods are. Two people can be born on the same day and still have different moon signs. Emotional differences run deep and may be present even when people seem similar on the surface.

The moon rules over the sensitive sign of Cancer and is exalted in luxuriant Taurus. However, it is in detriment under Capricorn's cold practicality, and its constantly changing nature is in fall under Scorpio's fixed intensity.

## ☿ Mercury

Mercury is named after the Roman god of knowledge, science, commerce, travel, and thievery, and it takes all of these qualities from its namesake. This planet rules over the intellect, communication of all kinds, technology, invention, voyages, money, and deception. Mercury is quick-thinking and quick-acting, but also volatile and indecisive. Psychologically, Mercury is the intellect.

In the Zodiac, Mercury rules two signs: double-minded Gemini and detail-oriented Virgo. Its connection with Virgo is doubled, as this is its sign of exaltation as well as its rulership. However, Mercury's intellectual and sometimes duplicitous nature is in detriment in honest Sagittarius and emotional Pisces—and again, the negative connection to Pisces is doubled, as this is also Mercury's sign of fall.

## ♀ Venus

In Roman mythology, Venus is the goddess of love and beauty, and these are the chief associations of this planet. Venus rules over everything beautiful and sensual: love, sex, art, music, design, glamor, friendship, and affection. All aesthetics fall under its domain, as do the things we indulge in simply for the sake of pleasure. Everything lavish, dazzling, and ornamental belongs to this planet.

Venus's signs of rulership are Taurus, with its love of material pleasures, and Libra, with its aesthetic eye for balance. It is exalted in Pisces, where it can express overflowing and abundant love. Conversely, its signs of detriment are unforgiving Scorpio and brash Aries, and its sign of fall is pedantic Virgo.

## ♂ Mars

Mars is the Roman god of war, and this planet lives up to its namesake. Astrologically, Mars is the planet of conflict, aggression, anger, strife, spite, war, destruction, division, and violence. It's not all bad—Mars can also represent vitality, power, and discipline—but conflict is at this planet's core, and those negative qualities are an inescapable part of what Mars represents.

It is unsurprising, then, that Mars has rulership over Aries and Scorpio. Aries is the sign of raw power; Scorpio is the sign of strength. Furthermore, Mars is exalted in ruthless Capricorn.

Its signs of detriment are diplomatic Libra and unshakable Taurus, and the vulnerability of Cancer makes that sign Mars's fall.

## ♃ *Jupiter*

In the Roman pantheon, Jupiter is the king of the gods. This translates to astrology, where Jupiter is the planet of kings. This planet signifies political power, ascendancy, and leadership. It also represents the things associated with kings, in reality or as an ideal: luxury, wealth, comfort, stability, generosity, justice, prodigiousness, charity, and compassion. Jupiter is the planet of all good things, and it's associated with fortune, luck, and beneficence.

Jupiter's qualities of idealism and empathy are easily seen in Sagittarius and Pisces, the signs of its rulership. It's exalted in Cancer, the kindest and gentlest of the signs. However, Jupiter's abundance doesn't do well everywhere. Gemini is inconstant, and Virgo is too focused on small details, making them Jupiter's signs of detriment. Meanwhile, Capricorn is restrictive and disciplined; as such, the lavish king of the planets is in fall in this sign.

## ♄ *Saturn*

Saturn is named after the Roman god who ate his own children. As such, it's a rather fearsome planet, associated with misfortune, disease, restriction, limitation, labor, suffering, imprisonment, malediction, and death. Like Mars, this planet is not all bad; it is also connected to hard work, physical accomplishment, agriculture, measurement, and containment. Nonetheless, its reputation is primarily malefic, and Saturn is most known for its binding and constricting qualities.

Saturn rules over Capricorn and Aquarius. Capricorn is more willing than any other sign to reckon with the limitations imposed by the world; Aquarius casts off those limitations, but imposes its own narrow view of how things should be. Saturn is exalted in Libra, the sign of measuring and apportioning. It is in detriment in gentle Cancer and optimistic Leo, and it is in fall in undisciplined Aries.

## Seven Planets Spread

The planets govern seven distinct areas of life. Much like the Zodiac, they can be used as the basis for a tarot spread that provides a snapshot of your (or your querent's) life at a given moment. The following spread can be useful if you want to look at a given issue from all angles, or even if you don't know specifically what you want to ask about and are just looking for a general "How do things look?" reading.

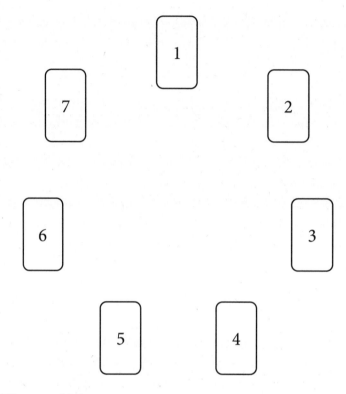

1. The Sun: The central issue

2. The Moon: How you feel about the issue

3. Mercury: What you think about the issue

4. Venus: A source of comfort and pleasure

5. Mars: A source of conflict and difficulty

6. Jupiter: What's working in your favor

7. Saturn: What's working against you

## The Planets in the Major Arcana

Just like the elements and the Zodiac, the planets appear in the Major Arcana. Of the twenty-two cards in the Major Arcana, four correspond to the elements and twelve correspond to the signs; that leaves six cards remaining that haven't got any correspondences yet. These connect to six of the seven planets. For the seventh planet, one card has to do double duty, corresponding to both a planet and an element. In this way, the twenty-two Major Arcana encompass the elements, signs, and planets altogether, which form the foundation of Western esotericism. The majors of the tarot deck are a symbolic microcosm of everything you need in order to do magic in the Western tradition.

### ☉ The Sun: The Sun

In perhaps the most obvious correspondence of all, the Sun in tarot corresponds to the sun in astrology. As a tarot card, the Sun represents truth, illumination, and the conscious mind; as a planet, it does the same. Wherever the Sun card shows up, it draws our attention and helps to shed literal and metaphorical light on the things surrounding it, making problems easier to understand and address. Both the card and the planet provide clarity and knowledge. It's important to be careful with the Sun, however; its light can be harsh and blinding, and sometimes it shows us truths that we might have preferred not to see.

### ☽ The Moon: The High Priestess

Like the moon, the High Priestess is the guardian of deeper secrets that are hidden from the conscious mind. She sits in front of a veil concealing the inner sanctum; the seeker can't know what lies behind that veil until after they have passed through it and experienced its mysteries for themselves. The High Priestess is a card of intuition and wisdom, the keeper of deep spiritual insights that can never be properly explained in the clear light of day. She is also the card of initiation, rebirth, and becoming something new—just as the moon is constantly reborn in its monthly cycle. Like the moon, the High Priestess encourages us to quiet the conscious mind and look inward for answers.

### ☿ Mercury: The Magician

Quick-witted Mercury finds itself in the Magician, the card of wonder-workers and hucksters alike. The Magician brings change through the application of his intellect and his will. He transforms himself and the things around him, changing as quickly and as easily as Mercury itself. Moreover, the Magician has a dual nature; while he is genuinely capable of miracles and magic, he is not above cheap tricks and deception. Mercury is the planet of liars, smooth talkers, and con men, all of which can also be represented by the Magician. Therefore, this card embodies both aspects of Mercury's nature: the miracle of transformation accomplished by a sharp mind, and the dangers of deception and duplicity.

### ♀ *Venus: The Empress*

The Empress lives in luxury, and as such she is associated with Venus, the planet of pleasure. The Empress is a warm, nurturing, generous figure; she embodies Venus by offering care, joy, and beauty to the people who encounter her. Although this card is not commonly associated with romantic love (the main theme people think of in connection with Venus), it represents the pleasure and beauty with which Venus likes to surround itself. If you are living an abundant, graceful life where you can enjoy art and the company of the people you love, you have been touched by Venus and the Empress alike. The Empress is one of the most propitious cards in the deck, shining with the benefic qualities of this planet.

### ♂ *Mars: The Tower*

The catastrophic Tower corresponds to Mars, the planet of strife and conflict. It's an unfortunate reality of life that sometimes things fall apart or blow up in our faces. Conflict is inevitable; often, the question before us is not how to prevent bad things from happening, but how to deal with them when they do. The Tower, like Mars, is unflinching in its message: It tells us that things have gone wrong and there is a problem that must be addressed. The only way to solve this problem is to face it directly, and the Tower instructs us to take on Mars's courage and strength. Mars brings problems our way, but it also gives us the power we need to confront those problems and rebuild from the rubble of the fallen Tower.

### ♃ *Jupiter: Wheel of Fortune*

One of Jupiter's chief associations is with luck, chance, and turns of fortune. The card that represents these themes *par excellence* is, of course, the Wheel of Fortune itself, which makes paupers into kings. Although the Wheel of Fortune does not only represent good luck—it turns kings into paupers just as easily—it still has a close connection with the planet of kingship and divine favor. The Wheel of Fortune reminds us that not everything is in our control, and sometimes the best we can do is to hope the winds of chance blow in our direction. Handing ourselves over to fate and hoping for the best means putting ourselves in the power of Jupiter, the planet that bestows divine gifts.

### ♄ *Saturn: The World*

Finally, we come to the World. This card does double duty in the Major Arcana; in addition to elemental earth, it corresponds to Saturn, the planet of limitation, constriction, and physical embodiment. At first, this correspondence may seem counterintuitive; the World is generally a positive card, and Saturn is often viewed as an unfriendly planet. It is helpful to remember, however, that the World is a card of endings. It brings the cycle of the Major Arcana to its natural close, allowing one thing to end so that another may begin. In this sense, it carries with it the serious nature of Saturn and the heavy responsibility of endings. This is a hefty card, and it is through the correspondence with Saturn that we can truly understand what it means to have the weight of the World on our shoulders.

## Tarot and Your Birth Chart

I first learned astrology through its correspondences to tarot. I found that my prior knowledge of the tarot deck made it easier for me to understand the planets and the signs, as I could connect them to the themes I already knew from my divinatory practice. I know others who have gone in the opposite direction, starting from a familiarity with astrology and using that knowledge as a point of access for tarot. In either case, the astrological connections in the tarot deck can help you leverage your familiarity with one subject as a way of getting more comfortable with the other.

Listing the astrological correspondences of the deck is a good starting point, but in order to properly understand these correspondences, you ought to put them into practice. I've found that one of the best ways to do this is by applying the correspondences of the tarot deck to your own astrological birth chart.

Your birth chart is a diagram of the position of the planets at the exact time and place of your birth: a snapshot of the heavens when you were born. By interpreting this chart, astrologers can tell you things about the circumstances of your life, your personality, and even when certain events are likely to happen for you. Through the astrological correspondences of the tarot deck, you can draw up something analogous: a tarot reading that is specific to you and to the astrological circumstances of your birth.

To do this, you'll need to start by obtaining a copy of your birth chart. Any astrologer will be able to do this for you, as will a variety of free apps or websites. Some of the more popular resources available include the websites astro.com and astro-seek.com, as well as the apps TimePassages, CHANI, and The Pattern. Using whatever resource you choose, input the exact date, time, and location of your birth in order to pull up your natal chart.

As a hypothetical example to illustrate how this process works, imagine someone named Javier was born in Fort Worth, Texas, at 9:19 a.m. on January 14, 1988. Javier's birth chart would look like this:

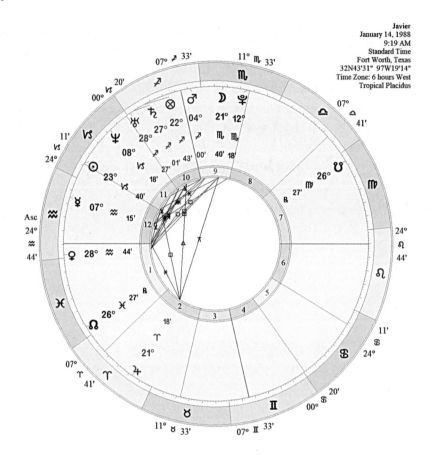

*Javier*
January 14, 1988
9:19 AM
Standard Time
Fort Worth, Texas
32N43'31" 97W19'14"
Time Zone: 6 hours West
Tropical Placidus

If you're new to astrology, a chart like this can look intimidating, but don't worry. You can break it down and focus only on certain relevant parts of it while using tarot as your guide. The first thing you need to do is find the degree of the Ascendant. This is the point in the Zodiac that was on the eastern horizon at the time and place of your birth; it's on the left-hand side of the chart, and it is marked with the letters *Asc*. In Javier's case, his Ascendant is 24 degrees into the sign of Aquarius.

Find the card in the Minor Arcana that corresponds to the section of the Zodiac where your Ascendant is located. (Refer to the chart in chapter 4 for guidance.) Pull this card out of your deck and set it on the far left-hand side of your reading space. For Javier, this is the Seven of Swords, which corresponds to the final 10 degrees of Aquarius.

Now, going counterclockwise around your reading space, lay out the rest of the zodiacal Minor Arcana in sequence. The final result should be a thirty-six-card circle. For Javier, the next cards would be the Eight through Ten of Cups (corresponding to Pisces), the Two through Four of Wands (corresponding to Aries), and so on.

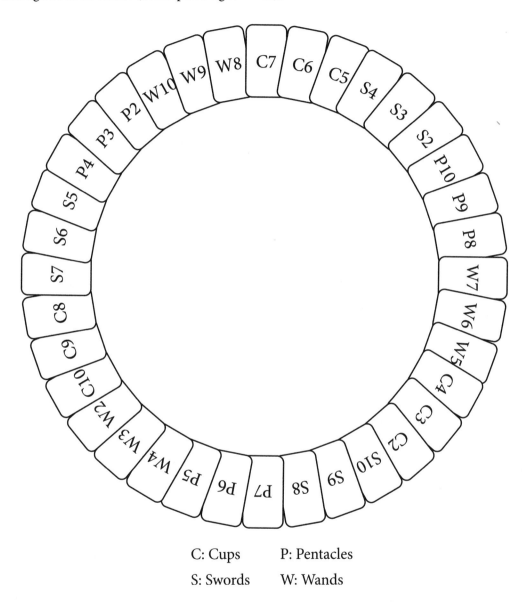

C: Cups     P: Pentacles

S: Swords    W: Wands

Once you've laid out the Zodiac for your birth chart, you need to fill it with the planets. Start with the sun. Look at your birth chart and take note of where the sun was placed in the Zodiac at the time of your birth. Now, find the Sun card in your deck and place it on your reading space, next to (or on top of) the card corresponding to that section of the Zodiac. Javier was born with the sun 23 degrees into the sign of Capricorn, so for him, we'll put the Sun card on top of the Four of Pentacles.

Now do the same with the remaining planetary cards of the Major Arcana, until you have placed all seven planets in the chart. Javier's completed chart would look like this:

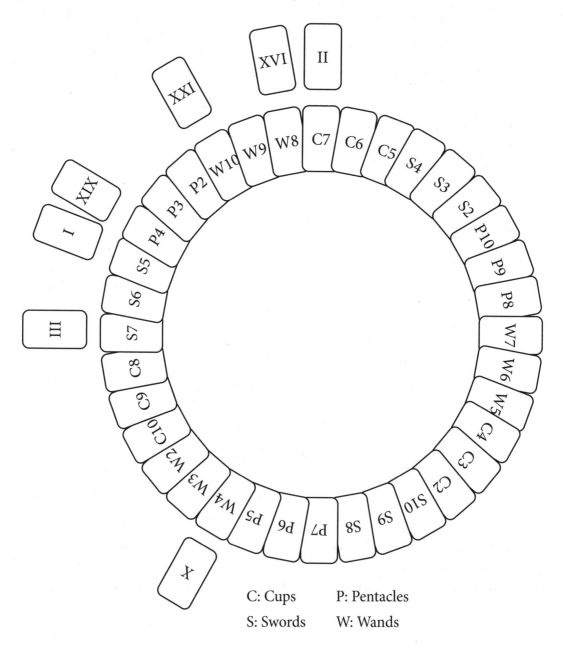

C: Cups        P: Pentacles

S: Swords      W: Wands

The spread on the previous page is Javier's natal chart translated into tarot; it's a snapshot of the sky at the time and place of Javier's birth, but using the symbolic language of tarot to express its central themes. Likewise, the spread that you generate using your own birth chart is an expression of who you are; it describes you specifically, based on the unique circumstances of your birth. Interpreting this tarot spread can give you fodder for introspection, reflection, and a deeper understanding of yourself in a way that is personalized and specific to the arc of your life.

In this spread, each major card is placed next to a card from the Minor Arcana; it is even possible for two or more majors to be next to the same minor card. The majors identify different areas of your life, and the minors next to them indicate the themes that are most important in each of those areas. Broadly speaking, the seven planetary cards represent:

1. The Sun: The central focus of your life

2. The High Priestess: Your emotions

3. The Magician: Your intellect

4. The Empress: Your relationships with others

5. The Tower: Your struggles

6. Wheel of Fortune: Your material circumstances

7. The World: Your limitations

This gives you a map of the key themes you can focus on in your life.
To wrap up our example, let's take a quick look at Javier's reading.

1. The Sun is next to the Four of Pentacles. A central concern in his life is the desire for stability and security.

2. The High Priestess is placed next to the Seven of Cups. Javier is a dreamer who fantasizes about the life he doesn't have.

3. The Magician is next to the Five of Swords. Words are a weapon for Javier, and he uses his intellect to cut down his competition.

4. The Empress is next to the Seven of Swords. Javier has difficulty trusting others and is always on guard against dishonesty and deceit.

5. The Tower is next to the Eight of Wands. Because Javier is so invested in stability, it is difficult for him to embrace rapid change.

6. Wheel of Fortune is next to the Four of Wands. Javier's material life is generally comfortable, and he has a great deal to be thankful for.

7. The World is next to the Ten of Wands. Javier can overcommit himself and take on too much work, and his chief obstacle is that he cannot do everything at once.

This description isn't just a static report on who Javier is; it also provides a guide for how he can look inward and do the inner work it takes to grow as a person. Seeing the Eight and Ten of Wands as problem areas in his life, Javier could start to think about how to address those problems. Seeing the Five of Swords in a prominent position, he could be more attentive to how he uses his words so that he doesn't inflict unintended harm on others. In this way, the birth chart reading provides guidance for who Javier is and for who he could choose to become.

Take a look at your own birth chart reading, and make note of the Minor Arcana cards associated with each of your seven planetary placements. What do these cards have to say about your life? How do they align with—or differ from—the impression you currently have of yourself? What practical advice might you take away from these cards as you think about how you want to live?

## Planets in the Minor Arcana

The final set of planetary correspondences in tarot is found in the Minor Arcana. To understand these correspondences, first you need to know about something called the *Chaldean order* of the planets. This is the order of the planets according to the apparent speed by which they move across the sky, from fastest to slowest. The fastest planet is the moon, which traverses the whole of the Zodiac in less than a month; the slowest is Saturn, which takes approximately twenty-eight years to complete a circuit through the signs. The full Chaldean order of the planets is: the moon, Mercury, Venus, the sun, Mars, Jupiter, and finally Saturn. This order structures the planetary correspondences of the Minor Arcana in the tarot deck. Each minor card with a zodiacal correspondence also has a planetary one, and those planetary correspondences are based on the Chaldean order.

We start with the Two of Wands. As the beginning of Aries, this card kicks off the sequence of the Zodiac, so it makes for a natural starting point. The planet associated with this card is

Mars, the ruler of the sign of Aries. From there, a planet is assigned to each card in the zodiacal sequence, working *backward* through the Chaldean order. That is to say, the next card is assigned to the sun, the card after that is assigned to Venus, and so on through the rest of the cards.

| ♂ MARS | ☉ THE SUN | ♀ VENUS | ☿ MERCURY | ☽ THE MOON | ♄ SATURN | ♃ JUPITER |
|---|---|---|---|---|---|---|
| Two of Wands | Three of Wands | Four of Wands | Five of Pentacles | Six of Pentacles | Seven of Pentacles | Eight of Swords |
| Nine of Swords | Ten of Swords | Two of Cups | Three of Cups | Four of Cups | Five of Wands | Six of Wands |
| Seven of Wands | Eight of Pentacles | Nine of Pentacles | Ten of Pentacles | Two of Swords | Three of Swords | Four of Swords |
| Five of Cups | Six of Cups | Seven of Cups | Eight of Wands | Nine of Wands | Ten of Wands | Two of Pentacles |
| Three of Pentacles | Four of Pentacles | Five of Swords | Six of Swords | Seven of Swords | Eight of Cups | Nine of Cups |
| Ten of Cups | — | — | — | — | — | — |

This schema allows us to map the thirty-six zodiacal cards in the Minor Arcana to the seven planets. As with the other correspondences in the deck, these planetary associations help to elucidate the themes of each card and to show connections between the cards that might not otherwise have been immediately apparent. If you do a three-card reading and draw the Two of Wands, the Ten of Cups, and the Three of Pentacles, your reading is dominated by the aggressive energy of Mars—highlighting potential conflicts in a way that you might not notice if you didn't pay attention to that planetary connection.

Each planet provides a common theme that unites the various cards corresponding to it. Those cards, in turn, offer variegated perspectives on that theme, exploring it through different lenses. By looking at all of a planet's cards together, you can gain a deep understanding of how they relate to each other as well as to the planet itself.

## ♂ *Mars*

The Mars cards all deal with conflict in some way. They're not all negative cards. Many of them express themes of overcoming or resolving conflict, and the question of how we face difficulties is present in all of these cards.

- The Two of Wands is the willpower required to solve a problem.
- The Nine of Swords is the card of anxiety, sleeplessness, and anguish.
- The Seven of Wands encourages perseverance in the face of adversity.
- The Five of Cups represents grief and prolonged suffering.
- The Three of Pentacles overcomes obstacles through teamwork and collaboration.
- The Ten of Cups is the resolution of conflict through love and community.

## ☉ *The Sun*

The solar cards are all concerned with culmination, completion, and fruition in some way. This can be good or bad—a happily ever after or an unpleasant comeuppance—but the sun shows us things building to a natural conclusion of some kind.

- The Three of Wands shows the early payoff of a well-executed plan.
- The Ten of Swords is a calamity and a betrayal as things end in the worst possible way.
- The Eight of Pentacles puts in study and hard work to achieve a happy outcome.
- The Six of Cups reflects back on a happy past that has come to an end.
- The Four of Pentacles believes it has achieved the most it can hope for and holds tightly to what it has.

## ♀ *Venus*

Venus's cards express themes related to love, companionship, and pleasure. Some of these (such as the Two of Cups) are obviously Venusian and about romantic or sexual desire; others are more oblique, dealing with themes of comfort, aesthetics, or enjoyment.

- The Four of Wands is a celebration of community and gratitude.
- The Two of Cups represents partnership and romantic love.
- The Nine of Pentacles is the enjoyment of luxury and ease.

- The Seven of Cups is what we wish for and fantasize about.
- The Five of Swords shows the way in which desire can hurt and undermine us.

## ☿ *Mercury*

Mercurial cards deal with change, often in big, rapid, and dramatic ways. Mercury is constantly adapting and never rests in one state for long. Because of its association with commerce, this planet's cards also often connect to themes of money, which changes hands frequently and is always coming and going—much like the planet itself.

- The Five of Pentacles shows the changes that bring loss and misfortune.
- The Three of Cups is the celebration of things changing for the better.
- The Ten of Pentacles is a sudden windfall and change in material circumstances.
- The Eight of Wands is the card of swiftness and motion toward something new.
- The Six of Swords is a personal change of perspective.

## ☽ *The Moon*

The lunar cards express themes that deal with emotional vulnerability and needing help. Whether by facing our own vulnerability or coming up against the vulnerability of others, the moon forces us to confront the softness and the emotional needs that all human beings have.

- The Six of Pentacles is about charity and meeting the material needs of others.
- The Four of Cups represents stagnation, sadness, and a feeling of being stuck.
- The Two of Swords is indecisiveness and uncertainty of oneself.
- The Nine of Wands is how we feel when we are worn down and need a respite.
- The Seven of Swords is the desire to dissemble and cover up our deeper feelings.

## ♄ *Saturn*

The Saturn cards all represent difficulty, often in conjunction with a sense of duty. These are hard cards, cards of work and obligation—and while obligation is not always a negative thing, it is never easy. The Saturn cards demand that we do the things that must be done, even when they aren't comfortable.

- The Seven of Pentacles represents hard work and toil requiring patience.
- The Five of Wands represents competition and the need to overcome.

- The Three of Swords is a card of pain, suffering, and heartbreak.
- The Ten of Wands is about being overburdened and overtaxed.
- The Eight of Cups represents setting down a burden and choosing to walk away.

## ♃ *Jupiter*

The Jupiter cards deal with the theme of success. Whether it's success achieved or success denied, whether it is exactly what we had hoped for or somehow looks different than what we had expected, success is at the heart of Jupiter and its connection to the Minor Arcana. These cards invite us to consider what accomplishment really looks like.

- The Eight of Swords presents blockages to success, which often come from our own self-doubt.
- The Six of Wands is the card of crowning victory.
- The Four of Swords is about respite and rest, a ceasefire rather than a decisive victory.
- The Two of Pentacles represents bringing things into balance.
- The Nine of Cups symbolizes joy and emotional fulfillment.

Some of the correspondences detailed in the previous chapters may have seemed a bit obscure; I presented each card and its various elemental and astrological connections, but why should certain cards have these connections and not others? Why does the astrological moon correspond to the High Priestess and not the Moon card? Why does the Hanged Man correspond to elemental water? Couldn't there be other ways to assign these correspondences, which might in some instances be more intuitive?

The answer is that all of these correspondences were developed within the context of a larger system called Qabalah. This system—used by the Hermetic Order of the Golden Dawn—sought to unite all the disparate components of Western mysticism, including the elements, astrology, alchemy, and ceremonial magic. The Golden Dawn aimed to create a single unified system for all magic so that their astrological practices would relate to their evocation of angels, to their personal meditative work, and to everything else they did. They used the tarot deck as a touchstone for all these correspondences, embedding their complex metaphysical worldview into the symbolic structure of the tarot.

The Qabalah used by the Golden Dawn has its roots in Kabbalah, a form of mysticism that emerged in medieval Jewish communities. Kabbalah synthesized Jewish religious tradition with alchemy, astrology, Neoplatonism, and various other strands of esoteric thought extant at the time, producing a body of received wisdom designed to facilitate an intimate, mystical experience of God, his connection to the Jewish people, and the mysteries of scripture. This Kabbalah still exists as a living tradition in Judaism today.

Shortly after Jewish Kabbalah emerged, Christian mystics and magicians decided to appropriate a version of it for themselves, stripping it of its cultural and ethno-religious context to create a form of mysticism that superficially resembled Kabbalah but was not oriented toward Judaism. Over the course of several centuries, this Christianized version of Kabbalah worked its way across the European continent, becoming a staple of occultism and magic in the Western world and eventually developing into the magical Qabalah used by the Golden Dawn in the late Victorian period. Some writers, myself included, use a spelling distinction to differentiate the Golden Dawn's magical Qabalah from the living Jewish tradition of mystical Kabbalah.

The legacy of magical Qabalah is messy, and it necessarily provokes a discussion of the long history of European antisemitism. Throughout European history, Jewish people have been pariahs as members of an ethnic and religious minority. They suffered from systematic discrimination, second-class legal status, and outright violence. Jewish communities were subject to blood libel—the pernicious lie that claimed Jewish people murdered Christian children as part of their religious rites—and when antisemitism came to a head, it often culminated in mass violence against entire communities in the form of pogroms and ethnic cleansing. Although the most devastating instance of antisemitic violence was the genocide of the Holocaust, antisemitism by no means ended with the defeat of the Nazi regime, and Jewish people today continue to face the discrimination, marginalization, and violence that has threatened Jewish communities for millennia.

This is the backdrop against which we must understand the Qabalah of the Golden Dawn. Part of the appeal of Qabalistic magic for gentile European magicians was that it looked exotic; it came from an "other," a group of people who were unlike the magicians using it. Qabalah was presumed to be especially mystical because of its apparent foreignness. Although much of its Jewish content had been stripped away, Qabalah still looked superficially Jewish in certain ways, especially because it involved the use of Hebrew, a language that most gentile magicians didn't speak and that had an alphabet and structure totally different from those of Germanic or Romantic languages.

Even as these magicians fetishized the apparent exoticism of Jewish mystical wisdom, they participated in a society that excluded actual Judaism and marginalized Jewish people. In many cases, these magicians were themselves overtly antisemitic even as they chanted Hebrew in their magic. Because of this, Qabalah sits at an uncomfortable crossroads: non-Jewish magicians took ostensibly Jewish magical practices for themselves while at the same time discriminating against actual Jewish people for similar practices.

None of this is to say that practicing magical Qabalah is inherently bad or that no one should do it; it's just to say that practitioners should be aware of Qabalah's complicated context. History can sometimes be uncomfortable, but we have a responsibility to engage with it head-on despite the discomfort it might cause us. If we're going to engage with magic that has been influenced by Qabalah, we have to contend with its legacy.

Magical Qabalah is a major part of the landscape of occultism today; not all magic relates to Qabalah, but much of it does, including the magical structure of tarot. As we'll see shortly, Qabalah structured how the Golden Dawn used tarot, providing a robust system and a set of magical correspondences that underlie how tarot is used to this day. I firmly believe that there's no way to put that genie back in the bottle. Different tarot decks may be more or less overtly Qabalistic—it varies from one deck to another—but all contemporary tarot is touched by Qabalah. The question, then, is what to do with that fact.

Some people are uncomfortable incorporating Qabalah into their magic precisely because of the way it intersects with a legacy of antisemitism. If you're one of those people, that's perfectly okay. You by no means have to use Qabalistic magic in conjunction with your tarot practice. However, I would still encourage you to read this chapter all the way through. Qabalah was central to the Golden Dawn, and the Golden Dawn was the biggest influence on the development of modern tarot. Even if you don't want to use Qabalah, it's worth your time to understand how it underlies the structure of a modern tarot deck. If nothing else, that knowledge will help shed some light on tarot's other magical correspondences.

If you do want to use Qabalah as part of your magical work with tarot, that's legitimate too. Think about the lessons you can learn from history and how you can approach magical Qabalah in the best way possible. The problem wasn't the Golden Dawn's use of magical ideas that had originated in another culture; it was the antisemitism underlying the way they often interacted with those ideas. Today, working with Qabalah is an opportunity to confront that antisemitism as it existed then and continues to exist now. The Golden Dawn's magical Qabalah is in tarot's bones, but antisemitism is not. It's up to us as modern practitioners to learn how to disentangle one from the other.

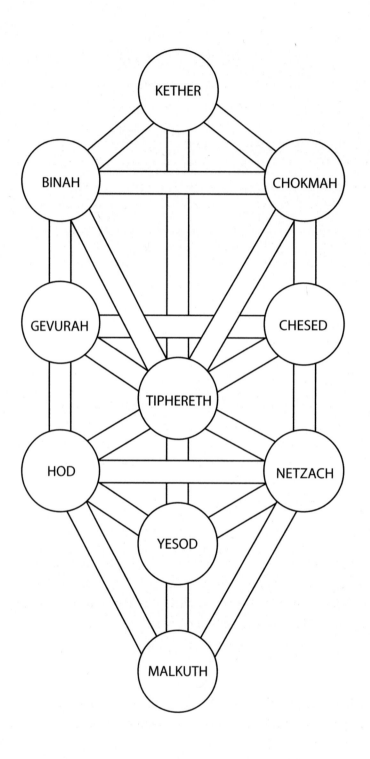

## The Ten Sephiroth

The center of the Golden Dawn's Qabalah was an image known as the Tree of Life, which originated in the Jewish Kabbalistic tradition. The Tree of Life is many things at once: an allegory about the creation of the world, a diagram of different magical energies and how they interact with each other, and a map to guide practitioners exploring planes beyond the physical world. More than anything else, the Tree of Life serves as a repository of information; every magical concept can be connected to some part of the Tree, so by learning its basic structure, Qabalistic magicians give themselves a shorthand way to reference anything they might encounter in their magic.

The Tree of Life is organized into ten *Sephiroth* (singular: *Sephirah*), or "spheres." Each Sephirah represents a different kind of magical energy. Taken all together, the ten Sephiroth show ten different magical themes as well as interconnections between them. Moreover, each Sephirah corresponds to other items and concepts that can be used in magic, including numbers, colors, plants, stones, animals, planets, and (of course) tarot cards. As a brief overview, here are the core themes of each of the Sephiroth.

### Kether

Kether is the original divine spark—the source of magical power that precedes all creation. It represents absolute unity. Kether is the complete dissolution of the ego, the elimination of boundaries between one thing and another, resulting only in a sense of pure oneness. This is the Sephirah of potential and new beginnings. Magically, it's the Godhead and the transcendent consciousness toward which mystics are perpetually striving.

In tarot, Kether corresponds to the Aces.

### Chokmah

The second Sephirah is Chokmah, which represents a chaotic outpouring of power. Chokmah is expansive, energetic, and dynamic. It is bursting forth, full of change, but it is also undirected; because Chokmah is trying to go everywhere all at once, it is going nowhere in particular. Magically, Chokmah is the force of change and movement.

Chokmah's tarot cards are the Twos and the Kings.

### Binah

Where Chokmah is energy without shape, Binah is shape without energy. This Sephirah represents form, shape, and manifestation—as well as limitation and the creation of boundaries.

Binah is the Sephirah of moving from what things *could* be to what they *are*. Magically, Binah is the power to create, giving things concrete form.

In tarot, Binah corresponds to the Threes and the Queens.

### Chesed

Chesed is the Sephirah of compassion, mercy, and mildness. It is a pleasant Sephirah that offers stability, grounding, and protection. More than any other sphere on the Tree of Life, Chesed represents abundance, wealth, prosperity, happiness, and fulfillment. It also connects to interpersonal themes of forgiveness and generosity, as we find the power within ourselves to extend good favor to others. Magically, it is good fortune and the power to bless.

In tarot, Chesed corresponds to the Fours.

### Gevurah

By contrast, Gevurah is the Sephirah of severity, harshness, and discipline. Associated with struggle, conflict, anger, and strife, this Sephirah has hard lessons to teach. It demands strict accountability, and it punishes those who fail to live up to their obligations. Gevurah is a hard sphere; it reminds us that life often isn't fair. Magically, Gevurah is the power to exact justice and inflict harm.

The tarot cards associated with Gevurah are the Fives.

### Tiphereth

Tiphereth sits at the center of the Tree of Life, representing balance and harmony. This is the Sephirah of enlightenment, the complete integration of the self, and of harmony in the external world. In Tiphereth, all things are brought together in concert with each other so that each plays its appropriate part and no one thing dominates another. It is a joyful sphere associated with success and completion. Magically, Tiphereth is the cycle of death and rebirth.

In tarot, Tiphereth corresponds to the Sixes and the Knights.

### Netzach

In Netzach, we find beauty, pleasure, and luxury. This Sephirah rules over interpersonal connections, a feeling of social belonging, and anything that is *we* rather than *I*. It also corresponds to love and affection of all kinds. Netzach is the sphere of all things that bring us pleasure or that put us in connection with other people. Magically, Netzach is the attractive force that draws beauty and love.

Netzach's tarot cards are the Sevens.

## *Hod*

Whereas Netzach is emotional and collective, Hod is intellectual and individual. This is the sphere of science, writing, thought, experimentation, mathematics, scholarship, and rationalism. It is associated with the ego and the conscious self. Hod is the ability to shape reality by analyzing it: taking it apart to see how it works and then putting it back together again. Magically, Hod is the power of the written and spoken word.

The tarot cards for Hod are the Eights.

## *Yesod*

Yesod is the mysterious Sephirah of dreams, myths, symbols, and stories. In Yesod, nothing is ever as it seems; reality becomes an illusion, and we have to trust in a deeper knowledge that belies the deceptive power of the senses. Yesod speaks to the transformative power of symbolism and allegory, the inherent magic of allowing one thing to represent another. Magically, Yesod is psychism and intuition.

In tarot, Yesod corresponds to the Nines.

## *Malkuth*

Finally, Malkuth is the Sephirah of the material world. It is associated with completion, fulfillment, and manifestation. This sphere rules over the physical body as well as everything material we do and experience: It governs health, wealth, logistical planning, geography, and physics. Malkuth shows us that nothing is ever really mundane or ordinary, because a spark of life exists in everything we see and touch. Magically, Malkuth is the presence of the divine in the ordinary world.

The tarot cards of Malkuth are the Tens and the Pages.

## The Sephiroth in the Minor Arcana

The Sephirothic correspondences of tarot cards bring out surprising nuances in the cards, often highlighting aspects of them that escape popular notice. Each card has a title derived from its Qabalistic correspondences, which illuminates how it manifests the energy of its particular Sephirah. Some of these titles will seem evident and familiar to most tarot readers, while others may be surprising—but in all cases, they add another layer of depth and meaning that you can use in your readings.

The titles given for the Minor Arcana are taken from the Thoth deck, a Qabalistic tarot deck conceived by Aleister Crowley and illustrated by Lady Freida Harris. They reflect Crowley's understanding of how the energies of the Sephiroth appear in the Minor Arcana. However, it's worth noting that different tarot readers throughout history have given their own Qabalistic interpretations of the Minor Arcana and offered alternative titles for them based on their connections to the Sephiroth; the titles and themes given by Crowley are not the only or definitive way to make sense of tarot's Qabalistic connections.

In designing the Thoth deck, Crowley retitled and reordered the court cards, creating a whole world of trouble for anyone after him who wanted to write about the Qabalistic connections of the tarot court. For the sake of simplicity and clarity, I've retained the more familiar Rider-Waite-Smith ranks of the court cards here, and I give their Qabalistic titles as used by the Hermetic Order of the Golden Dawn rather than Crowley's reordered version.[12] For anyone who wants to delve more deeply into the Crowley-specific versions of the court cards, I recommend Lon Milo DuQuette's *Understanding Aleister Crowley's Thoth Tarot*.

### Aces

In the Thoth deck, the Aces have no particular title, but because of their correspondence with Kether, they represent origination and beginnings: the roots of elemental power.

- The Ace of Pentacles is the *Root of the Powers of Earth*.
- The Ace of Swords is the *Root of the Powers of Air*.
- The Ace of Cups is the *Root of the Powers of Water*.
- The Ace of Wands is the *Root of the Powers of Fire*.

### Twos

The Twos each encapsulate the dynamism of Chokmah, expressed through the elemental energy of their respective suits. They are forceful, energetic, and expansive.

- The Two of Pentacles is *Change*.
- The Two of Swords is *Peace*.
- The Two of Cups is *Love*.
- The Two of Wands is *Dominion*.

---

12. Mathers, *Book T*, 3–4.

## Threes

Binah gives things shape and form, and accordingly the Threes are associated with things taking shape and becoming real—sometimes for the better, sometimes for the worse.

- The Three of Pentacles is *Work*.
- The Three of Swords is *Sorrow*.
- The Three of Cups is *Abundance*.
- The Three of Wands is *Virtue*.

## Fours

The Fours are associated with the abundant, beneficent energy of Chesed. Qabalistically, these are positive cards that represent good fortune, clemency, and kindness.

- The Four of Pentacles is *Power*.
- The Four of Swords is *Truce*.
- The Four of Cups is *Luxury*.
- The Four of Wands is *Completion*.

## Fives

The harshness of Gevurah makes the Fives difficult, challenging cards. They bring conflict to their suits, representing the obstacles and challenges we have to overcome.

- The Five of Pentacles is *Worry*.
- The Five of Swords is *Defeat*.
- The Five of Cups is *Disappointment*.
- The Five of Wands is *Strife*.

## Sixes

Harmonious Tiphereth makes the Sixes cards of balance, equilibrium, and order. These cards signify putting things to rights and making everything as it should be.

- The Six of Pentacles is *Success*.
- The Six of Swords is *Science*.

- The Six of Cups is *Pleasure*.
- The Six of Wands is *Victory*.

## Sevens

Connected to Netzach, the Sevens represent desire—both in its fulfillment and in its frustration. The Sevens show the tension between what we want and what we actually get.

- The Seven of Pentacles is *Failure*.
- The Seven of Swords is *Futility*.
- The Seven of Cups is *Debauchery*.
- The Seven of Wands is *Valor*.

## Eights

The Eights correspond to intellectual Hod, showing our mental activity. These cards are the mind at its best and worst, showing how it can help or hinder us.

- The Eight of Pentacles is *Prudence*.
- The Eight of Swords is *Interference*.
- The Eight of Cups is *Indolence*.
- The Eight of Wands is *Swiftness*.

## Nines

Yesod is the unconscious mind, and the Nines show parts of ourselves that belong to the unconscious: things that come from instinct or intuition rather than conscious thought.

- The Nine of Pentacles is *Gain*.
- The Nine of Swords is *Cruelty*.
- The Nine of Cups is *Happiness*.
- The Nine of Wands is *Strength*.

## Tens

Physical Malkuth brings a grounded, real-world energy to the Tens. These cards represent the big things we seek and fear in our material lives.

- The Ten of Pentacles is *Wealth*.
- The Ten of Swords is *Ruin*.
- The Ten of Cups is *Satiety*.
- The Ten of Wands is *Oppression*.

## Pages

Corresponding to Malkuth, the Pages are the most grounded of the court cards—the ones who take care of practical details overlooked by other personalities.

- The Page of Pentacles is *The Princess of the Echoing Hills* and *The Rose of the Palace of Earth*.
- The Page of Swords is *The Princess of the Rushing Winds* and *The Lotus of the Palace of Air*.
- The Page of Cups is *The Princess of the Waters* and *The Lotus of the Palace of Floods*.
- The Page of Wands is *The Princess of the Shining Flame* and *The Rose of the Palace of Fire*.

## Knights

The Knights are idealistic and hopeful, aspiring to perfection and constantly on a quest of some kind. As such, they correspond to the perfection of Tiphereth.

- The Knight of Pentacles is *The Prince of the Chariot of Earth*.
- The Knight of Swords is *The Prince of the Chariot of the Winds*.
- The Knight of Cups is *The Prince of the Chariot of the Waters*.
- The Knight of Wands is *The Prince of the Chariot of Fire*.

## *Queens*

Corresponding to Binah, the Queens understand the importance of carefully shaping their plans, evaluating what can and can't be done in order to accomplish their goals most effectively.

- The Queen of Pentacles is *The Queen of the Thrones of Earth.*
- The Queen of Swords is *The Queen of the Thrones of Air.*
- The Queen of Cups is *The Queen of the Thrones of the Waters.*
- The Queen of Wands is *The Queen of the Thrones of Flame.*

## *Kings*

The Kings are forces of nature. They're the most powerful court cards, corresponding to the undirected energy of chaotic Chokmah, and they can accomplish anything.

- The King of Pentacles is *The Lord of the Wide and Fertile Land* and *The King of the Spirits of Earth.*
- The King of Swords is *The Lord of the Wind and the Breezes* and *The King of the Spirits of Air.*
- The King of Cups is *The Lord of the Waves and the Waters* and *The King of the Hosts of the Sea.*
- The King of Wands is *The Lord of the Flame and Lightning* and *The King of the Spirits of Fire.*

## Tree of Life Spread

The ten Sephiroth of the Tree of Life can be made into a useful tarot spread. This spread identifies a core theme in Kether—the source of divine energy at the top of the Tree of Life—and then shows you a variety of perspectives on that core theme, drawing it down through the other Sephiroth the same way the spark of Kether is pulled through the Tree down to Malkuth.

1. Kether: The subject of the reading

2. Chokmah: The driving force in the situation

3. Binah: The overall shape of the situation

4. Chesed: The resources available to you

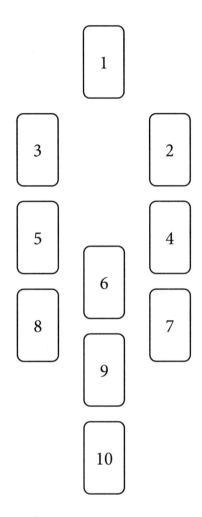

5. Gevurah: The obstacles you face

6. Tiphereth: What you should strive for

7. Netzach: What you want from the situation

8. Hod: What you think about the situation

9. Yesod: What your gut is telling you

10. Malkuth: The practical reality you have to face

## The Twenty-Two Paths

Looking at the Tree of Life, you'll notice that it's not just made up of the ten Sephiroth. There are also lines drawn between them: a set of twenty-two paths connecting the spheres of the Tree. These paths represent the way that divine or magical energy flows through the tree, progressing from one Sephirah to another. Some spheres are directly connected, representing a direct transition from one kind of magical energy to the next; for example, there is a close relationship between the self-oriented energy of Hod and the other-oriented energy of Netzach. It is easy for divine power to flow back and forth between these two states of being. Other spheres, however, share no direct connection; to get from the divine unity of Kether to the manifest reality of Malkuth, you have to pass through intermediary stages in other spheres on the Tree of Life. If the Sephiroth are the landmarks on the Tree, the paths are the map showing how to get from one to another.

The twenty-two paths connect to the twenty-two Major Arcana of the tarot deck. Throughout history, there have been different ways of assigning those correspondences, but the most common way in magical Qabalah is to start at the top of the tree and progress through the Major Arcana from top to bottom. The Fool is the path between Kether and Chokmah at the top of the Tree, while the World is the path between Yesod and Malkuth at the bottom. Thus, the Tree of Life reflects not only the Minor Arcana and the court cards, but the majors as well:

- The Fool connects Kether and Chokmah.
- The Magician connects Kether and Binah.
- The High Priestess connects Kether and Tiphereth.
- The Empress connects Chokmah and Binah.
- The Emperor connects Chokmah and Tiphereth.[13]
- The Hierophant connects Chokmah and Chesed.
- The Lovers connect Binah and Tiphereth.
- The Chariot connects Binah and Gevurah.
- Strength connects Chesed and Gevurah.
- The Hermit connects Chesed and Tiphereth.

---

13. In the Thoth deck, Aleister Crowley swaps the paths for the Emperor and the Star. Unless you're working specifically with the Thoth system, I'd recommend sticking to the correspondences given here.

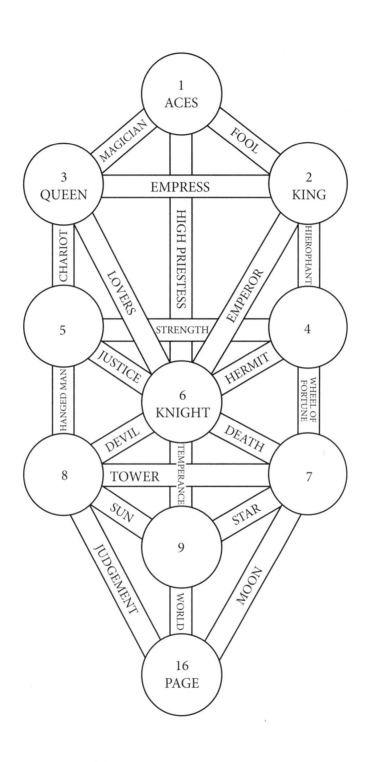

- Wheel of Fortune connects Chesed and Netzach.
- Justice connects Gevurah and Tiphereth.
- The Hanged Man connects Gevurah and Hod.
- Death connects Tiphereth and Netzach.
- Temperance connects Tiphereth and Yesod.
- The Devil connects Tiphereth and Hod.
- The Tower connects Netzach and Hod.
- The Star connects Netzach and Yesod.
- The Moon connects Netzach and Malkuth.
- The Sun connects Hod and Yesod.
- Judgement connects Hod and Malkuth.
- The World connects Yesod and Malkuth.

Each card in the Major Arcana corresponds to a path between two Sephiroth. This isn't just a pretty visual arrangement; it has deep significance for the meaning of the cards. A path on the Tree of Life allows us to transmute the energy of one sphere into another. To get from one Sephirah to another, we have to traverse a particular path. That path—along with its associated tarot card—tells us something crucial about the relationship between those two spheres.

### The Fool

On the path between Kether and Chokmah, the Fool mediates between divine unity and the undirected power of creation. This is the card of absolute potential.

### The Magician

The Magician is creative like the Fool, but he is much more concrete and directed; he brings the potential of Kether into the form of Binah.

### The High Priestess

The High Priestess brings the Godhead down the Tree into Tiphereth, where we can experience it as a religious mystery. She is the card of initiation and revelation.

### The Empress

The unity of force and form between Chokmah and Binah is the ultimate act of creation and fecundity, belonging to the nurturing power of the Empress.

### The Emperor

The Emperor unites forceful Chokmah with harmonious Tiphereth; he is the imposition of order through the application of dynamic personal power.

### The Hierophant

The Hierophant unites the chaotic force of Chokmah with the calming, gentle energy of Chesed, finding wisdom in going slowly and doing things the established way.

### The Lovers

Binah makes the equilibrium of Tiphereth real and concrete through the Lovers, the card of perfect matches and complementary halves that fit together to make a whole.

### The Chariot

The Chariot is a destabilizing card, moving from the known, settled world of Binah to the uncertainty and challenges of Gevurah.

### Strength

Strength overcomes the strife of Gevurah with the equanimity of Chesed, finding inner strength that brings peace to difficult situations.

### The Hermit

Between well-ordered Tiphereth and mild Chesed, the Hermit finds equanimity through introspection, quiet reflection, and the search for inner peace.

### Wheel of Fortune

The Wheel of Fortune occupies the path between beneficent Chesed and pleasurable Netzach, representing the good fortune we hope will come our way.

### Justice

The path between Gevurah and Tiphereth is Justice, which reminds us that balance requires impartiality and that fairness can sometimes be harsh.

### The Hanged Man

The Hanged Man sits between Gevurah's challenges and Hod's consciousness, showing us that many difficulties can be overcome with a change in perspective.

### Death

Death releases the pleasures found in Netzach in order to achieve the harmony of Tiphereth. It reminds us that even good things naturally come to an end.

### Temperance

Sitting on the middle of the Tree, Temperance brings Yesod's mysterious, symbolic nature to the harmony of Tiphereth, becoming a card of true alchemical transmutation.

### The Devil

The Devil shows the tension between egocentrism in Hod and a greater sense of perfection in Tiphereth. In order to achieve happiness, the self has to be relinquished.

### The Tower

Catastrophe brings people together, and the cataclysmic events of the Tower are an impetus that can help connect the self in Hod with the community in Netzach.

### The Star

The Star uses Yesod's intuition to find renewal and rebirth in the pleasant domains of Netzach. This card dreams of a better life in order to find healing.

### The Moon

The Moon connects what we want in Netzach with what we actually have in Malkuth. It bridges the gap between the real and the imagined, reality and fantasy.

### The Sun

The Sun provides illumination, making the unconscious conscious. It's the path of enlightenment from the sleeping mind of Yesod to the waking mind of Hod.

## *Judgement*

Judgement, likewise, is a card of awakening—from the unthinking, corporeal nature of Malkuth to the curiosity, intellect, and analytical probing of Hod.

## *The World*

Finally, the path from protean Yesod to manifest Malkuth is the path of the World, the ultimate card of completion and fulfillment, where things become the most real.

# The Paths and Other Correspondences

The paths on the Tree of Life are the basis of just about all of the correspondences of the Major Arcana as used in the Golden Dawn or other Qabalistically oriented magical systems. Through the paths, the Golden Dawn associated each major card with particular plants, animals, gemstones, deities, incenses, and more. Of particular note, however, are the astrological and elemental associations of the cards—the very same ones that you've read about in earlier chapters of this book. The structure of those correspondences comes from the Qabalistic Tree of Life.

The correspondences are based on a Jewish Kabbalistic text called the *Sefer Yetzirah*, which describes God's creation of the world through the twenty-two letters of the Hebrew alphabet. These letters are divided up into groups based on their phonetic and linguistic properties in medieval Hebrew—although Hebrew pronunciation has shifted since the time of the *Sefer Yetzirah*'s writing.

- Three of the letters are known as the *mother letters* because they're taken to be the most basic sounds from which the rest of language is born.
- Seven of the letters are known as the *double letters* because these letters could each be pronounced two different ways.
- The remaining twelve letters are known as the *single letters* because they each have only one pronunciation.

Each of these letters is associated with a path on the Tree of Life and its associated tarot card: Aleph (א), the first letter, corresponds to the Fool, while tau (ת), the last letter, corresponds to the World. This division forms the basis of the magical correspondences for the Major Arcana: The twelve single letters are associated with the twelve signs of the Zodiac, the seven double letters are associated with the seven planets, and the three mother letters are associated with the elements (plus one double letter that—appropriately enough—does double duty as both elemental and planetary). These letters give their correspondences to the paths on the Tree of Life as well as to the tarot cards associated with them.

Thus, the Fool is associated with aleph (א), a mother letter connected to the element of air; the Magician is beth (ב), a double letter connected to the planet Mercury, and so on through the rest of the Major Arcana and the Hebrew alphabet. You can find a complete list of the Hebrew letters and their corresponding tarot cards in chapter 12.

This is why the correspondences of the tarot deck to the Tree of Life are so worth knowing. They don't just provide an overtly Qabalistic layer of meaning to the cards—they are the foundation upon which the rest of magical tarot rests. If you want to understand the tarot through the lens of astrology or the elements—to *really* understand it structurally, and not just by memorizing a list of cards—Qabalah can reveal the inner logic that holds together the magic of tarot. The correspondences of each card aren't just accidents of fate; they're part of a larger, coherent system where each part fits into a unified whole.

## Using Qabalah in a Reading

How can Qabalistic correspondences actually help in the process of interpreting a tarot reading? Let's look at a couple of key examples. Suppose a client comes to you because she's having difficulty with an overbearing boss at work. You do the following four-card reading, using no particular spread:

There's a lot to discuss in a reading like this. The most obvious figure who leaps out is the Hierophant: the micromanaging leader who insists on everything being done a certain way, whose attitude is taking an emotional toll on the querent. We see the specifics of the toll in the cards above the Hierophant, where the Four of Pentacles and the Four of Swords express the querent's feelings of being overpowered and needing a break. However, all is not lost. To the Hierophant's right is the Two of Wands: a plan of action for improvement and development.

Importantly, the Hierophant sits between these negative and positive cards—not just physically, but Qabalistically. The Fours are Chesed and the Two is Chokmah, and the Hierophant occupies the path between them. Looking at the reading from a Qabalistic point of view, an important—and surprising—theme comes to the fore. The manager's overbearing style is difficult and even oppressive, but it's not all bad. Despite the interpersonal conflict it generates, it is also helping the querent develop professionally; she is learning a lot from this manager and moving forward in her career toward the better and brighter things represented by the Two of Wands. She just hasn't been able to see the ways in which that development is happening.

In trying to improve her professional relationship with her boss, the querent can focus on the genuinely good work that is being produced. It is frustrating for her to feel like she's not being listened to, and that needs to be addressed—but at the same time, the advice her boss gives her is genuinely good, and it is making her work better. Her focus should be on improving the communication between them so that managerial intervention doesn't undermine her autonomy, but she shouldn't be trying to shut down her boss's advice entirely.

Looking at a reading through a Qabalistic lens, the Minor Arcana represent fixed points, the way that things *are*. The Major Arcana, on the other hand, are pathways of transformation, allowing one thing to become another. By paying close attention to which spheres and which paths are present in a reading, you can get a strong sense of what things look like now, where they're changing, and what they're changing into.

Take a look at the following Past/Present/Future spread.

At first glance, this spread looks really rough. Things have been bad in the past, are worse now, and seem like they might get even worse in the future. We see themes of grief and bondage in all three of these cards, and it's clear that the querent is dealing with some heavy problems that aren't going to go away overnight. Some things are serious and hard, and they may take years to work through properly; this reading reflects just such a situation. However, if we're adding in a layer of Qabalistic interpretation, we can see a glimmer of light at the end of the tunnel.

Look at the cards in terms of progression through the Tree of Life. In the past, the querent was in Gevurah, the Sephirah of difficulty and harshness. In short, something bad happened to them in the past, and they're still processing and working through that pain. In the present, they've moved out of Gevurah and into Hod. This is progress—they're no longer trapped in the immediacy of their pain, and they've successfully moved out of Gevurah. But the healing arc still isn't complete. In Hod, we see a withdrawal into the self; the querent is isolating themselves and turning inward. This is further borne out by the specific meaning of the Eight of Swords. The Eight of Swords is not necessarily a bad card here, because it shows a necessary step in the process of healing, but it can't be the end point. Eventually, the querent needs to open up to other people again.

Surprisingly enough, this is where the Devil comes in. The Devil is the path that connects Hod to Tiphereth. Here, with a querent who is stuck in Hod and needs to find a way to restore balance to their life, the Devil represents their way out. There is still some hard work ahead of them, and they're not out of the woods yet; the Devil, by his nature, is going to force them to come to terms with some hard truths that they've been avoiding. The short-term future still has a lot of difficulty in it, and that's unavoidable in interpreting a reading like this one. However, the Devil also shows movement—and specifically, movement in the direction of Tiphereth. The road ahead is hard, but it promises to take the querent somewhere better. If the querent does the hard work the Devil demands of them, there is a promise of healing on the other side.

Try this for yourself. Do a reading using whatever spread you prefer. Once you've laid out the cards, do a first-pass interpretation as you normally would, without looking at the Qabalistic correspondences of the cards. Then, go through and take note of how the cards match up with the Tree of Life.

First, identify every card that corresponds to a Sephirah on the Tree of Life. Which Sephiroth are present in your reading? Take particular note of any spheres that are represented by multiple cards in the reading and have a dominant presence in the spread overall. How do the energies of these spheres relate to the question you've asked?

Next, identify every card corresponding to a path and note which paths they correspond to. These cards show the parts of your reading where something significant is transforming. They are the key points of flux and change. What do these points have to say about the reading overall?

Third, for each major card, identify the two spheres that it connects on the Tree of Life. The card itself is a transformation; the two spheres show you what things are transforming *from* and *to*. Do any of the paths in your reading connect to each other? Do they connect to Sephiroth that are represented by Minor Arcana or court cards elsewhere in the reading? Take note of these connections.

Finally, using all of the above information, see if you can trace a dynamic trajectory on the Tree of Life. Do the cards of the Sephiroth and paths come together in such a way that you can describe motion across the Tree of Life from one sphere to another? If so, what is the starting point of that motion, what parts of the Tree does it pass through, and where does it appear to end? This is the core Qabalistic interpretation of your reading. Think about how that journey through the different energies of the Tree could be interpreted as the answer to the question you asked.

This will be difficult at first, but it gets easier with practice. As with all of the reading techniques discussed in this book, the Qabalah is only one tool in your interpretive toolbox. Some readings will be well suited to Qabalistic interpretation, and others might be less so. Over time, you'll get a sense of when Qabalistic connections are apparent and potentially useful for your readings. For now, try applying the above procedure to your readings and make a record each time you do. Sometimes it'll be useful and sometimes it won't, but by using it regularly you'll become more confident with it and will be able to develop an intuitive sense of when to put it to use.

*part two*

# Tarot in Magic

# chapter seven
# Pathworking and Meditation

In part I, I gave you a survey of fundamental magical correspondences and techniques for reading tarot through a magical lens. Here in part II, we're going to flip that on its head. Instead of looking at how to use magical perspectives to help with reading tarot, we're going to use tarot as a tool in magic.

There are countless ways to incorporate tarot into a magical practice; with magic, anything you can think to try is fair game, and there's room for a great deal of experimentation. The techniques presented in the following chapters are all things I have used in my own magical work and found successful, but that's not to say they're the be-all and end-all of tarot in magic. Use what you like, but feel free to add, cut, rework, or innovate any and all of the magical techniques I present here. It may be the case that something works well for me but isn't suited to your approach to magic, and you may think of magical ways to use tarot that would never have occurred to me. The most important rule of all is simply to do what gets you results.

Tarot is useful in magic because its language is symbolism. In tarot, every image is meaningful, representing something more than what it initially seems. Every detail of a card tells you something deeper about its meaning; in tarot, a cigar is never just a cigar. The same is true in magic. Whether your magic is primarily sympathetic or intercessional, everything you do in a magical context—every object, word, and gesture—has symbolic significance. It's the easiest thing in the world, then, to bring symbol-laden tarot into a magical context and draw on tarot imagery in order to achieve magical goals.

There's no universal approach to magic, but as I discussed in chapter 2, there are some broad structural similarities. One of those similarities is an emphasis on meditation or other skills that train the mind. If you open up just about any introductory book on magic, you'll see the author recommending a meditative practice of one kind or another. Meditation trains you to clear your mind of distractions and to focus your intention. This is a valuable skill in general, but it's particularly helpful for magic; it allows you to immerse yourself fully in the magical work that you're doing.

Whether your magic is working primarily through sympathy or through intercession, it requires focus. In order to build a strong sympathetic link or to make an effective request of a spirit, you need to be able to direct your attention to the task at hand without letting other thoughts or worries get in the way. Meditation can help you do that.

There are countless ways to meditate. Most people think of meditation as something done by anchorites sitting cross-legged on remote mountaintops—people who have removed themselves entirely from the world and who have succeeded in completely silencing their conscious minds so that they can become one with the universe. This is a noble image, and I don't fault anyone who wants to pursue that kind of meditative practice, but it's not the only thing meditation can be. Some people meditate every day, but others meditate less often. Some people sit in one place, but others meditate while exercising, playing music, or doing some other activity that helps them still their minds. Some types of meditation emphasize emptying the mind, but others emphasize focusing the mind and drawing the thoughts together. All of these forms of meditation are legitimate, and each person will have success with some and difficulty with others.

The following are a variety of techniques for building or strengthening a meditative practice using tarot. These techniques can help you if you're just starting out and trying to establish a habit of regular meditation. They can also serve particular purposes: connecting to individual cards, exploring magical correspondences, opening up to spirit communication, and even achieving specific magical goals.

## A Simple Tarot Meditation

This meditation is designed to help you familiarize yourself with a tarot card, especially one that you struggle to understand and interpret. For this exercise, you'll need:

- A tarot card of your choosing

- A blank sheet of paper and a pen

- A comfortable place to sit

- Candles for illumination as needed

- A fifteen-minute timer

Choose a card from your deck that you want to get to know better. Remove it from the deck and set it on top of the sheet of paper. Now, take a few minutes to think about what you associate with this card. What are the major themes, interpretations, and symbols that this card has? What does it make you think of? Write these things down on the paper surrounding the card. This is an exercise in free association, and there are no right or wrong answers. You can use keywords you've learned from a book—including the ones included in the appendix of this book—but you should also feel free to write personal interpretations, insights, and associations. The goal is to write down what the card means to *you*. By the time you're finished, your card should be surrounded by a "frame" of paper filled with your thoughts and keywords.

Once you've written as much as you can think of, find a place where you can sit comfortably, and set the card and paper in front of you. Light your candle(s) to illuminate the space. You should have enough light that you can turn off the electric lights in your room but still see the card and read the keywords you've written.

Sit in a comfortable position in front of the card. Say:

*I seek knowledge of the hidden mysteries of tarot.*
*I seek the wisdom of [the name of the card].*

Set your timer for fifteen minutes. During that time, keep your gaze focused on the card and its surrounding word cloud. Focus your thoughts on the card and its meaning. What does this card mean to you? What are the things about it that you struggle to understand, and why? Does it make you think of anything in your life: people you know, memories, favorite books or movies, problems that you're currently facing, and so on? How does its imagery make you feel, and which parts of its picture stand out to you the most?

Your thoughts will wander while you're doing this. That's as it should be. The point is to allow your mind to roam free and make connections to the card, and your thoughts may take you to some surprising places. If you realize that the Knight of Swords makes you think of your third-grade teacher, fantastic! That's a new insight into the card that will help you understand it on a more personal level.

If you find that your thoughts are wandering too far afield and you're no longer thinking about the card at all, that's okay. It's totally normal, and it doesn't mean you've failed at the meditation. It happens to everybody, especially when first starting out with a meditation practice. When you notice that your thoughts have left the card behind, just pause, take a deep breath, and re-center yourself, bringing your attention back to the card. It's okay for your mind to drift, but when you notice that it has done so, bring it back to where it's supposed to be. Over time and with experience, it'll get easier and easier to catch your thoughts and maintain focus for longer periods of time.

When your fifteen-minute timer is up, say:

> *I have sought the wisdom of [the name of the card]. I go now, grateful for*
> *the knowledge I have found and aware that there is always more to know.*

Extinguish the candles. Your meditation is now complete. I recommend writing down any insights or new associations you've found over the course of your meditation, as well as keeping the word cloud that you wrote. These records are useful to have on hand so that you can look back at the development of your relationship with a particular card.

I recommend using this meditation at least once for every card in your tarot deck. I know that sounds like a lot—seventy-eight meditations in a row!—but I'm not suggesting you do them all at once. Learning how to read tarot is a lifelong process; I've been reading the cards since I was eleven years old, and I'm still finding new insights, techniques, and ways of relating to tarot's imagery and symbolism. Meditating on the cards is one way of building a deeper connection with them, and it can take months or even years to work through the whole deck. Working at a pace of one card per week, it would take you about a year and a half to go through the whole deck. This is a project that I've found immensely valuable for my own understanding of the cards, but it's perfectly okay if you prefer to focus on a few cards rather than tackling the whole deck.

It's also worth noting that you may want to meditate on a given card more than once. A meditative session may yield new perspectives on a card, but there will always be new things to discover. Particularly if there's a card you're struggling to connect to, one fifteen-minute session will probably not be enough to develop a deep understanding of the card's themes and symbolism. You may want to revisit the same card multiple times in meditation in order to explore it as much as possible.

Finally, note that the fifteen-minute time limit is a recommendation, not a hard-and-fast rule. Some people have difficulty sitting still for extended periods of time, and newcomers to meditation may find fifteen minutes exhausting or overly taxing. Conversely, some people may feel that fifteen minutes is not enough time for them, and they may want to meditate in greater depth and for a longer period of time. Feel free to adjust the timing of this exercise to suit your own needs.

## Pathworking the Tarot

Magical practitioners will often talk about a particular kind of meditation known as *pathworking*. The term comes from Golden Dawn Qabalistic magic and refers to the paths on the Tree of Life. In the original Golden Dawn usage of the word, a pathworking was a guided meditation or visualization that used tarot symbolism to help a magician explore one of the paths on the Tree. Over time, the word began to be applied more loosely, and you'll now hear people talk about pathworking in reference to just about any guided meditation, especially those involving tarot.

Pathworking tends to be a highly structured form of meditation organized around a thematic journey. Rather than stilling and emptying your conscious mind, it directs you to imagine and experience a particular symbolic narrative. A pathworking is narrated from a pre-written script and instructs the meditator to imagine themself as the protagonist of a story that takes place in the world of tarot, featuring characters and scenery from a particular card. The goal of a meditation like this is for someone to be able to experience the energy of a card directly—not just thinking about what a card means, but stepping into the world of that card and feeling it for themself. Different pathworkings may emphasize different features of the cards, pulling forward particular symbols or Qabalistic correspondences depending on what the author of the pathworking is trying to convey.

There are both advantages and disadvantages to pathworking as an approach to meditating on tarot. On the plus side, pathworking gives structure and direction to a meditative experience. Particularly for people who have less experience with meditation, it can be helpful to have something to focus on, walking through a pre-written story where you know what you are supposed to be thinking and feeling every step of the way. Freeform meditation of the "sit still and empty your mind" variety can be intimidating for newcomers, and pathworking provides an easy point of entry to meditation and other mental exercises. Moreover, because the script for a pathworking is written in advance, any pathworking experience will have clear, deliberately chosen symbolism. You don't have to worry about what you're going to get out of a pathworking or whether you will experience something significant—you know from the outset what's going to happen.

On the downside, the structure of pathworking can be rigid and even constrictive at times. Pre-written guided meditations are consistent and reliable, but they also leave less room for spontaneity. In a pathworking, you're less likely to encounter something genuinely unexpected: a flash of insight, an unfamiliar symbol, or a new way of interpreting a card. Pathworking is more about mapping the territory you already know than about discovering new terrain.

Pathworkings are typically written as guided visualizations. A narrator describes events while the meditator (or meditators, if multiple people are doing the pathworking simultaneously) tries to imagine what's being described as vividly as possible. Not everyone has an inner eye that allows them to visualize in this way, but that doesn't mean they can't do pathworkings. If you struggle to visualize but would still like to try pathworking, you can simply treat pathworking as a narrative to listen to, much like listening to a podcast or audiobook. If you do this with pathworkings that other people have written, you may need to retouch the language a bit in order to remove instructions that emphasize visualization, but it's generally fairly straightforward to adapt a script in this way. If you do go this route, still try to consciously engage with the symbolism and themes described; the goal is to be an active participant, even if you can't mentally see the things being described.

## The Astral Temple

Pathworking is an imaginative journey you take through the tarot deck. As with any journey, it's helpful to know your starting and ending points: Where are you journeying from and to? Over the course of a pathworking, you step out of the ordinary world and into the rich, symbolic world of the tarot—and then at the end of your journey, you return to the mundane. No matter what magical, imaginative things you encounter along your trip, the journey starts and finishes in regular, everyday reality.

Because of this, it's helpful to have a consistent procedure for transitioning from the ordinary to the extraordinary and back again. One of the most effective ways of doing so is by constructing something known as an *astral temple*. This is a space that you build in your imagination and can visit any time you like. It belongs only to you, and every detail of its construction is your design. Your astral temple is meant to be a place that feels familiar and safe—somewhere in the landscape of the imagination that is decidedly your turf. You then start and end every pathworking in your astral temple so that regardless of what else you encounter in your meditative explorations, you have a familiar anchor point. This makes it easier to transition between waking consciousness and the daydreaming reality of a pathworking.

Moreover, an astral temple serves as an escape hatch of sorts. Pathworking the tarot is an opportunity to explore the full range of tarot's symbolism and meaning, and that includes some potentially dark and heavy topics. It sometimes happens that someone will be halfway through a pathworking and suddenly realize they're not emotionally equipped to deal with that pathworking's themes. If that happens, you can immediately mentally evacuate to your astral temple, putting yourself back in a place where you feel safe and secure.

Some people use astral temples for a variety of purposes beyond pathworking, including visiting the temple in their imagination and performing spells or other rituals there. There are even magical groups that collectively establish an astral temple together and use that space for their magic rather than performing physical ritual. Personally, I've never enjoyed that approach to magic—if I'm casting a spell, I want to do it physically and not just in my imagination—so my own use of an astral temple is almost exclusively relegated to pathworking. However, it's worth noting that the possibilities are not limited to meditation, and if you want to explore using an astral temple for other kinds of magical work, you are heartily encouraged to do so.

### Building an Astral Temple

This is a brief guided meditation to help you visualize your astral temple for the first time and design it to your liking. Before doing this meditation, I'd recommend reading through it once to familiarize yourself with it. Then, you can either record yourself reading it or ask a friend to read it aloud while you meditate. That way, you have an external narrator and can devote your focus entirely to the work of building your astral temple.

The astral temple is intimate and personal, belonging to you alone. As such, what it looks like is entirely up to you. The only real requirements are that it be yours, that it feel safe, and that you be able to consistently recreate it in your imagination. Your astral temple is a place you'll return to again and again, so it should be something you can easily imagine or describe. Don't create a mental space with a thousand elaborate details that you won't remember on your next visit.

Sit comfortably and close your eyes. Take a deep breath in, hold it for a moment, and then let it out. Again: Breathe in, hold, breathe out. In. Hold. Out.

Continue to breathe in this pattern, and as you do so, allow your mind to clear of distractions. Your scattered thoughts, worries, and problems from everyday life all begin to fade into the background. You are wholly present here, now, in this moment. You are at the center of yourself. Be aware of the air filling your lungs and the heart pumping blood through your veins. Allow your consciousness to venture beyond your body, feeling your connection to the earth beneath you and the sky above you. You are part of the living universe, and the beating of your heart is part of the eternal song of the cosmos. Listen to that song. Hearing it, you feel a sense of deep completion and belonging.

Focus on that sense of belonging and let it fill you up. You are safe. You are at peace. You are whole. Gradually, you begin to be aware that you are in a new place, a place no one else has ever been before. This is a safe place, a refuge where you can come any time you need to feel peace and security. Look around you. Where are you? Are you indoors or outside?

If you are inside, take note of the room you are in. How big is it? What is it shaped like? How is it illuminated? If you are outside, pay attention to the landscape. What geographic features do you notice? Are there any plants or animals nearby? What time of day is it?

As this place takes shape around you, you begin to walk around it, taking it in with all your senses. You take a deep breath in and notice the pleasant smell of the air here. You reach out with your hands and feel the textures of everything that surrounds you. Notice the colors, the way light and shadow play across the ground. Be still for a moment and listen for the distinct sounds that make this place unique.

Explore for as long as you wish. When you are done, return to the center of the space. You are going to place an altar here, to ground your temple and serve as a locus for any magic you do. As you watch, a tall, square table appears in the space before you. Reach out and place your hands on the table, feeling its cool, smooth surface beneath your palms. What color is this table? What material is it made out of? You run your hands along it, noticing how sturdy it is.

Now, one by one, you notice that your four elemental tools begin to appear on your altar. First, your earth pentacle. Lift it off the table, noticing its heft as it catches the light. As you hold the pentacle, you feel your feet rooted to the ground, supporting you, keeping you steady. You know that with the strength of earth, nothing can move you from this spot against your will.

Replace the pentacle on the altar. Next to it, your air blade appears. Lift the blade and swish it through the air, feeling a gust of sudden wind blow down your arm. Your mind is sharp and clear, full of fresh ideas and knowledge. With the wisdom of air, there is nothing you cannot discover.

Replace the blade. Third, your water cup appears, filled with cool, clear water. Lift it up to your lips and drink deeply. The water is sweet and refreshing. It nourishes and replenishes you. As you drink, allow your heart to open; feel insuppressible joy welling up within you. With the grace of water, the whole world is a source of bliss to you.

Put your cup back on the table. Finally, your fire wand appears on the altar. Pick it up and brandish it before you. As you watch, a flame appears at the tip of the wand. It dances brightly, casting off light and heat without burning you or your wand. Looking at the flame, you feel excitement and confidence blaze within you. With the courage of fire, you can face every challenge.

Put your wand back on the altar and watch its flame extinguish. Survey all four of your elemental tools. These tools will remain here, on the altar in your astral temple, ready for you to use whenever you need them. With them, you may work any magic you choose, and you can accomplish wonders in the astral realm that would be impossible in the physical.

Look up and survey your astral temple. Remember this place: how it looks, how it feels, all the little details that make it unique. You can come back here any time you choose. The temple will be here waiting for you, exactly as you left it— but this is your space, and you can make changes to it as you please.

You will need a way to enter and exit the temple. Look around for an egress. It might be a door, a pathway, a shimmering portal, or something else. If you do not see one already present in the temple, choose a place to put your exit. No matter what it looks like, this is a magical portal. When you pass through it, you can return to the physical world or go anywhere in the astral. Approaching the exit, you feel a warm, soft glow radiating from it, like the heat cast off by a campfire.

Turn and look at your astral temple one last time. You lift a hand and wave farewell, then take the passage out from the temple. As you do so, you find yourself in your body once again, sitting comfortably with your eyes closed. Your chest rises in deep, even breaths. Wiggle your fingers and your toes, feeling sensation return to them. Stretch out your arms and roll your shoulders back. You are feeling more and more settled in your body as you return to ordinary consciousness. Focus on what it feels like to be back in your body, in this world, wholly present in the current moment. When you are ready, open your eyes.

## An Elemental Pathworking: The Hanged Man

This sample pathworking explores the symbolism of the Hanged Man through his connection to elemental water. This is only a demonstration of the sort of imagery you can explore through tarot pathworking; after you work through this one, I encourage you to write your own. As with the meditation to build your astral temple, you should either have someone read this pathworking aloud to you or pre-record yourself reading it so that you can listen to it as you meditate.

Begin by closing your eyes, breathing deeply to relax, and situating yourself in your astral temple. Once you are comfortable there, picture yourself walking out through the portal to a new, unknown location. The pathworking begins as you are exiting the temple.

You find yourself in a shadowy grotto. The rocky walls are dimly lit by light coming from the distant mouth of the cave, and they're slick with water that drips in a slow, steady rhythm. You smell the sharp brine of seawater. Farther away, you see that the cave floor disappears beneath dark waters. The water churns and bubbles, roaring with noise as it washes in and out of the cave. Rest in this cave for a few moments. Take in the sound of the waves, the taste of salt on each breath you take. Reach out to touch the cave wall and feel the cool, wet rock beneath your palm.

When you are ready, you walk to the edge of the water. If you are wearing shoes, remove them. Step into the water. You shiver as the cold water laps around your ankles. The cave floor slopes gently beneath you as you wade deeper into the sea. It comes up to your knees, then to your waist, your chest, and finally up to your shoulders as you fully enter the water. Although the cold water is shocking at first, you find that your body begins to grow comfortable in it. Lift your feet off the cave floor and allow yourself to float in the water, moving gently back and forth with the ebb and flow of the waves.

The currents surrounding you are strong but not rough. You find yourself pulled with the flow of the water, but you are in no danger. You are safe as you yield yourself to the tide. Close your eyes and release your mind into the eddying currents that swirl around you. Allow yourself to become one with the expanse of the sea.

Gradually, the currents pull you farther and farther into the cave, away from the point where you entered the water. As you are pulled deeper into the water, you find yourself at the mouth of the cave. Outside, you see a dazzling blue sky lit by the midday sun. The water extends as far as you can see, a line of deep sapphire extending across the horizon, punctuated by occasional white caps on the waves. In the distance, you hear seagulls calling.

As you pass the mouth of the cave and emerge into the sunlight, look around you. Off to your right, you see a rocky coastline. To your left, the rocks give way to a white, sandy beach that curves in a wide crescent around a gentle bay. Beyond the beach, you see a dark green tangle of trees leading into a deep jungle.

Swim in the direction of the beach. As you begin swimming, you find that the water parts smoothly before you, and a current at your back speeds you on your way. Duck your head beneath the water and glide forward with gentle, easy strokes. Keep swimming until the water becomes more shallow beneath you and you are able to stand comfortably. Walk out of the surf and feel the hot sun beating down on your body, drying the beads of saltwater from your skin. As you walk up onto the beach, the fine sand clings to your feet, giving you a pleasant sensation of warmth. The sound of the waves recedes behind you, still present but no longer deafening.

"Hello, there!" calls a voice off to your left.

Turn to look in the direction of the voice. At first, it's difficult to see who spoke to you because he's obscured by the shadows at the edge of the tree line. As your eyes adjust, though, you see a man hanging upside-down from a branch on one of the trees, suspended by a rope tied around his ankle. He is dressed in a blue shirt and a pair of red trousers. He hangs with his hands folded behind his back and his head swaying just barely above the ground.

Walk over toward the man. As you get closer, he flashes you a smile.

"It's a beautiful view, isn't it?" he calls out to you. "Of course, I'd rather not be stuck here at all, but one learns to appreciate what one has."

He cocks his head on an angle, looking up at you.

"I would ask you to untie me, but I'm afraid it's no use," he says. "I can't be released until I've served my time. But I would be grateful if you could sit for a while and keep me company."

He pulls a hand from behind his back and gestures to a log lying in the sand nearby. You sit on the log, facing out toward the waves.

"I've been here a long time," says the Hanged Man once you've settled yourself, "Watching the waves every day. At first I hated it; I was dreadfully bored. I have to admit, though, it is rather peaceful after a while. Once I let go of wanting to be elsewhere, I learned to appreciate where I am."

He turns his head to look at you.

"What's your prison?" he asks. "Everyone is stuck somewhere."

Take a moment to reflect on his question as you watch the rising and falling of the waves. The sound of surf on the shore is hypnotic, a continuous beat of water rising from the depths and crashing upon the sand. You think about your own life and the challenges you have been facing. What has been restricting and confining you? What shackles have you been struggling against? Listening to the waves, you become aware of the answer to the Hanged Man's question. Tell him about the area of your life where you feel stuck.

He thinks for a moment, swaying gently back and forth as he ponders in silence.

"It's hard," he says at last. "I know how hard it is to feel helpless. You want to do something—anything—to change the way things are, but it feels like nothing you do can have any effect. All you can do is wait."

As he speaks, you realize that he is swaying like a pendulum, rocking back and forth in perfect unison with the sound of the waves.

"I've learned a few things in my time here," he continues. "The first is that everything changes eventually. Change is the nature of life. It's like the ocean: The tides ebb and flow, new waves are always breaking, and there are currents swirling deep beneath the surface. Even when the ocean looks perfectly still, it's not. Things are changing even when you can't see the change."

He falls silent again, collecting his thoughts. You look at him and realize he is much older than he had initially appeared. There is a deep wisdom behind his eyes. You wonder exactly how long the Hanged Man has been waiting here, and what he is waiting for.

"The second thing I've learned is how to surrender," he says. "Water takes the shape of the vessel it fills. It flows with its environment instead of resisting it. Sometimes, relinquishing control is the best thing you can do. That doesn't mean that you give up on wanting things to change, but you realize when change is beyond your power. It's okay to accept that this is where you are for now, knowing that it won't be forever."

He gestures up at his bound ankle.

"I've been hanging here for longer than anyone can remember, and no one but me knows why. It hasn't always been pleasant, especially when storms roll in from the ocean. Still, I'm here through fair weather and foul, and I yield to whatever comes. One day, I hope, I may be released, but until then, I have found the wisdom of surrender. Even through all the suffering, there's something you can learn if you choose to."

With that, he folds his arms behind his back and turns his gaze back to the ocean. You get the sense that the conversation is over. Remain on the log a while longer, watching the tide come in alongside the Hanged Man. If you wish, you may ask him a question, and he may answer, but he may also remain silent; he has shared his wisdom with you, and the rest is for you to discover yourself.

When you are ready, stand up from the log. Bid the Hanged Man farewell and return to the water. Wade back into the ocean, allowing the cold water to lap around your ankles, your knees, your waist, your chest, and finally your shoulders. As you lift your feet up from the sandy ocean floor, a current catches you and begins to pull you deeper into the bay. Duck your head beneath the waves, feeling the refreshment of cool water against your hot skin. Swim farther into the bay in the direction of the cave.

Although you are returning to where you have already been, it looks different now. In the time you were speaking with the Hanged Man, the sun has moved in the sky, and the change in light is evident as you swim. The sky is a richer shade of blue, with tints of purple becoming evident as the sun falls nearer to the horizon. Deep shadows play among the rocks ahead of you, hinting at hidden depths you hadn't noticed before.

You are moving away from the beach, farther and farther into the water. As you come to the edge of the bay, you see the mouth of the cave you had emerged from. The current picks you up and carries you toward the grotto. Yield to it, allowing it to bring you back to your beginning. The current is strong and forceful, but you feel no danger. You know that you are safe as you float in with the tide and toward the deeper part of the cave.

Listen as your ears fill with the echoing sound of waves against the rocks. Follow the water deeper, deeper into the cave, returning to your point of origin. Gradually, you find that the cave floor is beginning to slope up beneath you. You are able to set your feet down and you emerge from the water: first your shoulders, then your waist, then your knees and your ankles, until finally you have stepped out of the ocean altogether. You are back in the cave where you began.

If you had shoes and left them here, put those shoes back on. Walk farther into the cave and notice how the changed light catches on the glimmering water drops covering the ceiling and walls. Within the cave, you recognize the entrance to your astral temple. Take one last look around the grotto, then walk through the entrance. You find yourself back in your astral temple, safe and sound.

Walk over to your altar. Lift your water cup and drink deeply from it. When you have finished drinking, replace the cup on the altar and watch the water settle inside it, noting how it takes the shape given to it by the cup. Contemplate what the Hanged Man told you as you watch the water return to a state of tranquility.

You may remain in your astral temple as long as you like. When you are ready, walk to the exit and return to your physical body.

## Active Imagination

The final type of meditation I'll discuss here is *active imagination*. This is very similar to path-working in that you go on an imaginary journey where you encounter arcane images and symbols, but it differs in one important respect: Whereas pathworking is pre-scripted, active imagination is freeform. With active imagination, you place yourself in an imaginary situation and then interact with your environment as if it were real—and that means there's no script to follow. The onus is on you to imagine how you would act if placed in a particular setting, as well as how other characters in that setting would react to you.

You'll sometimes see people using the word *pathworking* to describe this unscripted type of meditation as well as pre-written guided meditations, but the two are different enough that I find it helpful to have separate terms for them. The phrase *active imagination* comes from the work of Swiss psychoanalyst Carl Gustav Jung, who developed the technique as a means of engaging with esoteric symbolism in a therapeutic setting. Jung suggested that by engaging in childlike play and participating in an extended fantasy or daydream, people could come face to face with meaningful images that would help them integrate the unconscious parts of their psyches.[14]

Active imagination can be a bit intimidating, because there's no real guide to tell you how it's supposed to go. Each session of active imagination is its own unique experience, and you never know what to expect going into such a session. Because you treat your environment as real, the other people and spirits in that environment will act of their own accord, often doing things that surprise you. They may even act in ways that you dislike or disapprove of.

The key is to imagine them as separate from yourself, as beings with their own agency. You are not creating a passive daydream where everything is exactly how you want it to be—you are actively entering into a magical environment where you will interact with other beings, each of whom has their own personality and desires. With active imagination, you are not merely fantasizing; rather, you are using fantasy as a technique to facilitate a trance journey. The result of that journey will be an encounter with magical symbols and personalities that are much larger than you and that are ultimately beyond your control, and the goal is to walk away from that encounter changed in some deep way.

Active imagination is a technique designed for people with an "inner eye"—that is to say, those who can easily reproduce images in their thoughts. As I've previously noted, some people struggle with this or are altogether unable to visualize, and if you're one of those people, this

---

14. See *Jung on Active Imagination* to learn more.

technique may not be the most useful for you. Still, if you want to give it a try, I encourage you to do so. To do active imagination without visualization, focus on being able to describe what happens. Rather than picturing an encounter for yourself, narrate it out loud, as if you are telling the story of something that is currently happening.

To perform active imagination with the tarot, choose a card you want to explore in depth. Sit in a comfortable place with the card set in front of you so that you can see it. I like to work by candlelight because I find electric lights distracting, but that's a matter of personal preference. Examine the card closely. Take note of every detail—every shape, line, and color. Who are the people depicted on this card? Where are they? What time of year is it? Are there any animals? For the time being, refrain from thinking about what these images may symbolize. Try to just absorb the picture shown on the card. Focus on it so intently that you can reproduce it perfectly in your mind's eye, down to the smallest detail. If you have no mind's eye, focus so intently that you can perfectly describe what the card looks like.

When you feel that you have captured the essence of the card in your mind, close your eyes.

Go to your astral temple. Visualize the card as vividly and in as much detail as possible. Walk through the exit of your astral temple, and on the other side of the exit, imagine finding yourself in the scene depicted by the card. You are now present in that image, alongside the characters and objects already populating it.

From this point on, there is no road map. Explore the landscape of the card. Speak with the people there. You may ask them for wisdom or for help with a particular problem—or, conversely, you may find yourself enlisted to help them with their problems. You may participate in an ordinary, quiet conversation, or you may go on an epic quest. You may even receive an object of some special significance, which you can take back to your astral temple with you after your journey is done. Whatever happens during your active imagination session, it will be significant and will relate to a lesson that this particular card has to teach you.

Active imagination is a skill, and like every other skill, it's difficult the first time you try it. Don't be discouraged if you have difficulty imagining yourself entering into a card, or if you don't know how to act once you do. Like all things, it gets easier with practice.

When you have finished your journey, return to your astral temple and take some time to recenter yourself before coming back to ordinary life.

Importantly, don't just do the meditation and then go about your day as if nothing happened. Allow this meditation to sink in. Take some time to reflect on the journey you just experienced. What did you see? What did you do? What parts of it were unexpected or surprising to you? What can you learn or take away from this session, and how does it relate to your ordinary life? If you keep a tarot journal or magical diary, I would heartily recommend taking the time immediately after your active imagination to write about it in your journal. That way, you can revisit it further on down the line, with fresh perspective on its significance.

## chapter eight
# Stacking the Deck

Reading tarot is already such a powerful practice. Using a deck of images printed on ordinary card stock, you can reach across time and space to find answers to your biggest questions. Because of this, it's surprisingly simple to use a tarot reading as a magical tool in its own right—engaging in active change rather than merely passive divination. You can choose not only to receive answers, but to decide what those answers are going to be. You can use the framework of a tarot reading to exert magical change on the world around you.

The basic technique for doing this is stacking the deck: choosing in advance which cards you're going to turn up. By consciously selecting the symbols that go into a tarot reading, you turn the reading into a type of sympathetic magic. You create a symbolic narrative that represents the outcome you want to see—by creating the outcome in symbol, you also create it in reality. This turns tarot reading into an act of co-creation with the universe, where you take an active role in shaping the future rather than confining yourself to predicting it.

## The Basic Procedure

To stack the deck for a magical reading, begin by thinking about the outcome you want to achieve and how you might get there. In the center of a blank piece of paper, write a word or a short phrase describing your magical goal. If you're trying to get a certain amount of money in order to make rent, you might write *$600*; if you are looking for a romantic partner, you might write *love*.

Circle that word or phrase, and then take ten minutes to make a word cloud surrounding it. What other words, emotions, ideas, or accomplishments go alongside it in your mind? Fill up the paper with as many ideas as you can, and don't be afraid to get specific. Keywords like *partnership* or *success* are great, but so are *cooking dinner together* or *a 5 percent salary raise*.

When you have finished your word cloud, take a minute to look it over. This is a scattershot look at your magical goal: the outcome you are trying to achieve through your reading. Some words are going to seem more important than others; underline those words to add emphasis to them. These words represent the focus of your magic.

Your task now is to reverse-engineer a tarot reading based on this word cloud. Imagine that this word cloud is your set of notes after performing a tarot reading. What would the reading have looked like? What is the question you would have asked? What spread might have been used, and what cards would have been drawn in order to produce this final message?

Take a fresh sheet of paper. At the bottom of the sheet, write a sentence that summarizes your outcome; this is the "answer" to the question posed in your reading. At the top of the sheet, write the question that goes with that answer. For example, if your answer is "I will be in a relationship within six months," the question might be "What does my love life look like in the year ahead?" If your answer is "I will receive a 5 percent raise," the question could be "How will my boss respond to the work I've been doing recently?"

Now, think about the spread you would use to answer this question. In the middle of the paper, list out all the card positions for the spread you would use. Then, go through the list one by one and write down the ideal card for each position. If you were performing a reading for your chosen question and everything turned up exactly as you hoped it would, what cards would you see?

When you have finished selecting your cards, sort through your tarot deck and pull out all of the cards you've written down. Arrange them on the top of the deck so that you can draw them in order to lay them out in the spread you've arranged. Your deck is now stacked and ready for magical use. When you are ready, you can perform a staged reading with it as an act of sympathetic magic, spinning the wheel of fate with your own hand.

## A Ritual Framework

When performing a magical reading with a stacked deck, it's helpful to have a ritual frame for your work. Establish a particular magical space and time in which you're going to do your reading. In doing so, you demarcate your magical work from the flow of your day-to-day life, emphasizing that your reading is something special and set apart from the ordinary world. Different practitioners have their own preferences for the ritual frameworks of their magic. Some people prefer an elaborate setup with a carefully dressed altar, incense blended specially for the occasion, ceremonial garments, and magical sigils drawn on the ground; others prefer something simple like lighting a candle and taking a moment to center themselves psychically before beginning magical work. Regardless, it's good to have something.

The following procedure is a basic setup you can use for magical readings, which is a bit more on the low magic end of things. Try it out for yourself, and feel free to tweak it according to your preferences. You can make it simpler or more elaborate, change the words, and add elements as you see fit. The goal is to use my sample to develop a framework that fits into your own magical practice—and that will look different for each person. You will need:

- A clear, flat surface on which to read
- Your stacked tarot deck
- A bowl of soil
- A hand fan
- A bowl of water
- A candle
- Matches or a lighter
- Your four elemental tools

Situate yourself in front of your reading space. Take a few deep breaths and center yourself, allowing thoughts of your everyday life to fade into the background. Focus on the task at hand and the magical work you are about to do. Place your tarot deck in the center of your reading space and say:

> *Great powers of magic, bear witness! I come before you with the*
> *tools of fate, not to see the future but to choose it for myself.*

Pick up your bowl of soil. Holding it cupped in both hands, say:

> *May the element of earth bless my magic with stability.*

Take a small pinch of soil from the bowl and carefully sprinkle it around the perimeter of your reading space. Be sure to leave plenty of clean room in the center of your space to lay out your cards. When you have completed your circuit of the space, take your earth pentacle and place it in the front left-hand corner of your reading space. Place the bowl with the remaining soil on top of your pentacle.

Now, pick up your fan. Holding it with both hands, say:

> *May the element of air bless my magic with inspiration.*

Use the fan to waft air around the perimeter of your reading space. When you are done, take your air blade and place it in the front right-hand corner of the space. Lay the fan alongside your blade.

Third, take your bowl of water in both hands and say:

> *May the element of water bless my magic with love.*

Sprinkle a little bit of water around the perimeter of your reading space, being careful to leave plenty of dry room in the middle. When you are done, place your water cup in the back left-hand corner of the space. Pour the remaining water into the cup, then set the empty bowl alongside it.

Finally, light your candle. Hold it in both hands and say:

> *May the element of fire bless my magic with power.*

Hold the candle steady as you pass it around the perimeter of your reading space. When you are done, place the candle and your fire wand in the back right-hand corner of your reading space. Say:

> *I call the elements to bear witness to the magic that is about to be performed here. Bless this tool of fate, that I may shape my own destiny. In this place and time, I choose the future of [the thing you are doing magic for].*

Now, pick up the tarot deck. Lay out the cards according to the spread and order you have predetermined. As you place each card down, identify it out loud and declare its significance:

> *In the position of [spread position], I draw [card]. This signifies [what you have chosen the card to mean].*

Finish laying out all the cards. Then, extend your hands over the reading surface. Concentrate on the outcome you are trying to produce, and see how that outcome is represented in the cards you have chosen. Say:

*I desire [outcome], and the cards show my true desire. It is written now*
*in the book of fate. This is what I wish. It must be! It shall be! It is!*

Spend some time in this space reflecting on your desired outcome and how you plan to achieve it. If you like, you may take this time to sing, meditate, journal, or do other activities so long as they are related to your magical goal. When you are ready, say:

*The cards have borne witness. It is done.*

Extinguish the candle. The ritual is now complete. Leave the ritual space—including the tarot spread—in place and untouched until your result is achieved.

## The Ethics of Stacking the Deck

As soon as we introduce the idea of curating cards—as opposed to drawing them at random—an ugly dragon rears its head. Tarot readers are already mistrusted in popular culture, thought of as charlatans and hucksters. Indeed, the unfortunate reality is that there are con artists out there who see tarot as an opportunity to prey on vulnerable people and defraud them of thousands of dollars. These are the sort of people who will pull cards for a new client and say, "I drew the Ten of Cups and the Four of Wands. This means there is a terrible curse on you, and the only way to remove it is with a very costly ritual that only I am qualified to perform." This is a far cry from the sincere tarot divination that you'll read about in this or other books, but it does happen, and it casts a shadow over the reputation of all tarot readers.

When someone comes to you for a tarot reading, they are placing a great deal of trust in you. Depending on the circumstances, they may be disclosing intimate details of their personal life, making themself vulnerable in a way that people rarely are when talking to strangers. People seek out tarot readers when they have questions they want answered, and they place trust in a reader's skill at drawing and interpreting the cards to supply those answers.

It is critically important that you never abuse the trust that a querent places in you. Therefore, allow me to say this in no uncertain terms: **Do not *ever* stack the deck in a situation where you have been asked to perform a divinatory reading.** Divinatory tarot relies on randomness: You draw cards without knowing in advance what they're going to be, and you find the answer to your question through interpreting those randomly selected cards. When someone asks you for a divinatory reading, they are trusting that divinatory process. If you remove the element of randomness by intentionally tampering with the cards you draw, you are deceiving your querent and breaking faith with them. This is bad. Don't do it.

If you read tarot for long enough, you will eventually come up against cards that say things you and your querent don't want to hear. In times like these, it can be tempting to fudge a bit: to reshuffle and draw the cards again, to draw a "clarifying" card in the hopes that it will change the timbre of the reading, and so on. But this is fundamentally dishonest and unethical. Your responsibility as a tarot reader is to interpret the cards that you draw, even when they have unpleasant truths to share.

I had to learn this lesson the hard way. Many years ago, I was performing a reading for someone who was dealing with an intense personal crisis. We had talked through some very heavy topics, and I wanted to leave the reading on a positive note.

"Let's draw a final card," I said. "Are you going to be okay?"

The card I drew was the Devil.

I stared at the card for a long while, and then I made a bad decision (and one I have never made again since).

"You know what?" I said. "Let's redraw that card."

I put the Devil back into the deck and pulled a second card. This time, it was the Nine of Swords. Feeling frantic, I replaced that card as well and drew a third. This one was the Hanged Man.

I'd received my answer with the first card and chosen to ignore it—my querent was *not* going to be okay. But I didn't want to admit that and didn't know how to have a delicate conversation about it with the querent, so I tried to change the reading. Luckily, in this case, my deck kept spitting out cards with painful themes until I got the message, but I shouldn't have tried to change the reading in the first place. My querent deserved my honesty; they had asked me what the cards said about their situation, and I had a responsibility to tell them. In this case, it turned out the situation was worse than my querent had disclosed to me. They urgently needed the intervention of a trained professional. Because I finally had the guts to be honest about the reading, the querent did reach out for help and did end up being okay, but if I had kept redrawing until I pulled a happy card, they might not have.

The moral of the story: Don't futz with the cards when you're doing divination.

Stacking the deck is a wonderful and effective magical technique, but it's important to maintain a boundary between the divinatory and magical uses of tarot. The two are closely related and may look similar from the outside, but there is a fundamental difference in orientation between them. Divination relies on passively receiving the message that comes your way; magic relies on actively changing it. If you try to do one when you're supposed to be doing the other, you're going to land yourself in hot water.

Because of this, I only use magical deck-stacking techniques in situations where I have deliberately set out to do so. I have to know that I'm doing magic before I even pick up the cards. If I start a reading as divination and see it going in a direction I don't like, I never change course halfway through and decide to start tweaking the reading magically. Instead, I'll complete the reading, interpret it thoroughly, and take notes. Then, at some later date, I will sit down and perform a conscious act of magic to change the result of the reading. By maintaining separation between divinatory sessions and magical ones, I help to preserve the ethical boundary and ensure that I'm never tempted to redraw cards in a divinatory reading just because I don't like what they have to say.

## Spreads for Stacking the Deck

The following are a few sample spreads that you may wish to use for magical readings. These are designed for predictive questions with a range of time frames and subject matters. Each of them can be used in a divinatory context, but I also find them exceptionally useful for magical deck-stacking readings. If you find that none of these spreads meet your needs, you can always use other spreads (from this or another book) or design your own spread from scratch.

### *Year Ahead Spread*

This twelve-card spread is large, but it's actually quite simple to interpret. You draw one card for each month of the coming year, giving you a full twelve-month forecast of the future. This spread is useful for magical readings when you want to establish that something will happen by a particular date.

1. January (or the first month after the reading is performed)
2. February (or two months after the reading)
3. March (or three months after the reading)
4. April (or four months after the reading)
5. May (or five months after the reading)
6. June (or six months after the reading)

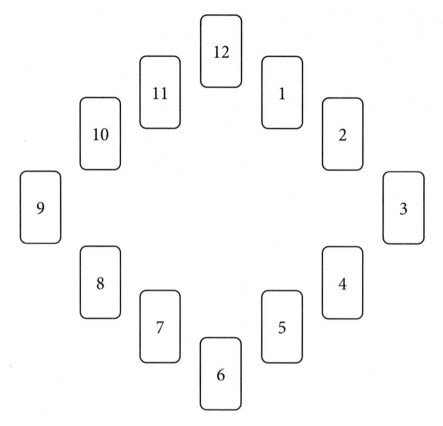

7. July (or seven months after the reading)

8. August (or eight months after the reading)

9. September (or nine months after the reading)

10. October (or ten months after the reading)

11. November (or eleven months after the reading)

12. December (or twelve months after the reading)

## Obstacles and Resources Spread

This is a simple spread designed to help you overcome a particular obstacle. It identifies your current circumstances and the challenge you're dealing with, then points you to the resources or allies you need in order to surmount that challenge. Finally, it shows you the outcome of the situation if you make the best use of the tools available to you. This is an ideal spread to use for magical readings aimed at solving a specific problem.

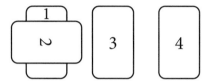

1. Your current situation
2. The problem you face
3. The resources that can help you
4. The final outcome

## Depth of the Future Spread

This is similar to the Past/Present/Future spread in that it shows you three different moments in time. Rather than looking into the past, however, it shows you the future at varying distances: how things will look in the short-term, the medium-term, and the long-term. This gives you a more nuanced and complex look into the future, showing how future events may evolve and change over time. You can use this spread for magical readings that deal with multiple future events in sequence, or when you are trying to cause a progression or development of some kind.

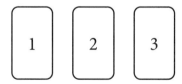

1. The near future
2. The middle future
3. The distant future

## Growth Spread

This spread identifies something in your life that is going to grow over time. It's particularly useful for magical readings when you are embarking on something new and want to see it flourish—whether that's a creative endeavor, a financial venture, a new relationship, or something else entirely.

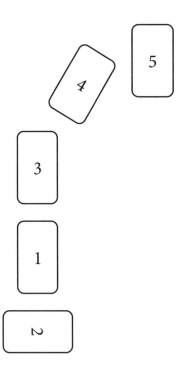

1. Seed: The potential for new growth

2. Root: What nourishes that growth

3. Sprout: The early stages of growth

4. Flower: The first visible reward of growth

5. Fruit: The final product of the growth

## Connections Spread

This spread explores the resolution of interpersonal conflict. It is useful for magical work to heal relationships of all kinds, whether those relationships are friendships, professional connections, family ties, or romantic partnerships. This magical work requires honesty and introspection on the part of everyone involved—it aims at genuine mutual understanding, not just magically steamrolling other people and getting your own way—but it is worthwhile for those willing to undertake it. The spread is designed for two people, but it can be expanded to explore connections between three or more.

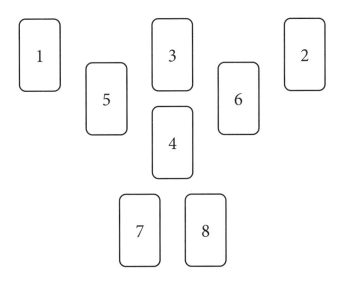

1. Person A

2. Person B

3. The apparent conflict

4. The deeper cause of the conflict

5. What person A needs to understand

6. What person B needs to understand

7. The path to reconciliation

8. The outcome

## Course Correction Spread

Sometimes you know you need to make a change because your current plan just isn't working. This simple spread shows where you're headed now and how to redirect to another path. It's good for magical readings when you are trying to make a significant change in your life and want some magical assistance to make sure that your new plan of attack goes better than the old one.

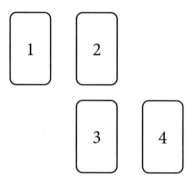

1. Your current plan of action

2. The likely outcome

3. How to change your action

4. The outcome after the change

## Choosing the Right Cards

When you're stacking the deck, the real magic is in the symbolism of the cards you choose. Deck stacking is a type of sympathetic magic, and it relies on the similarity between your magical goal and the story you tell with your cards. While the ritual framework of performing the staged reading is important—that's the actual magical act—most of the hard work in this type of magic goes into the preparation you do beforehand. How good your spell is depends almost entirely on whether you choose the cards that best represent the outcome you're trying to effect.

So, how can you make sure that you choose the right cards?

The most important card, of course, is the outcome card. Whatever card in your spread represents the future or final resolution will set the tone for the rest of your magic and for the reading as a whole. This is the card to start with. Ask yourself, *What is the best possible outcome card I could draw if I did a reading about this?* Keep in mind that there may be multiple good candidates in the deck depending on the result you're trying to achieve, but each card will carry its own particular nuances. A card may capture one aspect of the desired result but leave off other important features; if that's the case, you have to decide what your top priority is and choose your card placement accordingly.

To start with, then, it's best to think about the desired result and brainstorm three to five cards that represent that goal. From there, narrow in on which one is best suited to your magical needs, and select that as the outcome card for your reading.

Let's suppose you're doing a reading to accelerate your divorce proceedings. There are several cards you could choose for the final result. These include (but are not limited to) the Eight of Wands for speed, the Eight of Cups for leaving something behind, or Strength for independence. Each of these captures something that the others do not: The Eight of Wands says that something is happening swiftly, but doesn't specify what; the Eight of Cups indicates a separation, but doesn't guarantee a time frame; Strength shows you happily on your own, but doesn't clarify how you get there.

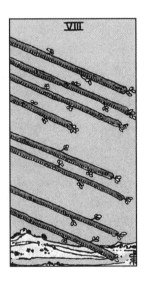  

Which card you choose will depend on what you most want to prioritize. If what you care about most is getting out as fast as possible, the Eight of Wands might be your best bet. If you want to focus instead on the self-sufficiency you'll have post-divorce, Strength would be a better way to go.

However, regardless of which card you choose, you may still want to incorporate the others into your reading. All of the candidate cards you selected represent other important aspects of your desired outcome. You can place them elsewhere in your spread in order to bring their energy into the magical reading; even if they're not in the outcome position, they can still contribute to the overall magical effect of the work you're doing.

Continuing with the divorce example, let's suppose that you decide to use the Growth spread. After deliberation, you decide that Strength is most representative of the final outcome you want: to be on your own and thriving. Therefore, you'll place Strength in position 5 of the spread, "Fruit." It represents the overall result of the growth you're going through. Now, think about where in the spread you might want to put the Eight of Wands and the Eight of Cups. How can these cards contribute to the reading if they're not the final outcome? The Eight of Cups might be a good fit for position 1 of the spread, "Seed." There, it represents the thing that you are trying to cultivate—namely, getting out of your current marriage. Likewise, the Eight of Wands would be a good fit for position 3, "Sprout," in order to represent the divorce moving as quickly as possible once it's initiated.

There are other ways you could arrange these cards. Each different arrangement will provide a similar overall message, but with subtle differences in emphasis and framing. How you choose to lay out your cards is entirely up to you. Do what feels right and looks like it best represents the kind of reading you want to receive.

Once you've placed those cards, you can look at the remaining spread positions and think about what's missing. What information have you not yet put into the reading? With the positions you have left over, how can you flesh out your reading in order to make it say exactly what you want it to say?

In our example, there are two unused spread positions: position 2 ("Root") and position 4 ("Flower"). Looking at the cards selected so far, the reading talks about walking away from something, moving quickly, and achieving independence. The reading does not yet specify what you're walking away from, nor how you're going to achieve it. Those are probably good themes to bring in with the remaining cards. In position 4, you might place the Two of Cups in reverse; this makes it abundantly clear that as a result of your growth, a romantic connection is coming to an end. In position 2, you would place a card that represents how you're hoping to get through this divorce; for example, you might pick the Ten of Cups to represent community. The final reading can be seen on the following page.

This is a clear reading that identifies the key themes of the magic being done, and it shows a narrative progression toward a quick resolution in the divorce and a happy life afterward.

Once you have chosen your cards (and before you perform your stacked reading), take a moment to consider the spread as a whole, looking at it through the various magical lenses discussed in part I of this book. What is the balance of the four elements? Are there predominant astrological influences in the reading? How does the reading fit onto the Tree of Life? You don't have to design your reading around those considerations, but they can be a helpful way of packing in more symbolism to align the spread with your magical goal—and they're a good way to make sure the cards say what you really want them to. A magical reading about schoolwork will likely have a predominance of airy Swords, while one about a job will generally be full of earthy Pentacles. If your reading is trying to establish peace and harmony, it probably won't be overwhelmed by cards that correspond to Mars. If you want to stabilize a situation and slow it down, you don't want too many Twos bringing in the Qabalistic energy of Chokmah.

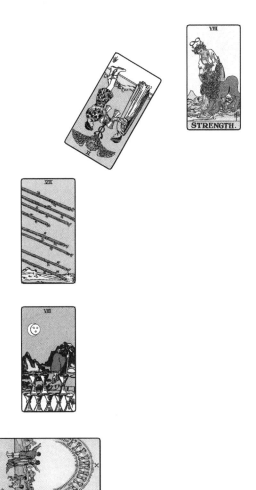

Again, none of these guidelines are hard and fast, and you don't have to structure your reading around these correspondences if you don't want to. Nonetheless, they are available to you. It wouldn't hurt to look at your tarot spread through these various magical lenses before performing a stacked reading.

| CARD | ELEMENT | ZODIAC | PLANET | TREE OF LIFE |
|------|---------|--------|--------|--------------|
| Eight of Cups | Water | Pisces | Saturn | Hod |
| Ten of Cups | Water | Pisces | Mars | Malkuth |
| Eight of Wands | Fire | Sagittarius | Mercury | Hod |
| Two of Cups (reversed) | Water | Cancer | Venus | Chokmah |
| Strength | — | Leo | — | Chesed → Gevurah |

Looking at the sample reading in this way, a few significant patterns jump out. Three of the five cards correspond to elemental water, which is fitting for a reading about interpersonal relationships. Two of the five are associated with Pisces, showing the need for clarity and distance in an emotional relationship that has become unhealthy. There is no dominant planetary presence, but two of the five cards connect to Hod, the Sephirah of independence and the self. Thus, examining the reading through these various magical lenses, we see that it reinforces key themes about emotional needs, boundaries, and self-sufficiency. These themes align perfectly with the magical intent behind the reading.

## Altering a Previous Reading

As a variant on this technique, you may choose to magically alter a previous divinatory reading that you've performed. Divination gives you a glimpse into the future; if you don't like that future, magic gives you the power to change it. There is tremendous magical potency in mindfully rewriting a narrative that you've been given in divination—rejecting one vision of the future and instead substituting your own.

To alter a reading magically, you will ritually replace some of the cards in the spread with others of your choosing. The goal is not to perform an entirely new reading, but to adjust the existing one in order to avoid the problems you've foreseen. Because of this, the goal is to change the reading as little as possible. You want to leave the shape of the original reading intact, surgically altering one or two cards rather than throwing everything out and starting over from scratch.

There's also a practical reason for this. Remember that magic can't make impossible things possible. You can use magic to apply pressure and alter the course of events, but it's important to maintain perspective on what is and is not achievable. A reading that says "Your trip to Hong Kong is going to be troubled by logistical delays" is much easier to rewrite than one that says "Your trip to Hong Kong is going to be terrible and you should cancel it altogether." The smaller the change you make, the easier your magic is to accomplish; replacing one card is easier and more targeted than replacing every card in the spread.

If you alter a reading, it's still important to maintain a boundary between divinatory and magical tarot reading. Don't perform a reading, see that you dislike it, and then immediately redraw the cards to try to change them. Instead, if you receive a divinatory reading and want to alter it magically, sit with the reading for a while before taking any magical action. Write down the spread you used, the cards you drew, and your interpretation of the reading. Then, walk away from the reading and give yourself a few days for your head to clear.

When you come back to the reading, ask yourself what exactly you disliked. What were you unhappy with? What do you want to change? And importantly, is it something you *can* change? Try to identify the points where you want to apply magical pressure. Which specific cards are causing problems for the reading? These are the cards you're going to replace. Try to be as narrow in scope as possible. Ideally, you'll change only one card in order to achieve your magical outcome.

Once you've identified the cards you want to change, think about what you want to change them to. Again, the smaller your change, the easier the magical work. Turning the Seven of Swords into the Queen of Pentacles is a drastic change, because those two cards have basically nothing to do with each other. Turning the Seven of Swords into the Seven of Pentacles, on the other hand, is a smoother transition, because those two cards have at least a little bit in common: They're both Sevens with a numerological and Qabalistic connection to Netzach. Try to choose cards that have at least some kind of connection to each other, whether that's elemental, numerological, Qabalistic, astrological, or simply thematic. The less jarring your magical change is, the more likely you are to have success.

When you have finished choosing your new cards, stack your deck. Set it up with the cards from your first reading on top so that you can draw and place them exactly as they were originally. Then, place your selected cards beneath those so that they will be the next cards you draw from the stack. Your deck is now ready for magical use.

## A Ritual for Altering Readings

This is an adaptation of the deck-stacking ritual for use in magically amending a previous divinatory reading. It follows the same basic outline as stacking the deck, but with slightly different words and steps. You will need:

- A clear, flat surface on which to read
- Your stacked tarot deck
- A bowl of soil
- A hand fan
- A bowl of water
- A candle
- Matches or a lighter
- Your four elemental tools

Situate yourself in front of your reading space. Take a few deep breaths and center yourself, allowing thoughts of your everyday life to fade into the background. Focus on the task at hand and the magical work you are about to do. Place your tarot deck in the center of your reading space and say:

> *Great powers of magic, bear witness! I come before you with the tools*
> *of fate so that I might change the hand that fortune has dealt to me.*

Pick up your bowl of soil. Holding it cupped in both hands, say:

> *May the element of earth bless my magic with stability.*

Sprinkle the perimeter of your reading space with soil, then place the bowl and your earth pentacle in the front left-hand corner of your reading space.

Pick up your fan. Holding it with both hands, say:

> *May the element of air bless my magic with inspiration.*

Use the fan to waft air around the perimeter of your reading space. When you are done, place the fan and your air blade in the front right-hand corner of the space.

Third, take your bowl of water in both hands and say:

*May the element of water bless my magic with love.*

Sprinkle water around the perimeter of your reading space, then place your water cup in the back left-hand corner of the space and pour the remaining water into the cup.

Finally, light your candle. Hold it in both hands and say:

*May the element of fire bless my magic with power.*

Pass the candle around the perimeter of your reading space, then place the candle and your fire wand in the back right-hand corner. Say:

*I call the elements to bear witness to the magic that is about*
*to be performed here. Bless this tool of fate, that I may change*
*the shape of my own destiny. In this place and time, I choose to*
*alter the future of [the thing you are doing magic for].*

Now, pick up the tarot deck. Say:

*Here is the hand that fortune dealt.*

Lay out the cards to match your previous reading. As you place each card down, identify it out loud and declare its significance:

*In the position of [spread position], I draw [card].*
*This signifies [how you interpret the card].*

When you have finished laying out all the cards, pick up the first of the cards you intend to replace. Say:

*Hear me, [card], signifying [how you interpret the card],*
*you belong here no more. I release you from my fate.*

Turn the card face-down so that it is no longer visible. Draw the card from your deck that you are using to replace this card. Holding the card over your reading space, say:

*In your place, I welcome [card], signifying [what you have*
*chosen the card to mean]. This is now my fate.*

Place the card face-up on top of the card it is replacing. If you have multiple cards to replace, repeat this process until you have laid them all out. Then, extend your hands over your altered reading. Concentrate on the outcome you are trying to produce, and see how that outcome is represented in the cards you have chosen. Say:

*I deal my own hand. I change my fate. This is what*
*I wish. It must be! It shall be! It is!*

Spend some time in this space reflecting on your desired outcome and how you plan to achieve it. If you like, you may take this time to sing, meditate, journal, or do other activities so long as they are related to your magical goal. When you are ready, say:

*The cards have borne witness. It is done.*

Extinguish the candle. The ritual is now complete. Leave the ritual space—including the tarot spread—in place and untouched until your result is achieved.

*chapter nine*
# Tarot Talismans

A *talisman* is a magical object consecrated to the accomplishment of a particular goal. Talismans are designed to draw in a certain kind of magical energy: attracting abundance, love, popularity, and the like. Once made and consecrated, a talisman is placed in a particular location or carried on your person so that the power it attracts can have the greatest possible effect on you or your environs.

Everyone is familiar with talismanic magic, even if they don't think of it in those terms. A talisman can be elaborately constructed out of expensive materials at a carefully selected time, but it can also be incredibly simple. A horseshoe nailed over a door for protection is a kind of talisman; so is a pair of fuzzy dice hung from the rearview mirror to bring a driver luck on the road. We all share an instinct that some objects are just *good* and that their goodness will rub off on us if we keep them nearby. That's the law of magical contact at work. Talismanic magic picks up on this instinct and makes it more conscious and deliberate.

When making a talisman, you imbue a particular object or image with magical potency and symbolism. With a tarot deck in hand, you have seventy-eight symbolically rich, magically potent images premade and ready to go. Over the course of this chapter, I'll look at some more sophisticated ways of using tarot cards for talismanic work, but the simplest way is to pick a card that represents the energy you want and then carry that card with you, letting it do its thing.

When I'm going on a date, I'll pull the Two of Cups out of a tarot deck and slip it into my coat pocket. On a recent cross-country road trip, I put the Chariot in my car's glove compartment. The night before a big race, I stick the Eight of Wands into my running shoes. All of these cards have distinct meanings, carrying the weight of over a century of occult tradition. Because of this, each tarot card can act as a ready-made piece of sympathetic magic, influencing the world around it through magical contagion.

This is perhaps the simplest way to use tarot cards in magic. The cards already mean something; all you have to do is carry that meaning with you, both figuratively and literally, allowing it to affect the rest of your life.

If the cards I'm choosing for talismanic work are from the numbered Minor Arcana, I like to look at their Qabalistically inspired titles (see chapter 6). This gives me a clear, one-word focus for the magic, and it tells me in unambiguous terms what the talisman is going to accomplish. If I'm doing magic for wealth, I'll use the Ten of Pentacles, which is called *Wealth* in the Thoth system. If I'm trying to finish a long-running project, I use the Four of Wands, which the Thoth deck calls *Completion*.

This method is entirely a matter of personal preference, and you can and should choose the cards in the way that makes the most magical sense to you. An approach like this is really only suited to the numbered pip cards; the majors already have clear titles, and the court cards have complicated Qabalistic titles like *The Princess of the Rushing Winds*, which aren't useful in a talismanic context. Those other cards can still be used for talismanic work, of course, but you'd need to look elsewhere to find inspiration for how to make talismans from them. You may prefer to pick talismanic cards according to different keywords, or even according to visual imagery—especially if you are unfamiliar with the Thoth system of tarot. That's perfectly fine. What matters is that you draw on the power and symbolism latent in the tarot deck for the creation of your talismans.

It's also worth noting that pulling a physical card from your deck is not the only way to use tarot imagery for talismans. You can print a copy of a tarot card, draw it by hand, or even use a digital image. As I write this book, I'm in the process of hunting for a new job. To help with that process (and particularly to boost phone interviews with potential employers), the home screen on my phone is an image of the Ace of Pentacles. This is not exactly a talisman if we want to get finicky about definitions—it's not a physical object—but it effectively works in the same way. I keep the image of a particular tarot card close to hand at all times, allowing that card to affect my life through magical contagion. I have a friend who got the Two of Cups tattooed on his arm when he got married, with a similar idea in mind.

Using tarot cards in talismanic magic is a wonderful, effective, and extraordinarily straightforward way to bring together the worlds of tarot and spellcraft. In the rest of this chapter, I'll look at some more complex and sophisticated techniques you can use for tarot talismans, but the core of it is always the same: Take a card that aligns with the change you want to cause, put it in the place where that change will happen, and then step back and let it do its work.

## Talismanic Uses of the Major Arcana

The great Qabalistic magician Aleister Crowley used tarot as one of the principal lenses through which he viewed his magic. As part of his work, he listed out a series of magical goals and practices corresponding to the paths on the Tree of Life—and, consequently, to the Major Arcana of the tarot.[15] These magical goals represent particular things that you might want to do magic for, linking each goal to a particular card. Crowley's list is imperfect and ambiguous in places, but it serves as a great starting point for talismanic magic with the Major Arcana.

Each of the major cards can symbolize a wide variety of things, and you can use them creatively for talismanic purposes other than the ones given here. If you're looking for inspiration, though, this list can help you see which card or cards might be best suited for your magical purposes.

### The Fool

The Fool is associated with divination—trying to make sense of the great unknown. You can keep a Fool talisman near where your tarot decks or other divinatory tools are stored.

### The Magician

The Magician can be used for talismans involving healing, languages, or science, all of which connect to this card's planetary correspondence with Mercury.

### The High Priestess

Through its association with the moon and psychism, this card makes a good talisman for anything connected to dreams, the unconscious, or clairvoyance.

### The Empress

The Empress corresponds to Venus, the planet of love. Because of this, Crowley suggests this card (rather than the Lovers) as the Major Arcanum most connected with love magic.

---

15. Crowley, *777*, col. XLV.

### The Emperor

The Emperor is suited to talismanic magic surrounding consecration. Aries is the beginning of the Zodiac, and the Emperor helps in any magic having to do with consecrating or dedicating a new beginning.

### The Hierophant

Taurus is the bull, the symbol of strength. Because of this, the Hierophant connects well to any magic involving the body, physical prowess, and athleticism.

### The Lovers

Corresponding to Gemini, the two-bodied Lovers can help with magic where you're feeling stretched thin and overworked, like you need to be in two places at once.

### The Chariot

Crowley unhelpfully associates the Chariot with "casting enchantments."[16] I like to use this card to bless physical objects and make them work as desired, especially anything having to do with transportation.

### Strength[17]

Because this card depicts a maiden taming a lion, it's excellent for any magic that involves working with animals—especially to calm them or train them.

### The Hermit

The Hermit is a solitary, hidden figure. This card can be used for talismans to conceal things, hide them from view, or distract attention from them.

### Wheel of Fortune

Through its connection to Jupiter—the king of the planets—the Wheel of Fortune is good for talismanic magic involving politics, ambition, and ascendancy of any kind.

---

16. Crowley, *777*, col. XLV.

17. Some of the Major Arcana are titled differently in Crowley's work than what you might know from other decks. I've retained the more mainstream titles here for the sake of consistency and accessibility.

## Justice

Justice is the card most suited to magical work aimed at, well, justice. Use this card for talismans aimed at equilibrium and fairness. Be careful, however: What's *really* fair is often not exactly what we hope for.

## The Hanged Man

The Hanged Man is useful for magic aimed at transcending the individual ego and acquiring deeper wisdom. This is the card of what's sometimes called the "great work" of the magician— not practical low magic, but high magic aimed at self-development.

## Death

The Death card is useful for talismans pertaining to any magical work with the dead. You can use this card to open channels of communication between the world of the living and the spirits of the dead.

## Temperance

Crowley associates Temperance with the magic of transmutation: refining base materials into something better. Use this card for talismans of aspiration and improvement.

## The Devil

Magically speaking, this is a nasty card. It's really only suited to selfish and spiteful magic—things like the Evil Eye and other acts of malice.

## The Tower

Again, this is an unpleasant card. Its connection to Mars links it with wrath, vengeance, and magic done out of anger. It's suited for talismans made with the intent to raze and destroy.

## The Star

Crowley connects the Star with the stars above, linking this card to magic involving astrology. Personally, I like to use the Star for talismans involving forgiveness, renewal, and healing.

## The Moon

The inconstant Moon is a card of illusion and deception. This card makes a good talisman for glamor, disguise, and making things seem different than they actually are.

### The Sun

The golden Sun has connotations of joy and prosperity. This is an excellent card for money talismans, as well as for happiness and success in general.

### Judgement

Through its correspondence to elemental fire, Judgement makes an excellent elemental talisman for the things fire represents: passion, creativity, willpower, and ambition.

### The World

Crowley associates this card with cursing and death because of its connection to Saturn. However, the World also relates to elemental earth, and it can be used for talismans around completion, fulfillment, and abundance.

## A Talisman Blessing Ritual

As with all magic, talismanic work can be elaborate or simple depending on your preferences. Tarot cards are extraordinary magical objects in their own right, and it doesn't take much extra to make them pack a magical punch. Simply placing a card and letting it do its work can be an effective piece of magic, but if you like, you can do a more formal consecration of the card to its magical purpose. The following ritual is a sample consecration that you can adapt to your own taste. You will need:

- Your chosen card
- Dragon's blood incense and a censer to burn it in
- Matches or a lighter

Hold the tarot card in your hands and say:

> *I hold fate in my hands. I hold [card name], the card of [magical goal].*
> *[Card name], open the way! [Card name], share your magic with me!*

Set the card down and light the incense. Dragon's blood incense corresponds to Aries, the Emperor, and magical works of consecration, so it's well suited to consecrating a tarot talisman. Once the incense is lit, waft the smoke toward you, taking in the deep, earthy scent. Say:

> *May this sacred smoke cleanse and consecrate my talisman.*

Pick up the card and pass it through the incense smoke. As you do so, say:

> *[Card name], I consecrate you to a new purpose. You are now a sacred*
> *and magical object, and you will bring [the energy you want to draw]*
> *wherever you go. [Card name], help me achieve [your goal]!*

Set the card down again and extend both hands over it. Chant the name of the card repeatedly, holding your magical purpose firm in your mind. When you feel you have reached a peak, clap your hands together above the card. Say:

> *The talisman is consecrated. Its work is begun. Let it be so!*

Your tarot card has now been consecrated as a magical talisman. Keep it in a place where you want it to have a magically contagious effect. If you are using the talisman for a long period of time, you may wish to re-perform this consecration periodically (for example, once per year) or whenever you feel that its power has started to wane.

## Magical Timing for Talismans

You may wish to consecrate a talisman at a particular time determined by astrological considerations. Doing this allows the talisman to capture something of the astrological atmosphere at the time of its creation—adding to its magical contagion by emphasizing certain planetary or zodiacal energies. Magical timing is a common feature across just about all types of occultism, but the depth and precision of that timing varies from one practice to the next. Some traditions see magical timing as a helpful guideline, a "nice to have" rather than a "need to have." Other traditions have such exacting requirements that they only allow a window of a few minutes within which to perform a piece of magical work. The following are a few different ways you might approach magical timing; I'd recommend that you experiment with them and see what fits best within your own magical practice.

### *Moon Phases*

Doing magic by the phases of the moon is a classic, and for good reason. The moon is one of the most visible celestial bodies—and unlike its solar counterpart, it's in a constant state of flux and reflux. The moon is ever-changing, never in a constant state of being but always becoming. Its essence is transformation, and so it lends itself beautifully to the transformative work of magic. The waxing and waning of the moon is like the ebb and flow of the tides: If you sail with the tide, your ship will move more swiftly and smoothly, and if you set your magic with the moon, your spellwork will do the same.

Generally speaking, lunar magic is straightforward and intuitive. When the moon is waxing, its light is increasing, so the waxing moon is ideal for magic aimed at growth and increase. Conversely, the waning moon (when light is decreasing) is good for magic aimed at diminishing, banishing, and decrease. When the moon is full, its light is at a peak, and it becomes magically suited to work for abundance, accomplishment, and fullness. Finally, when the moon is new, it gives off no light whatsoever, making it good for magic around secrecy and the unknown.

## Planetary Days

Western astrological magic commonly features the use of a system of *planetary days*, wherein each day of the week is associated with a particular planet. This is an old system—so old, in fact, that it provides the structure to our calendar. The names of the days of the week in English are derived from the names of the planets and the Roman or Anglo-Saxon deities associated with them. The scheme of planetary days is as follows:

| MONDAY | TUESDAY | WEDNESDAY | THURSDAY | FRIDAY | SATURDAY | SUNDAY |
|--------|---------|-----------|----------|--------|----------|--------|
| Moon | Mars | Mercury | Jupiter | Venus | Saturn | Sun |

These planetary days may seem arbitrary at first, but they're actually based on the Chaldean order of the planets. Arrange the seven planets in a circle following the Chaldean order: the moon, followed by Mercury, Venus, and so on until you reach Saturn and then come back to the moon. Now, draw a single line connecting all seven planets in the shape of a seven-pointed star. As your line moves from one planet to the next, it follows the order of the planetary days. Starting from the moon (Monday), the next point you hit will be Mars (Tuesday), followed by Mercury (Wednesday), Jupiter (Thursday), Venus (Friday), Saturn (Saturday), and the sun (Sunday). In this way, there is a hidden, elegant structure to the order of the planetary days, derived from the speed at which the planets appear to move across the sky.

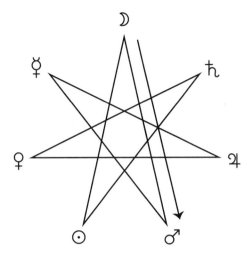

If you are making a tarot talisman and want to draw on the energies of one of the seven classical planets, one of the easiest ways to do so is by consecrating your talisman on the appropriate planetary day. This is especially helpful if you're using a tarot card that already has planetary associations. For example, if you're making a Two of Cups talisman for love, you could amplify that card's planetary association to Venus by making the talisman on a Friday.

### Planetary Hours

Even more specific than the planetary days, there is a set of planetary hours for magical timing. Not only is each day of the week associated with a planet, but each hour within each day has its own planetary correspondence as well.

The term *planetary hours* is a bit of a misnomer and can be confusing if you're not already familiar with the concept. We typically think of an hour as a standardized unit of time that's sixty minutes long, but planetary hours are variable in length. They are based on the amount of time that the sun spends in the sky each day; that amount of time changes from one day to the next, and therefore so do the planetary hours.

Each day is divided into twenty-four planetary hours: twelve for the daylight and twelve for the nighttime. The cutoff points between day and night are sunrise and sunset. To calculate planetary hours for a given day, take the total number of minutes between sunrise and sunset, then divide that into twelve equal segments; for the planetary hours of the night, do the same with the time between sunset and sunrise. As the days grow longer and shorter with the passing of the seasons, the length of the planetary hours will change as well: Longer days mean longer planetary hours by daylight; shorter nights mean shorter planetary hours by darkness. In this way, the system of planetary hours reflects the natural changes happening in the relationship between the earth and the cosmos as we revolve around the sun.

As an example: If the sun rises at 6:30 a.m. on a given day and sets at 4:18 p.m., that day has 588 minutes of total daylight. Dividing this by twelve, we find that each "hour" lasts exactly forty-nine minutes. Thus, the first "hour" runs from 6:30 to 7:19 a.m., the second is from 7:19 to 8:08 a.m., and so on through the day until sunset. The next day's "hours" will be marginally longer or shorter due to an incremental change in how much time the sun spends in the sky.

Each of the twelve "hours" is then assigned to a particular planet, following a simple pattern. The first hour of the day—starting from sunrise—corresponds to the same planet as the day itself. That is to say, the first planetary hour on Monday corresponds to the moon, the first hour of Tuesday corresponds to Mars, and so on. From there, each subsequent hour progresses from slower planets to faster ones: Saturn, Jupiter, Mars, the sun, Venus, Mercury, and finally the moon. After the moon, the cycle starts over again with Saturn.

The pattern of daylight planetary hours (from sunrise to sunset) is as follows:

|  | MONDAY | TUESDAY | WEDNESDAY | THURSDAY | FRIDAY | SATURDAY | SUNDAY |
|---|---|---|---|---|---|---|---|
| 1ST HOUR | Moon | Mars | Mercury | Jupiter | Venus | Saturn | Sun |
| 2ND HOUR | Saturn | Sun | Moon | Mars | Mercury | Jupiter | Venus |
| 3RD HOUR | Jupiter | Venus | Saturn | Sun | Moon | Mars | Mercury |
| 4TH HOUR | Mars | Mercury | Jupiter | Venus | Saturn | Sun | Moon |
| 5TH HOUR | Sun | Moon | Mars | Mercury | Jupiter | Venus | Saturn |
| 6TH HOUR | Venus | Saturn | Sun | Moon | Mars | Mercury | Jupiter |
| 7TH HOUR | Mercury | Jupiter | Venus | Saturn | Sun | Moon | Mars |
| 8TH HOUR | Moon | Mars | Mercury | Jupiter | Venus | Saturn | Sun |

|  | MONDAY | TUESDAY | WEDNESDAY | THURSDAY | FRIDAY | SATURDAY | SUNDAY |
|---|---|---|---|---|---|---|---|
| 9TH HOUR | Saturn | Sun | Moon | Mars | Mercury | Jupiter | Venus |
| 10TH HOUR | Jupiter | Venus | Saturn | Sun | Moon | Mars | Mercury |
| 11TH HOUR | Mars | Mercury | Jupiter | Venus | Saturn | Sun | Moon |
| 12TH HOUR | Sun | Moon | Mars | Mercury | Jupiter | Venus | Saturn |

And the pattern of nighttime planetary hours (from sunset to sunrise) continues:

|  | MONDAY | TUESDAY | WEDNESDAY | THURSDAY | FRIDAY | SATURDAY | SUNDAY |
|---|---|---|---|---|---|---|---|
| 13TH HOUR | Venus | Saturn | Sun | Moon | Mars | Mercury | Jupiter |
| 14TH HOUR | Mercury | Jupiter | Venus | Saturn | Sun | Moon | Mars |
| 15TH HOUR | Moon | Mars | Mercury | Jupiter | Venus | Saturn | Sun |
| 16TH HOUR | Saturn | Sun | Moon | Mars | Mercury | Jupiter | Venus |
| 17TH HOUR | Jupiter | Venus | Saturn | Sun | Moon | Mars | Mercury |
| 18TH HOUR | Mars | Mercury | Jupiter | Venus | Saturn | Sun | Moon |
| 19TH HOUR | Sun | Moon | Mars | Mercury | Jupiter | Venus | Saturn |
| 20TH HOUR | Venus | Saturn | Sun | Moon | Mars | Mercury | Jupiter |
| 21ST HOUR | Mercury | Jupiter | Venus | Saturn | Sun | Moon | Mars |
| 22ND HOUR | Moon | Mars | Mercury | Jupiter | Venus | Saturn | Sun |

| | MONDAY | TUESDAY | WEDNESDAY | THURSDAY | FRIDAY | SATURDAY | SUNDAY |
|---|---|---|---|---|---|---|---|
| 23RD HOUR | Saturn | Sun | Moon | Mars | Mercury | Jupiter | Venus |
| 24TH HOUR | Jupiter | Venus | Saturn | Sun | Moon | Mars | Mercury |

Using the system of planetary hours, every moment of every day is replete with astrological energy that can be used for magic. You can apply the planetary hours to elect an even more precise time to consecrate your talisman. If you're making a Four of Swords talisman and want to emphasize the planetary energy of Jupiter, you could consecrate your talisman on the day of Jupiter (Thursday), but you could also bring in that same planetary energy by consecrating it during the hour of Jupiter on any day of the week.

### Zodiacal Considerations

Astrological timing for talismans can be zodiacal as well as planetary. If you want to bring in the energy of a particular sign of the Zodiac, you can consecrate your talisman at a time when that sign is prominent. The easiest way to do this is to time your consecration by the sun's annual passage through the signs.

If you're making a talisman with the Strength card and want to emphasize its zodiacal connection to Leo, you could wait to consecrate that talisman until the sun is in Leo (roughly sometime between July 23 and August 22). Of course, timing like this may be inconvenient; if you need your Strength talisman *now* but the current date is August 30, you don't have the luxury of waiting a full eleven months for the best astrological timing. Another option is to use zodiacal timing based on the moon instead of the sun. The moon makes a full circuit through all twelve zodiac signs in the course of just one month. You can use the astrology software of your choice (or, if you're old school, you can use a printed ephemeris) to look up the next time the moon will be in the correct sign, and you can time your talismanic magic accordingly. Working by the signs of the moon, you'll never have to wait more than a couple of weeks for ideal zodiacal timing.

There is a third option available for zodiacal timing as well. Remember that most of the Minor Arcana correspond to both a planet *and* a sign of the zodiac. If you're making a Minor Arcanum talisman, you may choose to align the consecration of your talisman with a time when the corresponding planet is present in the corresponding part of the Zodiac. Doing this produces a set of astrological circumstances that deeply reinforce the particular magical energy of the card you're drawing on. For example, the Six of Swords corresponds to the planet Mercury and the second decan of Aquarius. If you wanted to make a Six of Swords talisman to help you expand your perspectives and learn something new, you could consecrate that talisman at a date and time when Mercury was between 10° Aquarius and 19° Aquarius, really driving home the card's astrological connections.

I've used this technique often and found it wonderfully effective. Again, though, this kind of timing may not be feasible depending on the card you're using and the timeline on which you need your talisman to take effect. For example, the Ten of Wands corresponds to Saturn in the final decan of Sagittarius. At the time of this book's writing, Saturn won't re-enter that part of the Zodiac until 2046. If you want your magic to take effect sooner than twenty years from now, this approach to magical timing won't always work for you.

There are a variety of options available to you for magical timing with the Zodiac. Use the ones that best suit your needs, and remember that what you need might change from one magical operation to the next.

### Combining Timing Techniques

Finally, it's worth noting that none of the timing techniques provided here are mutually exclusive. You can layer them over each other in order to provide a specific magical snapshot of the exact energies you want to bring into your talismanic work—and you can use as many or as few of them as you like. You don't have to adopt any of these timing techniques at all if you don't want to, and you can certainly just start using a talisman without any of this complicated astrological machinery. Conversely, you can use all of these techniques at once if you're so inclined. Use the following template to identify potential timing considerations for the card you're working with.

| CARD | |
|---|---|
| DESIRED MOON PHASE | |
| PLANETARY DAY | |
| PLANETARY HOUR | |
| ZODIAC | |

Then, you can elect a time to consecrate your talisman using any or all of those considerations. For example, let's suppose you're making a talisman to help you get a raise at work. You choose to use the Nine of Pentacles, which is titled *Gain* in the Thoth system and which signifies abundance and a reward for hard work. The Nine of Pentacles corresponds to Venus and the second decan of Virgo. Your timing chart for the card would look like this:

| CARD | Nine of Pentacles |
|------|-------------------|
| DESIRED MOON PHASE | Waxing (increase) |
| PLANETARY DAY | Friday |
| PLANETARY HOUR | Venus |
| ZODIAC | 10°–19° ♍ |

With this information in mind, there are countless ways you could time the creation of your talisman. You might make it on a Friday during the waxing moon, on the day and hour of Venus while the sun is in the second decan of Virgo, or on a day when the moon is waxing in the second decan of Virgo. Get creative with the possibilities here and see what works best for your situation. The world is your oyster.

## More Complex Talismans

While the heart of a tarot talisman is the card itself, that doesn't have to be the only component. You can experiment with making more complex talismans using other kinds of imagery or magical connections in order to deepen the talisman's symbolism.

You can build these connections intuitively, working from your personal understanding of a card's meaning and imagery. For example, if the Four of Wands in your deck features olive branches, you may decide to anoint your card with olive oil. Or, as an alternative, you can use the system of Qabalistic correspondences connected to each card. These correspondences will allow you to reinforce the magical significance of your talisman in more diverse ways, opening up new possibilities for your magic.

What follows are a few ideas for ways to make your tarot talismans more sophisticated by adding new ingredients or methods. Use as many or as few of these as you like, and don't hesitate to experiment and see what works for you. At the end of the section, I've provided a table with some relevant Qabalistic correspondences of the cards, which you may wish to draw on in your magic.

## Colors

Colors are intensely magical. They're one of the most immediately accessible forms of symbolism for many of us, and they provide a clear and direct way of setting the tone for magical work. Color symbolism is cultural, but at least within the context of the United States, there are widespread associations that can be used as touchstones in magical work: green for money, pink for love, purple for luxury, and so on. You may wish to incorporate color symbolism into your talismanic work. You could use one of these established cultural correspondences, or you could pull a color directly from the card you're using. For example, if the Two of Wands in your deck features a sunset with a red sky, you might pull that shade of red into your magic.

Perhaps the easiest way to use color when making a tarot talisman is to write on a card using a colored marker. For example, if you're making a talisman with the High Priestess, you might write *Intuition* on the back of the card with a silver Sharpie.

Alternatively, you could wrap your card in a handkerchief, napkin, or other piece of colored cloth in order to help contain its magical potency. Doing this has the added advantage of allowing you to include other ingredients (such as herbs or an intention written on a piece of paper) inside the cloth.

## Incense

In the consecration ritual shared earlier, I suggested using dragon's blood incense to consecrate your talisman. This is because dragon's blood corresponds to Aries, and thereby to the Emperor and to the magical work of consecration. However, you may wish to use an incense specifically tailored to the card you are working with or your magical goal. You can come up with your own incense blend if you like, or use a favorite incense with a particular magical significance. Re-censing the card periodically is a great way to keep your talisman active and to ensure its continued efficacy.

## Herbs and Other Plants

The use of herbs in magic is as old as magic itself. Some herbs are considered magical because they contain chemical compounds with genuinely medicinal properties. Others derive magical associations from the doctrine of signatures (see chapter 2). If you are familiar with magical herbalism, you may wish to incorporate herbs into the creation and consecration of your talisman. The simplest way to do this is to choose an herb with appropriate magical associations and then to sprinkle some of that herb on or around the location where you'll be placing the talisman. If you're keeping your card in a container of some kind, you could also put a pinch of your herb of choice inside that container.

Another option is to steep some of the herb in water to create a decoction. Then, when consecrating your talisman, you can gently brush or sprinkle some of the decoction across the surface of your card, imbuing the card with that herb's potency as part of your consecration.

Please do remember to exercise caution and common sense when working with herbs. Not all herbs are safe to ingest, and some cause irritation when they come in contact with skin. Always research a plant before using it in magic so that you know what its potential risks are, and never consume an herb if you don't know exactly what it is and what its medical effects are.

## Crystals

Full disclosure here: I rarely work with crystals in a magical context. They simply don't appeal to me much, and I haven't found that my magic benefits substantially from incorporating them into ritual and spellwork. That said, crystals are an important part of contemporary magic, and I think I'd be remiss if I didn't mention them here—especially because they can so easily be incorporated into talismanic work.

Crystals, like herbs, derive their magical properties largely from the doctrine of signatures. We identify their magical uses by looking at things like their color, crystalline structure, hardness, and origin, comparing these qualities with what we know about the rest of the magical world. Thus, a soft, white, water-soluble crystal like selenite has associations with the moon, while iron pyrite represents wealth because of its golden color.

Crystals are remarkably easy to use in tarot talismans. Choose a crystal that aligns with your magical goal, and then once you've prepared and consecrated your talisman, place the crystal on top of it. Talismans already work on the principle of magical contagion; by adding a crystal into the mix, you help to amplify that contagion, enhancing the talisman and allowing it to more easily produce its effect.

If you want to get slightly more elaborate, try constructing a crystal grid around your consecrated talisman. Lay out a number of crystals in a geometric pattern with the tarot card at their center. Structures of this sort allow you to incorporate different types of crystals in the same act of magic, and they allow you to visually emphasize your card as the center and focus of your magical work.

## Qabalistic Correspondences

Here are some of the classic Qabalistic correspondences for each of the types of magical connection I've discussed.[18] If you wish, you can draw on these correspondences to enhance your talismanic work with any card in the tarot deck. Note that some of these ingredients may be expensive or hard to obtain. If that's the case, you don't need to use them and can always use a substitute that fits your magical needs. Some of the listed plants here are toxic; please do not consume any of the plants listed, and always exercise caution when handling herbs.

| CARD | COLOR | INCENSE | PLANT | CRYSTAL |
|---|---|---|---|---|
| The Fool | Yellow | Galbanum | Aspen | Topaz |
| The Magician | Yellow | Mastic, white sandalwood, nutmeg, mace, storax | Vervain, herb Mercury, palm | Opal, agate |
| The High Priestess | Blue | Camphor, aloes | Almond, mugwort, hazel, buttercup | Moonstone, pearl |
| The Empress | Green | Sandalwood, myrtle | Myrtle, rose, clover | Emerald, turquoise |
| The Emperor | Red | Dragon's blood | Tiger lily, geranium | Ruby |
| The Hierophant | Red-orange | Storax | Marshmallow | Topaz |
| The Lovers | Orange | Wormwood | Orchid | Alexandrite, tourmaline |
| The Chariot | Yellow-orange | Onycha | Lotus | Amber |
| Strength | Yellow | Frankincense | Sunflower | Tiger's eye |
| The Hermit | Yellow-green | Narcissus | Snowdrop, lily, narcissus | Peridot |
| Wheel of Fortune | Purple | Saffron | Hyssop, oak, poplar, fig | Amethyst, lapis lazuli |

---

18. Crowley, *777*, col. XV, XVI, XLII, XXXIX, and XL.

| CARD | COLOR | INCENSE | PLANT | CRYSTAL |
|------|-------|---------|-------|---------|
| Justice | Green | Galbanum | Aloe | Emerald |
| The Hanged Man | Blue | Onycha, myrrh | Lotus | Aquamarine |
| Death | Blue-green | Benzoin, opoponax | Cactus | Ammonite |
| Temperance | Blue | Lignum aloes | Rushes | Jacinth |
| The Devil | Indigo | Musk | Hemp, thistle | Black diamond |
| The Tower | Red | Pepper, dragon's blood | Wormwood, rue | Ruby |
| The Star | Violet | Galbanum | Coconut | Glass |
| The Moon | Red-violet | Ambergris | Poppy | Pearl |
| The Sun | Orange | Frankincense, cinnamon | Sunflower, laurel, heliotrope | Chrysolite |
| Judgement | Red | Frankincense | Red poppy, hibiscus, nettle | Fire opal |
| The World | Indigo | Asafetida, scammony, indigo | Ash, cypress, yew | Onyx |
| Aces | White | Ambergris | Almond | Diamond |
| Twos and Kings | Gray | Musk | Amaranth | Star ruby, turquoise |
| Threes and Queens | Black | Myrrh | Cypress, poppy | Star sapphire, pearl |
| Fours | Blue | Cedar | Olive, shamrock | Amethyst, sapphire |
| Fives | Red | Tobacco | Oak, nettle | Ruby |

| CARD | COLOR | INCENSE | PLANT | CRYSTAL |
|------|-------|---------|-------|---------|
| Sixes and Knights | Yellow | Frankincense | Acacia, laurel, vine | Topaz, yellow diamond |
| Sevens | Green | Benzoin, rose, red sandalwood | Rose | Emerald |
| Eights | Orange | Storax | Entheogens | Opal |
| Nines | Purple | Jasmine, ginseng | Mandrake, damiana | Quartz |
| Tens and Pages | Citrine, olive, russet, black | Dittany of Crete | Willow, lily, ivy | Rock crystal |

## Writing Tarot Spells

*chapter ten*

Whereas a talisman is an object fashioned to accomplish a magical goal, a spell is a procedure. A spell is a set of symbolic steps that you ritually enact in order to produce a sympathetic magical result. Spells can be simple or complicated, incorporating whatever symbolism the practitioner finds appropriate. The most important thing is that the person performing a spell enacts a symbolic change that mimics the change they want to cause in the world.

Because tarot contains such a wealth of symbolism and imagery, it's ripe for adaptation in spellwork. You can design spells using tarot cards as your inspiration, drawing on particular themes, motifs, correspondences, and visual cues from the cards. The basic process of writing a tarot spell can be broken down into a few core steps.

### Identify Your Desired Outcome

Before you do any magic, you have to know what you want. What's the end result you're trying to achieve? Sit down and think concretely about what the world will look like if your magic is successful and you get your way.

## Identify Pressure Points

The next important question: Where can you take magical action in order to effect that desired outcome? A result like "I want to marry my soul mate" is fine as a long-term goal, but it doesn't give you much in terms of concrete magical action that you can take. Try to identify one place that you can apply pressure. What is one concrete, specific thing you can try to change that would help you achieve your stated goal? This is the focus of your spell.

I like to think about a spell's focus in terms of SMART goals (a term borrowed from the world of corporate HR).[19] A SMART goal is one that is specific, measurable, actionable, realistic, and timed:[20]

- **Specific:** What exactly are you trying to achieve?
- **Measurable:** By what metric can you judge whether you have or have not achieved your goal?
- **Actionable:** Can you do something about this goal? Is it in your power to affect?
- **Realistic:** Is this something that you can feasibly accomplish, or are you reaching for the impossible?
- **Timed:** When does it need to be accomplished by?

In the case of "I want to marry my soul mate," your first step would obviously be to meet someone. But just "I want to meet someone," is not, on its own, SMART enough. You might narrow it down as follows: "I want to meet someone on a dating app [specific, actionable] in the next four months [timed] who works in the arts and plays an instrument [measurable, realistic]." This is a concrete magical goal, and it's the sort of thing you can design a successful spell around.

## Find an Appropriate Card

Next, choose a card from your tarot deck that represents the SMART goal you're trying to achieve. There may be a couple of viable options, and you'll have to rely on your intuition for this step. Try to find a card that captures the essence of your stated goal. It may be that differ-

---

19. Leonard and Watts, "The Ultimate Guide to S.M.A.R.T. Goals."

20. You'll see variations on the SMART theme. Some sources identify A as *achievable* and R as *reachable* or *relevant*, for example. However, this is the version of the acronym that I find most helpful.

ent cards capture different aspects of that goal, in which case you have a choice between cards depending on what you want to emphasize.

Remember also that not every magical goal will be perfectly suited to working with the tarot, and that's okay. Tarot spells are one tool in your toolbox, but you don't have to use them for everything if you find that another magical approach is better matched to what you want to do.

In the example shared previously, the stated goal is to meet a particular kind of person. This seems well suited to magically working with one of the court cards. The profile of the desired person—someone who works in the arts and plays a musical instrument—resonates with the sensitive, artistic nature of the Page of Cups, so you might decide to build a spell around that card: a spell to bring someone like the Page of Cups into your life.

## Extract Relevant Symbols

Now, look at your card and identify the most relevant symbolism and imagery from it—the sorts of things that you could adapt into the symbolic framework of a spell. Two of the biggest and most important candidates are suit and number. If you're using a card from the Minor Arcana, which suit does it belong to? Right away, you should plan to incorporate the energy of that suit into your spell. Likewise, if your card is numbered, you'll want to find a way to bring that number into the spell somehow.

Other candidates include any of the magical correspondences we've already discussed for the various cards: planets, zodiacal signs, elements, colors, crystals, herbs, or incenses. All of these are quick and easy ways to draw on symbolism that is directly relevant to the magic of your chosen card.

Finally, remember that you can and should adopt imagery from your specific deck. In many decks, the Page of Cups is holding a cup with a fish leaping out of it; that is a striking detail that is unique to this card, and it is the sort of thing you might want to incorporate into a Page of Cups spell. This helps make your spell unique, creative, and personalized to you and your tarot deck.

PAGE of CUPS.

## Convert Symbolism to Action

Now that you've figured out the core symbols you want to use for your spell, you have to figure out what you're going to do with them. Remember, a spell is a procedure—it's a set of symbolic actions that you perform in order to sympathetically produce a desired change. You have your symbols, and now you need to figure out how to put them into action.

The core action of your spell should be something that mirrors the kind of change you are trying to cause. If you're causing something to increase, you might want to build something up; if you're banishing something, you could use the spell as an opportunity to destroy an object or throw it away. Around this core action, you can fill in the rest of the symbols that you've chosen specifically for your card.

Elemental suits make for excellent tools in a spell. If I'm doing a spell based on a card from the suit of Pentacles, you can bet your bottom dollar that I'm finding a way to involve my earth pentacle in that spell. Likewise, a card's number can be incorporated into a spell through the number of ingredients (e.g., an incense blend made with four herbs) or through repeated action (e.g., chanting an incantation four times). You can also think about creating (or recreating) particular objects or scenarios from your card.

In the case of the Page of Cups, I find the image of the cup with the fish in it quite striking. Because first dates often take place in a bar or coffee shop, I might structure this hypothetical spell around a beverage. I could place a fish (say, the sort of toy fish you can get for children's bath-time play) in my elemental water cup, fill the cup with an opaque beverage like wine, and then drink from it—"revealing" the sensitive soul of the Page of Cups waiting for me at the bottom.

## Write Your Script

Once you've outlined your core ritual actions, sit down and write out a script for the spell. This should include a list of all the ingredients and material tools you'll need, as well as a step-by-step walkthrough of what you're doing and when. It also helps to have scripted lines for the things you're going to say; some spells are done in silence and can be tremendously powerful, but I personally always find it helpful to have spoken lines where I declare what I'm doing and why.

Open the spell with a declaration of purpose. This could be your entire SMART goal ("I am here to work magic in order to meet…"), or it could be a distilled version of the goal you're trying to achieve ("I am here to draw a partner to myself"). Either way, you want to begin any magical enterprise by focusing yourself on the work at hand, and one useful way to do that is to state the nature of the work out loud.

As you proceed through your magical work, narrate the ritualized steps of your spell and explain the significance of each one. Every action you perform over the course of a spell has a symbolic meaning. By stating that meaning aloud (e.g., "I drink now from the cup of love!"), you reinforce it and bring it to the fore. This helps transform what you're doing into a magical act so that, in the case of my example, I'm not just some weirdo drinking wine out of a cup that has a bath toy in it; instead, I am a magician working wonders and bending the universe to my will.

Finally, remember to end the spell with a formal, spoken closing. This should reaffirm the nature of the magical work that you've performed, and it should assert the success of your work. It doesn't have to be fancy—something as simple as "Love comes to me. It is done!" will do. Whatever you say, it's useful to have that last verbal punch line to end your spell and mark the return from magical space to the mundane.

## Perform the Spell

Last, there's nothing left to do but to perform the spell. You can set your spellwork according to the magical timing techniques discussed in chapter 9 if you like. Gather all your materials, read through your script one more time to make sure you know what you're doing, and then away you go. Good luck!

## Sample Spells

In this section are a few examples of the ways you can adapt tarot symbolism to spellcasting. I've included a sample spell from each minor suit as well as the Major Arcana so that you can see tarot spells from all areas of the deck. Of course, these sample spells are not the be-all and end-all of tarot spellwork. They have worked for me, but they're included as samples here to help you figure out what tarot spells look like and how to design your own. Feel free to use any of these spells, but don't feel beholden to them. Adapt the words and actions as you see fit; for example, my spells tend not to rhyme, but many people find magical power in chanting rhyming verse. Do what gets results for you. Most importantly, please feel encouraged to write new tarot spells with cards other than the ones given here.

### A New Job: The Ace of Pentacles

This spell is good for new beginnings having to do with anything material: money, health, work, home, and so on. Personally, I've used it when job hunting, but you can apply it to other situations that fit with the theme of the Ace of Pentacles. You will need:

- A small potted plant
- An extra pot for the plant

- Potting soil
- A coin
- A permanent marker
- A watering can full of water
- Your earth pentacle

Set yourself up in a comfortable space where you can spread all of your materials in front of you. Close your eyes and take a few deep breaths. Let your stray thoughts drop away as you focus all of your attention on the magical work at hand. Open your eyes and say:

> *I begin the work of creation. I plant*
> *the seed of what is to come.*

Pick up the coin. Using the permanent marker, draw a pentagram on each side of the coin so that the coin looks like a pentacle. Hold the coin up high and examine it, saying:

> *One pentacle. One seed. As I plant you, so shall you grow, bring-*
> *ing me abundance and prosperity in a new job.*

Set aside the coin. Place your earth pentacle in the center of your space and set the empty pot on top of it. Pour a small amount of soil into the empty pot—just enough to cover the bottom. When you are done, place your coin in the center of the pot, pressing it down onto the soil. Say:

> *I plant this seed deep within the fertile earth. Grow! Grow! Grow!*

Add some more soil on top of the coin to bury it, continuing to chant "Grow!" as you do so. Keep up the chant as you carefully transfer your plant from its old pot to the new one, and then fill in the rest of the pot with fresh potting soil. Place your hands on either side of the pot and focus your attention on the plant growing and thriving, bringing you a new job as it does so. Holding this focus in your mind, bring your chant to a climax.

When you are done, say:

> *The seed of change is planted. I shall nourish it as*
> *it grows, bringing me the new job I seek.*

Use the watering can to water your plant. Say:

*It must be so.*

Set the plant somewhere it will get enough sunlight. Care for it regularly. Each time you water it, say:

*Bring me abundance and prosperity in a new job.*

Do this until your new job is secured. Then, if you like, you can transfer the plant to a fresh pot without the coin buried at the bottom.

### Making a Decision: The Two of Swords

The Two of Swords is the card of decision and indecision. When you are facing a difficult choice and need help determining the best course of action, you can draw on the symbolism of this card to magically show you the way. You will need:

- Your air blade
- A blindfold
- A piece of white chalk
- A pair of sturdy boots
- Someplace private and open with a clean, flat floor

Use the chalk to draw a line on the floor, dividing your space in half. Wearing the boots, stand with your feet straddling the line and place your air blade on the floor next to one of your feet. Make sure you know exactly where the blade is; you will have to be able to pick it up without looking at it.

Place the blindfold over your eyes and press your hands together in front of your chest. Say:

*I am lost in darkness and cannot see. Two roads diverge and a*
*choice must be made, but I do not know which path to take.*

Carefully pick up your air blade, making sure not to cut yourself on it. Hold the blade aloft and say:

*I call upon the powers of elemental air. Bring me cutting*
*discernment and piercing insight. Show me the way!*

Sweep the blade out in an arc to your right, saying:

*On my right hand is [your first possible choice].*
*Give me a sign if this is the way.*

Bring the blade back to center, then sweep it out in an arc to your left, saying:

*On my left hand is [your second possible choice].*
*Give me a sign if this is the way.*

Bring the blade to center again. Say:

*Though I cannot see, I listen to the wisdom of the wind. May*
*it guide me truly and bring the knowledge I seek.*

Set the blade down on the floor and remove your blindfold. Place the blade on top of the chalk line that you've drawn so that it is centered exactly on the line. Then, with a flick of your wrist, spin the blade. Be careful when you do this—don't send the blade careening into your feet. If you do accidentally hit your feet, the boots will protect you from cuts.

When the blade stops spinning, take note of the direction it is pointing. Whichever side of the chalk line it points to is the choice that you should make.

Pick up the blade again and stand facing in the direction it has indicated. Say:

*With the counsel of elemental air, I will [the choice you*
*have magically selected]. The choice is made!*

The spell is complete.

## Moving On: The Eight of Cups

This spell draws on the symbolism of the Eight of Cups to help you move on from a situation that is not serving you. You can use it to muster up the courage to leave or to heal from a past event that is still causing you pain. The spell is performed over the course of eight weeks, extended over a long time span because healing and moving on are emotional processes that work slowly. You will need:

- A pen and paper
- Your water cup
- Seven other cups
- Drinkable water

Begin with a short journaling exercise. Take some time to brainstorm the obstacles that are keeping you from moving on. These could be practical (such as a lack of security and resources) or emotional (such as self-doubt). Take as much time as you like to identify these obstacles. Then, choose the eight most significant ones. Arrange these eight obstacles in order from the least challenging (1) to the most challenging (8). Over the course of the spell, you are going to banish all eight of them.

Begin the spell on a Saturday at sunset. Find a windowsill or another place where you can line up all of your cups in a row; remember that this spell is going to take almost two months, so you want to pick somewhere you can leave the cups out for a long time without them being disturbed. Arrange the cups in a line with your elemental water cup on the far right. Fill all the cups with water.

Close your eyes and take a moment to collect your thoughts. Clear your mind of distractions and focus on the magical work at hand. Think about the situation you are trying to move on from and the challenges you face in moving forward. Open your eyes and say:

> *Tonight, I set my feet on the path that leads away from what I have known. Tonight, I choose to release the past and embrace hope for a better future. I begin the work of moving on from [your situation].*

Lift up the left-most of the cups in your line. Hold it close to your lips, but do not drink from it. Say:

> *[Obstacle 1], you have held me back, but you shall do so no more. I release you in peace and in love. Let the stagnant waters now flow freely, and let me be free as well.*

Silently take the cup outside and pour its contents onto the ground. Return inside and place the cup back in the lineup—but this time, place it upside-down. Say:

> *[Obstacle 1] is released. This is the path of healing.*

This is all the work you will do on the first night. You will return to the spell a week later. In the interim, you may notice that the water in your remaining cups starts to evaporate; if you see the level of the water dipping, just top it off with fresh, clean water.

The following Saturday, at sunset, return to your lineup of cups. Focus your attention again, then say:

> *Tonight, I continue on the path that leads away from what I have known. Tonight, I choose to release the past and embrace hope for a better future. I continue the work of moving on from [your situation].*

Take the second cup in your lineup and lift it to your lips, but do not drink from it. Say:

> *[Obstacle 2], you have held me back, but you shall do so no more. I release you in peace and in love. Let the stagnant waters now flow freely, and let me be free as well.*

Silently take the cup outside and empty it onto the ground. When you return inside, place the cup upside-down in its position and say:

> *[Obstacle 2] is released. This is the path of healing.*

Repeat this with a new cup and a new obstacle each successive week. On the eighth week, you will release your final and largest obstacle using the elemental water cup you made in chapter 3. When you return inside, place the cup upside-down and extend both hands over the row of cups. Proclaim:

> *The path ahead is clear. I walk it with trust and confidence, knowing that better things await me. I am free to move forward. The magic is done!*

Wash and put away your cups. The spell is now complete.

## Victory in Competition: The Six of Wands

The Six of Wands is a card of prominence and success, celebrating a crowning achievement. You can use it magically when you are preparing for a competition in order to bring yourself the victory that this card represents. You will need:

- A headband

- Six bay leaves

- A hot glue gun

- Frankincense and a censer to burn it in

- Your fire wand

- Matches or a lighter

For this spell, you will be making a laurel crown to signify your victory. Lay out all of your materials and take a moment to focus yourself. Clear your mind of distractions and center your attention on the competition you are going to participate in. Think about what victory looks like to you; it might not be a first-place trophy. If you're striving to set a personal record, that's also victory of a kind. What result will make you feel like you've accomplished what you set out to do?

When you are ready, light the incense. Frankincense is associated with Tiphereth on the Tree of Life, and thereby with the Sixes of the Minor Arcana. Extend your wand over the censer, holding the tip of the wand in the rising smoke. Say:

> *I kindle this sacred flame! Fire of ambition, fire of success, burn bright and burn long. Make me a champion!*

Pick up the first of your six bay leaves. Hold it flat in the palm of your hand and touch it with the tip of your wand. Say:

> *Sacred leaf of the laurel tree, bring me victory! I crown myself with thee.*

Pass the leaf through the incense smoke, chanting "Victory! Victory!" as you do so. When you feel that the leaf is sufficiently imbued with power, use the hot glue gun to affix it to the headband.

Take the second of your bay leaves and bless it as you did the first, but this time, imbue it with glory instead of victory:

> *Sacred leaf of the laurel tree, bring me glory! I crown myself with thee.*

Again, cense the leaf, chanting "Glory! Glory!" as you do so. Then, use the hot glue gun to affix it to the headband.

Bless the remaining four leaves in the same way, imbuing each of them with a different power: Bless the third leaf with success, the fourth with accolades, the fifth with achievement, and the sixth with triumph.

When you have blessed and attached all of the leaves, pick up the headband. Pass it through the incense smoke six times, saying:

> *Six times the crown is blessed. Six times my valor is*
> *assured. Behold the crown of the conqueror!*

The spell is complete. If you wish to decorate the headband further, you may do so to suit your aesthetic tastes, but it's not magically required. Wear the crown on the day of your competition, and don't take it off until the competition is about to begin.

### A Garden Blessing: The Empress

The Empress sits in a lush, verdant garden. She is surrounded by blooming life. Classically, this card connects to themes of nurturing, growth, and abundance—all of which are ideal for the aspiring gardener. This spell recreates the Empress's scepter to bring growth to your garden or lawn. You will need:

- Clippings from three plants in the garden
- A stick about the length of your forearm
- Three feet of copper wire

Perform this spell in your garden on a sunny day. Sit on the ground with your materials beside you. Take a few deep breaths, inhaling the scent of plants and fresh soil. Feel the sunshine on your skin. Using a finger, trace a circle on the ground in front of you. Say:

> *I invoke the Empress's power*
> *To make my garden grow.*
> *Fill this place with fruit and flower;*
> *Now it must be so!*

Place the stick in the center of the circle you've traced. Say:

*The scepter of the Empress! Bring me sovereignty over the land.*

Take the first of your plant clippings and lay it down next to the stick. Say:

*Green growth of [plant], you have blessed this gar-*
*den! Bless it anew and fill this place with life.*

Repeat this with the other two plant clippings. Then, take your copper wire and use it to wrap your stick and all three plant clippings together. Completely wrap the wire around the stick from top to bottom, and keep wrapping until you have used the entire length of wire. As you are doing this, sing or chant something related to gardening and growth; when I performed this spell, I used the "Mary, Mary, quite contrary" nursery rhyme. The choice of chant here is entirely yours.

When you have finished wrapping the scepter, stand up and hold it aloft in your dominant hand. Proclaim:

*By the power of the Empress, I hallow this ground! By the*
*power of the Empress, this garden shall grow!*

Walk around the perimeter of your garden, brandishing the newly made scepter. The spell is now done. Store the scepter with your other gardening tools, and bring it with you whenever you work in the garden.

## Multi-Card Spells

Sometimes, the magical work that you want to do cannot be appropriately captured by the symbolism of just one card. This is particularly true if you want to emphasize a transition from one state to another. If your current situation is the Eight of Swords and you're trying to shift your life over to the Nine of Cups, just one of those cards by itself won't really capture the symbolism of what you're trying to do. In cases like these, you may want to design a spell around multiple cards in succession: a whole spread rather than a one-card pull.

The basic process of this is the same as one-card tarot spells, except now you're incorporating the symbolism of two or more cards. The danger here is that things can get very complicated very fast. If you're trying to do a spell that draws on the Hierophant, the Nine of Swords, and the Star, all of a sudden you have a *lot* of symbolism you need to pack in. Your spell is going to get dense, elaborate, and murky if you're not careful.

That's not to say that you can never do multi-card spells, but if you're going to go down that route, I recommend a touch of restraint. Aim for as much simplicity as possible so that your spell can be clear and direct in what it's trying to achieve. In magic, it can be tempting to front-load as much symbolism as possible, making a spell so complex and overwrought that the script reads more like a dissertation than a piece of magic. Magic is symbolism, and following that logic, you may feel the urge to throw every imaginable piece of symbolism into your spell in order to make it perfectly reflect all the details of what you're trying to do. However, there's a trade-off here: The denser you pack the symbolism in your magic, the less room it has to breathe. The most effective symbols are clear and straightforward; trying to add too many will end up muddling the magic and detracting from the overall effect.

Because of this, it's important to think about simplicity and clarity when writing tarot spells. Don't build up an overwrought ten-card spell just so you can capture every nuance of your desired magical goal. Figure out what the most important thing is that you want the spell to convey, then build your magic around that. If you *really* can't fit your magical goal into the symbolism of a single card, it's okay to expand to more than one, but do so judiciously and with good reason.

If you do want to do one spell involving multiple cards, it's helpful to look for places where the symbolism of the cards overlaps. Find the common symbols between the cards you're using and build your spell around them. For example, if you want to do a spell to ensure that your current financial investments will pay off in the long run, you might pair the Seven of Pentacles and the Nine of Pentacles. These cards work well together in a single spell because they belong to the same suit and share their key symbol (the pentacle). It's easy to imagine a spell that ties these cards together. For instance, you could lay out seven coins to represent your current investments, then

ritually add two more coins to the set in order to symbolize your investments growing (bringing the total up to nine).

The procedure for writing a multi-card tarot spell is the same as for a single card. First, identify your outcome, then hone in on a magical goal, select your cards for the work, extract relevant symbolism, turn that symbolism into ritualized action, write your script, and perform the spell. The big difference is in that fourth step: finding the right symbolism. Here, you want to start with the commonalities between the cards; this lays a strong foundation for your magical work, uniting multiple cards in a single magical operation. Once you've established the common ground, you can figure out how to expand your symbolism in order to address each card individually (for example, by turning a pile of seven coins into a pile of nine).

However, sometimes your chosen cards don't have a lot of imagery in common, if any. In cases like these, the easiest thing to do is to break your project down into distinct spells. Let's say that you and your spouse have recently started marriage counseling, and you want to do magic together to help strengthen your relationship. Your magical goal might be twofold: to reopen lines of communication between you and to rebuild a lost sense of trust. For the former goal, you might choose the Ace of Swords; for the latter, you might choose the Ten of Cups.

There's no real overlap between these two cards. There's no common ground that you can use as the foundation for a spell that involves both of them. You *could* squeeze them both into the same spell, but the result would end up feeling disjointed and disorienting; you'd have

to act out communication with the Ace of Swords and then completely change gears to act out trust with the Ten of Cups. This is clunky at best and counterproductive at worst. Instead, you can choose to perform two separate spells: one for communication and one for trust. By performing these on separate occasions, you allow yourselves to fully dedicate your attention to each distinct goal rather than muddying the waters by trying to do everything at once.

## Tarot Cards as Spell Ingredients

There is another important way that tarot cards can be applied in spellcraft: not as the symbolic basis for a spell's outline, but as an ingredient or tool used in the magical work. There may be cases where you're designing a spell that isn't a tarot spell per se, but that incorporates a card or cards the same way you might incorporate herbs, crystals, or other physical objects in your magic.

Suppose you're doing a spell to get over your ex. One simple symbolic action you could perform in such a spell is to take a picture of your ex and tear it up, representing the destruction of your emotional attachment to them. Instead of a photograph, however, you might want to use a tarot card. If your ex always reminded you of the Queen of Swords and the Queen of Swords frequently shows up in readings to represent them, that card can work as an effective symbolic stand-in. You can tear up a copy of the Queen of Swords instead of tearing up a photograph, accomplishing the same sympathetic result.

Something like this really isn't a tarot spell; it's a breakup spell. The symbolic action of the spell is not rooted in the symbolism of the tarot deck. Nonetheless, it is a spell that uses tarot. The distinction may seem pedantic, but I think it's an important one. Your magic does not have to be completely centered on tarot in order for you to be able to incorporate tarot into it.

Because a tarot card is small and printed on card stock, it's easy to use as an ingredient in a spell. Each card represents a particular kind of energy. By acting on that card in a magical context, you are magically manipulating the associated energy. Here are a few ideas of ritual actions you could take as part of a spell, all of which have different symbolic and magical effects. Note that none of these actions is enough on its own to constitute a full-fledged spell; you would still need to flesh out a complete spell using the methods outlined earlier in this chapter.

### To Banish

If you are trying to banish something, choose a card that represents what you are trying to get rid of. Take that card, ritually declare what it represents, and then destroy it. The card can be torn, burnt, buried, or thrown in a trash can on the other side of town—dispose of it in whatever way feels most thematically appropriate to you.

### To Conceal

If you are trying to conceal something, a card can be folded, locked inside a box, or wrapped in cloth.

The counterpart to concealment is revealing, and you can use the reverse of this action in order to bring something previously hidden to light. For example: Start a spell with a card hidden away, then ritually remove it from its hiding place to make it visible and publicly known.

## To Enhance

You can also magically manipulate a card to enhance or augment the energy it represents. You might do this by writing keywords on the card or drawing on it with a specially consecrated pen; for example, you could exaggerate the abundance of the Ten of Pentacles by drawing even more pentacles on it, filling the card with symbolic wealth.

Another way to amplify a card is to enlarge it visually. You could use a magnifying glass or other lens to make the card seem bigger, or you could print out copies of the card at multiple sizes, ritually swapping out the smaller size for larger ones as the card symbolically grows.

## To Unite

Sometimes, you may wish to bring two things or disparate energies together, uniting them in magic. To do this, take two cards representing those energies and attach them to each other. You can glue them, tie them, staple them, or tape them—anything that forms a bond between them and turns two things into one.

## To Master the Elements

Finally, remember that the four suits of the Minor Arcana represent the four elements. You can use the Ace of any suit as a stand-in for elemental energy, the same way that you would use your elemental tools. Any time a spell might call for you to use an elemental tool, you can use the appropriate Ace instead. Likewise, you can incorporate the Aces into any spell where you want to boost a particular elemental energy.

*chapter eleven*
# Angels and Demons

Up to this point, we've largely looked at the use of tarot in sympathetic magic. Now, we're going to shift gears and look at some of the ways that tarot can be leveraged for intercessional magic, using the cards to call upon spirits for magical assistance. In this chapter, we'll look at two classes of spirits: angels and demons.

People sometimes get uncomfortable when this topic is brought up, for two primary reasons. The first is that magic involving angels or demons often has Christian overtones; after all, many of us are familiar with these sorts of spirits through Christian teachings and only know of them in a Christian context. The second reason people get uncomfortable is that they've seen too many horror movies, and they worry that this kind of magic will result in some kind of supernatural possession, haunting, or other dangerous event.

Angels and demons are simply classes of magical spirits. They—or spirits like them—are found cross-culturally around the world. Christianity usually describes them as "good" and "evil" spirits, respectively, but that's not the most helpful way to think about them. Angels are typically powerful, beneficent spirits that can be called on for help; they're the sort of spirits that you supplicate because they're more powerful than you and have your best interests at heart. Demons, on the other hand, are typically more interested in their own ends than in helping a magical practitioner. They're not necessarily outright hostile, but they're disinclined to provide magical assistance unless they're constrained to do so, or unless there's something in it for them.

In this sense, the difference between angels and demons is best understood not as a matter of morality (where one group is "good" and the other is "evil") but as a matter of the relationship the magician bears to the spirits in question. In chapter 2, I identified four basic types of relationships involved in intercessional magic: relationships of transaction, authority, affection, and supplication. When doing magic with angels, the magician offers prayers and pleas, relying on the angels' beneficence and inclination to provide help. The relationship involved here is largely one of supplication, although it may also involve some measure of affection (especially if you are calling on a personal guardian angel or other angelic spirit with whom you have an established relationship). By contrast, magic with demons often involves convincing or constraining them to do what the magician wants; the magician persuades demons either by offering them something in return or by establishing themself as a spiritual authority whom the demons are required to obey. In demonic magic, the relationship in question is one of transaction and authority.

There is a long history of magic that involves petitioning angels or demons to help the magician accomplish a particular task. The Solomonic grimoire tradition is replete with texts that offer techniques for persuading angels and demons, often involving elaborately consecrated tools and complex rituals that have to be performed at specific dates and times. Some of the most famous of these texts include works like the *Grimorium Verum*, the *Dragon Rouge*, and the *Lesser Key of Solomon*. These texts provide the foundation for much of this kind of magic in the Western world.

The techniques I'll share in this chapter are not Solomonic. They are my own. I take inspiration in many ways from the Solomonic tradition and the Qabalistic magic of the Golden Dawn and Aleister Crowley, but most of what you'll see here is experimental, based on my own process of trial and error. These days, the overwhelming majority of my magic is sympathetic; I favor its simplicity and symbolic elegance. However, when I first began practicing magic, I frequently used tarot as a means of working magic alongside many kinds of spirits including both angels and demons. This chapter is a glimpse into that practice.

## Tarot Tools and Intercessional Relationships

We've already identified four basic types of relationship that appear in intercessional magic. When I'm working with spirits in a magical context, I find it helpful to clarify what kind of relationship I'm trying to establish or draw on. I want it to be clear that I am offering a transaction, claiming authority, appealing to affection, or making a supplication. In my experience, one of the easiest ways to make this clear is through the choice of magical tools that I use in my practice.

Each of the four elemental tools of the tarot can be assigned to one of these four types of magical relationship. When I am working with a spirit and wish to set the tone for our magical partnership, I will choose to use a particular tool or tools to reflect that tone.

- The suit of Pentacles corresponds to commerce and trade. The earth pentacle can be used for intercessional magic when the fundamental relationship is one of transaction.
- The suit of Swords is rife with conflict and requires a clear head to navigate. The air blade relates to magical relationships of authority and command.
- The suit of Cups is harmonious and loving. The water cup can be used in magic when the magician is appealing to a bond of affection with the spirit being called upon.
- The suit of Wands deals in themes of higher aspiration. The fire wand is useful in magical relationships of supplication when the magician is calling upon a higher power.

When doing magic with demons, I am commanding them and offering some kind of tit-for-tat recompense for their aid. Because of this, I incorporate my pentacle and my blade into that magical work. By contrast, when I do magic with angels, I am nicely asking them to look favorably upon me, so I use my cup and wand.

This approach extends to other groups of spirits as well. I commune with ancestors and departed loved ones using my cup, I invoke deities with my wand, I direct elemental spirits with my blade, and so on. Having this taxonomy helps clarify the kind of relationship at stake and the nature of the work being done in partnership between the spirit and the magical practitioner. It will also help establish a basic framework for the magical work with angels and demons explored in the rest of this chapter.

## A Tarot Pentagram Ritual

The single most famous ritual to come out of the Hermetic Order of the Golden Dawn was a piece of Qabalistic and angelic magic known as the Lesser Ritual of the Pentagram. In this ritual, the magician places themselves at the symbolic center of the universe, calling on divine names, archangels, and the powers of the four elements in each of the four cardinal directions. By the power of these archangels, the magician can banish harmful magical influences, cleansing themself and their ritual space. The Golden Dawn's correspondences for each direction are:[21]

|  | EAST | SOUTH | WEST | NORTH |
|---|---|---|---|---|
| GOD NAME | YHVH | Adonai | Eheieh | Agla |
| ARCHANGEL | Raphael | Michael | Gabriel | Uriel |
| ELEMENT | Air | Fire | Water | Earth |

Like many magical practitioners, I began my foray into magic with the Lesser Ritual of the Pentagram. I performed this ritual every morning as a kind of magical hygiene, washing myself clean magically the same way that I washed physically at the start of each day. Over time, as I began to work more with tarot in a magical context, I developed an alternate version of the ritual using tarot cards to call upon the archangels.

For this ritual, you will need:

- A compass or GPS
- Four cards from your tarot deck: the Fool, the Hanged Man, Judgement, and the World
- Your elemental fire wand

Begin by tidying up the physical space where you're going to perform the ritual. It doesn't have to be as sterile as a hospital, but try to clear away clutter and sweep up any obvious dirt. You're performing a cleansing ritual—your space should be clean. Use your compass or GPS to identify your orientation in space and find out which way is east, south, west, and north.

Placing yourself at the center of the space, mark four equidistant points from you, extending in each of the cardinal directions. Lay your tarot cards on these points according to their elemental correspondences: the Fool (air) in the east, Judgement (fire) in the south, the Hanged Man (water) in the west, and the World (earth) in the

**BANISHING PENTAGRAM**

21. Regardie, *The Golden Dawn*, 93–94.

north. Stand at the center of these cards, holding your fire wand and facing east. Take a few deep breaths and clear your mind.

Now, extend the wand in front of you and draw a large pentagram in the air, starting from the bottom left-hand corner. As you do so, sing the name Raphael loudly, clearly, and slowly. Try to sing the name in a deep, resonant voice so that you can feel it vibrating in the center of your chest. In your mind, ask the archangel Raphael to clear away everything baneful to your east. When you have finished drawing the pentagram, stick the point of your wand through the center of the star you've drawn as if skewering it in place.

Turn to the south. Draw the pentagram again, but this time, sing the name Michael, again in a deep, resonant voice. Mentally ask the archangel Michael to clear away everything baneful to your south. Do the same with Gabriel in the west and Uriel in the north.

Turn to face east again, folding your arms over your chest. Take a moment to feel the presence of the archangels in the four cardinal directions, warding you and watching over you. Say:

> *Before me, the Spirit of Aether. Behind me, the Spirit of the*
> *Mighty Waters. On my right hand, the Spirit of the Primal Fire.*
> *On my left hand, the Great One of the Night of Time. By their*
> *power, the flaming pentagram protects me on all sides.*

Bow your head for a moment to thank the archangels for their assistance. The ritual is now complete; you can pick up your cards from the floor and go about your day as normal. You can perform this ritual daily as an act of magical hygiene, or simply whenever you want an additional bit of magical cleansing and protection.

## The Angels of Tarot

The pentagram ritual is a good all-around magical practice, but it's not designed to accomplish concrete magical goals. It's more general, drawing you to the archangels' attention and asking them to remove obstacles and harm from your way. For more specific magical purposes, you'll want to make a more directed appeal. In order to make such an appeal, you have to know who the angels are and how they connect to the tarot deck.

### Archangels in the Major Arcana

We've already explored the magical structure of the tarot deck at length, looking at how tarot overlays with the elements, the signs of the Zodiac, and the planets. Each of these, in turn, is associated with a particular set of angelic spirits. All of the angelic spirits of the Major Arcana belong to a particular group of angels known as archangels. These are understood to be more powerful than ordinary angels, and they have the authority to direct lesser angelic spirits. The four elemental cards of the Major Arcana are associated with the elemental archangels from the Lesser Ritual of the Pentagram: Raphael, Michael, Gabriel, and Uriel. Likewise, there are archangels associated with the remaining eighteen major cards through connections to the planets and the signs of the Zodiac.

The zodiacal archangels are:[22]

| SIGN | ARCHANGEL | CARD |
| --- | --- | --- |
| Aries | Melchiadel | The Emperor |
| Taurus | Asmodel | The Hierophant |
| Gemini | Ambriel | The Lovers |
| Cancer | Muriel | The Chariot |
| Leo | Verachiel | Strength |
| Virgo | Hamaliel | The Hermit |
| Libra | Zuriel | Justice |
| Scorpio | Barachiel | Death |
| Sagittarius | Advachiel | Temperance |
| Capricorn | Hanael | The Devil |
| Aquarius | Cambriel | The Star |
| Pisces | Amnitziel | The Moon |

And the planetary archangels are:

| PLANET | ARCHANGEL | CARD |
| --- | --- | --- |
| Moon | Gabriel | The High Priestess |
| Mercury | Raphael | The Magician |
| Venus | Anael | The Empress |

---

22. Crowley, *777*, col. CLXXVIII.

| PLANET | ARCHANGEL | CARD |
|--------|-----------|------|
| Sun | Michael | The Sun |
| Mars | Zamael | The Tower |
| Jupiter | Sachiel | Wheel of Fortune |
| Saturn | Cassiel | The World |

Many of these angelic names are unfamiliar, and they may be difficult for English-speaking practitioners to pronounce. By and large, they are taken from Hebrew; "Michael," for example, is a Hebrew name meaning "Who is like God." If you want to pronounce angelic names as authentically as possible, you'd do well to look at Hebrew pronunciation rules. Michael is pronounced "mee-khah-ELL," where the *kh* is a soft sound in the back of the throat, similar to the Scottish word *loch*. That said, throughout the history of European magic, people have largely learned these names by reading them in books. As a consequence, there's a great deal of variation in how the names are pronounced by magicians. Don't worry that pronouncing a name wrong will make it impossible for you to work with an angel magically. Just give it your best sincere effort.

You'll find some minor variations in the names of astrological archangels. For example, the archangel of Mars is often identified as Kamael rather than Zamael. If you already do angelic magic and are familiar with different archangel names for some of the planets or signs, feel free to use the ones you're comfortable with. Otherwise, you can stick with the names provided here and not worry too much about divergences in magical tradition.

These correspondences tell you which archangels to ask for help with different kinds of magical tasks. If you are doing magic to try to get a promotion at work, you might want to draw on the power of the Wheel of Fortune and its correspondence to Jupiter, so you could petition the archangel Sachiel for help. Likewise, if you wanted to boost your sex life, you might draw on the imagery of the Devil card, asking Hanael for assistance. Through the connection of archangelic spirits with particular elemental or astrological energies, you can identify the types of magical goal for which it would be most fruitful to petition their aid—and conversely, if you have a magical goal in mind, you can find the archangel who's most likely to help you with it.

### Angels in the Minor Arcana

The Major Arcana are not the only cards with angelic connections. Through their zodiacal correspondences, the Minor Arcana connect to a group of angels who rule over the decans of the Zodiac. Each of the thirty-six decans comprising the 360 degree arc of the Zodiac has two angels governing it: one for the first 5 degrees of the decan and one for the latter 5 degrees, making for a total of seventy-two decanate angels.

The names of these angels are derived from the *Shem Ha-Mephorash*, the seventy-two-fold name of God. Like many elements of European magic, this is taken from Jewish Kabbalah. In the biblical book of Exodus, there are three consecutive verses (Exodus 14:19–21) that are each made up of exactly seventy-two letters in the original Hebrew. Combining letters from each of these verses according to a particular formula produces seventy-two words of three letters each; these are taken to be names of God describing various attributes of divine splendor.[23] Each of these names, in turn, can be modified with a suffix to become the name of an angel. Thus, the seventy-two names of God give way to seventy-two angels who preside over the heavens with divine authority.

The seventy-two decanate angels of the tarot are:[24]

| DECAN | FIRST ANGEL | SECOND ANGEL | CARD |
|---|---|---|---|
| 0°–9° Aries | Vehuel | Daniel | Two of Wands |
| 10°–19° Aries | Hahasiah | Imamiah | Three of Wands |
| 20°–29° Aries | Nanael | Nithael | Four of Wands |
| 0°–9° Taurus | Mabaiah | Poiel | Five of Pentacles |
| 10°–19° Taurus | Nemmamiah | Ieialel | Six of Pentacles |
| 20°–29° Taurus | Harahel | Mizrael | Seven of Pentacles |
| 0°–9° Gemini | Umabel | Iahhel | Eight of Swords |
| 10°–19° Gemini | Anianuel | Mehiel | Nine of Swords |
| 20°–29° Gemini | Damabiah | Manakel | Ten of Swords |
| 0°–9° Cancer | Itaiel | Chabuiah | Two of Cups |
| 10°–19° Cancer | Rochel | Iabamiah | Three of Cups |
| 20°–29° Cancer | Haiel | Mumiah | Four of Cups |

23. Matt, *The Zohar*, 17.

24. Regardie, *The Golden Dawn*, 104–7.

| DECAN | FIRST ANGEL | SECOND ANGEL | CARD |
|---|---|---|---|
| 0°–9° Leo | Vehuaiah | Jeliel | Five of Wands |
| 10°–19° Leo | Sitael | Elemiah | Six of Wands |
| 20°–29° Leo | Mahasiah | Lelahel | Seven of Wands |
| 0°–9° Virgo | Achaiah | Cahetel | Eight of Pentacles |
| 10°–19° Virgo | Aziel | Aladiah | Nine of Pentacles |
| 20°–29° Virgo | Lauviah | Hahaiah | Ten of Pentacles |
| 0°–9° Libra | Iezalel | Mebahel | Two of Swords |
| 10°–19° Libra | Hariel | Hakamiah | Three of Swords |
| 20°–29° Libra | Lauviah | Caliel | Four of Swords |
| 0°–9° Scorpio | Leuviah | Pahaliah | Five of Cups |
| 10°–19° Scorpio | Nelebael | Ieiael | Six of Cups |
| 20°–29° Scorpio | Melahel | Hahuiah | Seven of Cups |
| 0°–9° Sagittarius | Nithhaiah | Haaiah | Eight of Wands |
| 10°–19° Sagittarius | Jerathel | Seeiah | Nine of Wands |
| 20°–29° Sagittarius | Reiiel | Ornael | Ten of Wands |
| 0°–9° Capricorn | Lecabel | Vasariah | Two of Pentacles |
| 10°–19° Capricorn | Iehuiah | Lehahiah | Three of Pentacles |
| 20°–29° Capricorn | Chevakiah | Menadel | Four of Pentacles |
| 0°–9° Aquarius | Aniel | Haamiah | Five of Swords |
| 10°–19° Aquarius | Rehael | Ieiazel | Six of Swords |
| 20°–29° Aquarius | Hahahel | Mikael | Seven of Swords |
| 0°–9° Pisces | Veuahiah | Ielahiah | Eight of Cups |
| 10°–19° Pisces | Sealiah | Ariel | Nine of Cups |
| 20°–29° Pisces | Asaliah | Michael | Ten of Cups |

This means that for each pip card in the Minor Arcana (except the Aces), there are two different angels you can petition to help you in magical work associated with that card. If you're looking to strengthen your relationship with your children and want to draw on the Six of Cups, you could ask either Nelebael or Ieiael for help—or you could ask them both.

Classically, these angels are each associated with half of a decan—the first 5 degrees or the last 5 degrees. Personally, I've had more success splitting them up by day and night. That is to say, rather than understanding Veheuel as the angel of 0°–4° Aries and Daniel as the angel of 5°–9° Aries, I approach them both as ruling over the full decan—but I petition Veheuel as governing the decan by day and Daniel as governing it by night. This is slightly unorthodox, but it's yielded good results for me.

The astrological correspondences of these angels are not merely an arbitrary organizational scheme that allows us to associate them with the tarot deck. These correspondences are, themselves, an indication of the best way to reach out to the angels. I talked in chapter 9 about various magical timing considerations using the astrological structure of the tarot deck; these considerations are particularly important when dealing with spirits who have astrological associations. If you're reaching out to an angel who governs a particular planet or part of the Zodiac, you're going to have an easier time communicating (and having your requests met favorably) if you take appropriate astrological considerations into account. For this reason, when working with decanate angels, I try to make sure that the sun or moon is located in the appropriate decan, and I work my magic during daylight or darkness depending on the specific angel I'm trying to reach.

## Sigils of Angels and Other Spirits

Once you know who the angels of tarot are, the question naturally arises: How are you supposed to communicate with them? How can you ask them for help in achieving your magical ends?

One of the classic ways to get an angel's attention is by using a sigil, a drawn image that is unique to a particular angel and that represents that angel's magical identity. An angelic sigil is something like a magical calling card. It allows you to identify and make contact with a specific angel so that you can direct your petition to them individually, rather than just asking for help from anybody who happens to be listening.

Many of the better-known angels and archangels have sigils that have been established over the course of centuries of magical tradition. If you looked up the sigil of the archangel Michael, for example, you would find a few common images that have been used by magicians. You could effectively use any of these in magic to contact Michael's spirit.

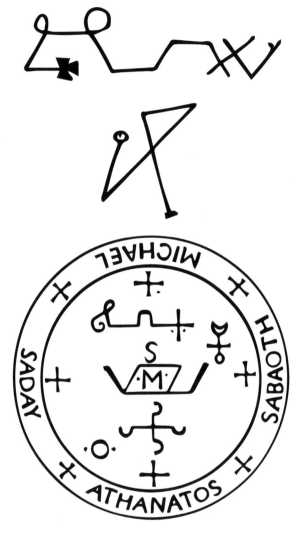

**SIGILS OF MICHAEL**

However, not all angels are as popular as Michael is. If you're unable to find a sigil for the angel that you want to petition, it's useful to know how to design your own to use in intercessional magic.

There are a number of different methods for creating magical sigils, and specifically the sigils of spirits like angels. The method that I like most is based on a geometric cipher taken from Freemasonry. The Masonic cipher assigns each letter of the Latin alphabet to a particular configuration of lines and dots.

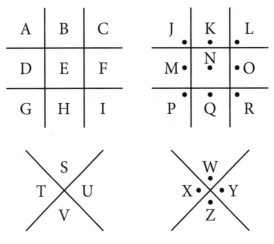

**THE MASONIC CIPHER**

So for example, the letter *D* is represented in the cipher by the shape ⊐, and the letter *M* is represented by the same shape with a dot in its center. To make a sigil using the Masonic cipher, first write out an angel's name and convert each of its letters using the cipher. For example, the name Mahasiah would look like this:

**MAHASIAH IN MASONIC CIPHER**

Then, draw the encoded name as a single, unbroken line, with the start of each letter connected to the end of the one preceding it. Joining together the letters of Mahasiah's name produces the following sigil:

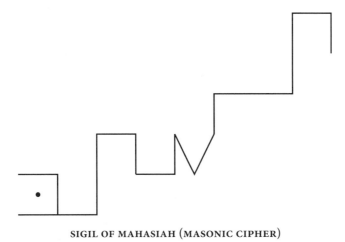

**SIGIL OF MAHASIAH (MASONIC CIPHER)**

You can use this method with any angelic name to create a sigil that is unique to an individual angel; that sigil will help you draw the angel's attention when you petition them for magical purposes.

The method shared here is my own method for making angelic sigils, although it does take some inspiration from a method developed by Cornelius Agrippa.[25] However, if you want to use a more common method, you can build angelic sigils using a magic square. A magic square is a tableau of numbers arranged so that every row, column, and diagonal adds to the same sum. These have a long history in magic—particularly in planetary magic, where each of the seven classical planets has its own magic square known as a *kamea*. The magic square most often used in making sigils takes the consecutive numbers from one to nine:

| 4 | 9 | 2 |
|---|---|---|
| 3 | 5 | 7 |
| 8 | 1 | 6 |

To make a sigil using this magic square, first assign a numerical value to each letter of the alphabet, ranging from the numbers one to nine.

25. Agrippa, *Three Books of Occult Philosophy*, 592–96.

| 1 | 2 | 3 | 4 | 5 | 6 | 7 | 8 | 9 |
|---|---|---|---|---|---|---|---|---|
| A | B | C | D | E | F | G | H | I |
| J | K | L | M | N | O | P | Q | R |
| S | T | U | V | W | X | Y | Z |  |

Then, write out your chosen angel's name and identify the numerical sequence it corresponds to. Mahasiah's name converts to the numbers 4-1-8-1-1-9-1-8. Place a sheet of paper over the top of the magic square and trace out a line connecting these numbers in order. If the same number occurs twice in a row, you can mark the repeated number with a small loop in the line. If a number appears in multiple nonconsecutive places, don't revisit the exact same point in the number's box. Instead, choose another point close by; otherwise, the sigil becomes too difficult to read. It's common to draw a small circle at the start of the line and a short perpendicular line at the end. Using this method, the sigil of Mahasiah would look like this:

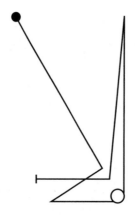

**SIGIL OF MAHASIAH (MAGIC SQUARE)**

Personally, I don't favor this method of sigil creation because the three-by-three magic square has strong planetary associations with Saturn. That's fine if I'm making a sigil for a saturnine spirit like Cassiel, but I don't necessarily want to bring the planetary power of Saturn into my work with other angels.

As an alternative, you may wish to design your sigils using the same method but with other magical squares: Reduce the alphabet to the numbers one through nine, convert the spirit's name to a series of numbers, and then draw a line connecting those numbers on the planetary kamea of your choosing. The numbers one through nine are used for their strong numerological and magical associations (such as their connections to the Sephiroth), but for a larger kamea, you could use the alphabetical values one through twenty-six instead if you prefer.

The kamea of Jupiter is a four-by-four magic square.

| 4 | 14 | 15 | 1 |
|---|---|---|---|
| 9 | 7 | 6 | 12 |
| 5 | 11 | 10 | 8 |
| 16 | 2 | 3 | 13 |

The kamea of Mars is five by five.

| 11 | 24 | 20 | 7 | 3 |
|---|---|---|---|---|
| 4 | 12 | 25 | 8 | 16 |
| 17 | 5 | 13 | 21 | 9 |
| 10 | 18 | 1 | 14 | 22 |
| 23 | 6 | 19 | 2 | 15 |

The kamea of the sun is six by six.

| 6 | 32 | 3 | 34 | 35 | 1 |
|---|---|---|---|---|---|
| 7 | 11 | 27 | 28 | 8 | 30 |
| 19 | 14 | 16 | 15 | 23 | 24 |
| 18 | 20 | 22 | 21 | 17 | 13 |
| 25 | 29 | 10 | 9 | 26 | 12 |
| 36 | 5 | 33 | 4 | 2 | 31 |

The kamea of Venus is seven by seven.

| 22 | 47 | 16 | 41 | 10 | 35 | 4  |
|----|----|----|----|----|----|----|
| 5  | 23 | 48 | 17 | 42 | 11 | 29 |
| 30 | 6  | 24 | 49 | 18 | 36 | 12 |
| 13 | 31 | 7  | 25 | 43 | 19 | 37 |
| 38 | 14 | 32 | 1  | 26 | 44 | 20 |
| 21 | 39 | 8  | 33 | 2  | 27 | 45 |
| 46 | 15 | 40 | 9  | 34 | 3  | 28 |

The kamea of Mercury is eight by eight.

| 8  | 58 | 59 | 5  | 4  | 62 | 63 | 1  |
|----|----|----|----|----|----|----|----|
| 49 | 15 | 14 | 52 | 53 | 11 | 10 | 56 |
| 41 | 23 | 22 | 44 | 45 | 19 | 18 | 48 |
| 32 | 34 | 35 | 29 | 28 | 38 | 39 | 25 |
| 40 | 26 | 27 | 37 | 36 | 30 | 31 | 33 |
| 17 | 47 | 46 | 20 | 21 | 43 | 42 | 24 |
| 9  | 55 | 54 | 12 | 13 | 51 | 50 | 16 |
| 64 | 2  | 3  | 61 | 60 | 6  | 7  | 57 |

The kamea of the moon is nine by nine.

| 37 | 78 | 29 | 70 | 21 | 62 | 13 | 54 | 5 |
|----|----|----|----|----|----|----|----|---|
| 6 | 38 | 79 | 30 | 71 | 22 | 63 | 14 | 46 |
| 47 | 7 | 39 | 80 | 31 | 72 | 23 | 55 | 15 |
| 16 | 48 | 8 | 40 | 81 | 32 | 64 | 24 | 56 |
| 57 | 17 | 49 | 9 | 41 | 73 | 33 | 65 | 25 |
| 26 | 58 | 18 | 50 | 1 | 42 | 74 | 34 | 66 |
| 67 | 27 | 59 | 10 | 51 | 2 | 43 | 75 | 35 |
| 36 | 68 | 19 | 60 | 11 | 52 | 3 | 44 | 76 |
| 77 | 28 | 69 | 20 | 61 | 12 | 53 | 4 | 45 |

You can use any of these magic squares to create an appropriate sigil for the angel you are trying to reach. Again, I tend to eschew this method unless I'm working with an explicit planetary connection, but the technique is quite common, and other people seem to have a lot of success with it. Try it out and see how it works for you.

These are far from the only ways of creating an angelic sigil, and you may already be familiar with other sigil-making techniques. If you are, feel free to apply those techniques to your work with angels here. The methods I've shared are a jumping-off point but are not meant to be restrictive, and you can certainly play around with other approaches that work well in your magical practice.

### An Angelic Petition Ritual

The following is a sample ritual to petition an angelic spirit for magical assistance using their name, sigil, and associated tarot card. Before conducting this ritual, you will want to determine your magical goal, identify the appropriate tarot card to represent that goal, find the angel associated with that tarot card, and find or create a sigil for that angel. You will need:

- Your chosen tarot card
- Appropriate incense for your chosen card and a censer to burn it in (see chapter 9)
- A copy of the angel's sigil
- A permanent marker
- Your fire wand
- Your water cup
- Wine or the beverage of your choosing
- A cauldron or other firesafe container
- Matches or a lighter

Choose a time to perform this ritual based on the astrological demesne of your chosen angel. Lay out all of your materials on a clean work space. Fill your cup with your beverage and light the incense. As the incense begins to burn, close your eyes and take a few minutes to clear your head. Focus on the magical task at hand, the angel you are going to petition, and the goal you are trying to achieve.

Open your eyes and say:

> *[Angel], I come before you as a humble magician to beg your assis-*
> *tance. I call upon you in your infinite beneficence and ask that you look*
> *favorably upon my work. Help me to achieve [your magical goal].*

Using the permanent marker, copy the angel's sigil onto the face of your tarot card. Softly repeat the angel's name aloud while you are drawing. When you've finished, pick up the card and waft it through the incense smoke, saying:

> *[Angel], hear my plea. [Angel], grant me [your magical goal].*

Set down the card and pick up your fire wand. Use the tip of the wand to trace the sigil on the card, repeating the refrain:

> *[Angel], hear my plea. [Angel], grant me [your magical goal].*

Keep doing this, allowing your voice to grow louder and more confident. Continue until you feel that the angel has taken notice of your request. This might come in the form of a physical sign—an unexpected breeze, a bird flying by your window, and so on—or it might just be a subjective inner feeling of satisfaction, an inexplicable knowledge that you've been heard. This may take a while, so have patience.

When you notice the angel's presence, lift up your wand and say:

> *[Angel], I have prepared this petition in your honor. I come before you*
> *in all your magnificence, a seeker after that which only you can give.*
> *[Angel], be kind unto me! Be merciful unto me! Hear my entreaty, I beg*
> *you, and find it in your infinite wisdom to grant that which I ask.*

Pass the tarot card through the incense smoke again. Then, place it in your cauldron and carefully set fire to it, allowing it to burn away completely. As it burns, say:

> *May this smoke carry my wishes to the heavens. By the*
> *power of the great and glorious [angel], let it be so.*

Once the card has burned away, lift your cup in a toast. Say:

> *[Angel], I thank you for hearkening unto me and for see-*
> *ing fit to aid me in my work. Let us drink now from the*
> *cup of fellowship, parting ways in love and peace.*

Take a sip from your cup to seal the petition. The ritual is ended, but you may remain here as long as you like, taking this time to meditate and drink from your cup.

## The Demons of Tarot

In addition to the seventy-two decanate angels of the Shem Ha-Mephorash, the Minor Arcana also correspond to a set of seventy-two demons. These demons are most famous from a grimoiric text known as the *Ars Goetia*, itself part of the *Lesser Key of Solomon*. The *Ars Goetia* and other grimoires provide an elaborate set of instructions for evoking these demons to appear and constraining them to execute the magician's will. A seventeenth-century magician named Thomas Rudd innovated on the tradition of demonic magic by associating these seventy-two demons with the seventy-two decanate angels.[26] Through this association, the demons became connected with the decans of the Zodiac and with the Minor Arcana of the tarot.

Just as with angels, there are many more historically attested demons than these seventy-two. The history of demons and demonic magic is complicated and often involves the cultural

---

26. Skinner and Rankine, *The Goetia of Dr. Rudd*, 72.

absorption and suppression of minority religions; some of these demons, such as Asteroth, take their names from the names of pre-Christian deities, as early Christianity literally demonized the religions it sought to replace. However, despite the shared names, these demons are properly treated as spirits in their own right and separate from their namesakes. The demon Asteroth is not the same as the goddess Astarte any more than a person named Mary is the same as the Virgin Mary of Christian mythology.

The seventy-two demons of the *Ars Goetia* and their connections to the tarot are:[27]

| DECAN | FIRST DEMON | SECOND DEMON | CARD |
|---|---|---|---|
| 0°–9° Aries | Bael | Phenex | Two of Wands |
| 10°–19° Aries | Agares | Halphas | Three of Wands |
| 20°–29° Aries | Vassago | Malphas | Four of Wands |
| 0°–9° Taurus | Gamigina | Raum | Five of Pentacles |
| 10°–19° Taurus | Marbas | Focalor | Six of Pentacles |
| 20°–29° Taurus | Valefor | Vepar | Seven of Pentacles |
| 0°–9° Gemini | Amon | Sabnock | Eight of Swords |
| 10°–19° Gemini | Barbatos | Shax | Nine of Swords |
| 20°–29° Gemini | Paimon | Vimé | Ten of Swords |
| 0°–9° Cancer | Buer | Bifrons | Two of Cups |
| 10°–19° Cancer | Gusion | Uvall | Three of Cups |
| 20°–29° Cancer | Sitri | Haagenti | Four of Cups |
| 0°–9° Leo | Beleth | Crocell | Five of Wands |
| 10°–19° Leo | Leraikha | Furcas | Six of Wands |
| 20°–29° Leo | Eligos | Balam | Seven of Wands |
| 0°–9° Virgo | Zepar | Alloces | Eight of Pentacles |
| 10°–19° Virgo | Botis | Camio | Nine of Pentacles |

27. Crowley, *777*, col. CLV, CLVII, CLIX.

| DECAN | FIRST DEMON | SECOND DEMON | CARD |
|---|---|---|---|
| 20°–29° Virgo | Bathin | Murmur | Ten of Pentacles |
| 0°–9° Libra | Sallos | Orobas | Two of Swords |
| 10°–19° Libra | Purson | Gamori | Three of Swords |
| 20°–29° Libra | Marax | Oso | Four of Swords |
| 0°–9° Scorpio | Ipos | Amy | Five of Cups |
| 10°–19° Scorpio | Aim | Oriax | Six of Cups |
| 20°–29° Scorpio | Naberius | Napula | Seven of Cups |
| 0°–9° Sagittarius | Glasya-Labolas | Zagan | Eight of Wands |
| 10°–19° Sagittarius | Bimé | Volac | Nine of Wands |
| 20°–29° Sagittarius | Ronove | Andras | Ten of Wands |
| 0°–9° Capricorn | Berith | Haures | Two of Pentacles |
| 10°–19° Capricorn | Asteroth | Andrealphas | Three of Pentacles |
| 20°–29° Capricorn | Forneus | Kimaris | Four of Pentacles |
| 0°–9° Aquarius | Foras | Amdusias | Five of Swords |
| 10°–19° Aquarius | Asmoday | Belial | Six of Swords |
| 20°–29° Aquarius | Gaap | Decarabia | Seven of Swords |
| 0°–9° Pisces | Furfur | Seere | Eight of Cups |
| 10°–19° Pisces | Marchosias | Dantalion | Nine of Cups |
| 20°–29° Pisces | Stolas | Andromalius | Ten of Cups |

Importantly, each of these seventy-two demons is paired with an angel. Bael is paired with Vehuel, Phenex is paired with Daniel, and so on through the decans. The angelic half of each pairing is a *thwarting angel*: the specific angelic being who has the power to command, coerce, or compel the demon in question. Like angels, each demon can be contacted using sigils; there are well-known sigils for each of these demons given in the *Ars Goetia*, which are easy to look up, or you can design your own sigils using one of the methods given in this chapter.

Demons are generally understood to be willful spirits who have the ability to intercede on a magician's behalf but are disinclined to do so; in order to direct demonic spirits, the magician must establish themself as having some kind of spiritual authority over the demon. Much like a middle school teacher staring down a room full of rebellious thirteen-year-olds, the magician has to establish that they are a figure worth respecting and listening to. One classic way to do this is for the magician to borrow the authority of a spirit whom the demon already knows and respects—in this case, the thwarting angel. By calling on the demon in the name of an associated angel, the magician can ensure that the demon listens to their request.

You may be wondering why it's worthwhile to call on a demon rather than an angel. If demons are generally unobliging and have to be browbeaten into providing magical assistance—and if demonic magic involves calling on angelic power *anyway*—then why not just petition an angel instead? Why go through the extra effort of seeking help from a demonic spirit?

The answer to this lies in the different natures of the relationships a magician has with angelic and demonic spirits. Doing magic with angels involves making a petition: The magician can request an angel's assistance, but they can't direct or command it. Ultimately, angels are more powerful beings with their own opinions and their own sense of what's best. A magician can ask angels for help, and angels are often inclined to give it, but an angel never has to do what the magician asks. Angelic magic is like asking someone for a favor: Sometimes you're told no, even if what you're asking for is well within their power to grant.

Demonic magic, on the other hand, is based on authority and command. When performing intercessional magic with demons, the magician doesn't ask the demon for help; rather, they tell the demon what needs to be done. In this relationship, the magician is in a position to give directions and to expect them to be followed. A magician's connection to a demon is like the relationship between a boss and an employee; as long as the magical request is within the demon's purview, it's the demon's responsibility to carry it out. There are limits, of course, just as there are with any relationship—but within those limits, there is a clear hierarchy and the demon acts as the magician's subordinate.

### The Circle and Triangle

In order to maintain this formal relationship of superior and subordinate, it's helpful to delineate physical boundaries in your ritual space. Demonic magic often involves the use of two geometric figures marked on the ground: a circle and a triangle. The circle is encompassed with divine names and symbols of power, and it represents the magician's home turf. This is the place where the magician keeps their tools and where they stand during magical work. The triangle, on the other hand, is placed outside of the circle. This represents the constraints put upon the demon. In the grimoire tradition, including in the *Ars Goetia*, a magician commonly evokes a demon to appear but constrains that demon to manifest only within the confines of the triangle. Doing this helps the magician maintain control over the dynamic between themself and the demon; the demonic spirit doesn't get free rein, but only appears and acts according to the specific constraints the magician has set down.

Horror movies have made a big deal of the importance of magic circles, giving many people the impression that disaster will result if a circle is imperfectly constructed—that if the magician leaves the circle or if there's so much as a letter out of place, untold evils will be unleashed on the world. The reality is much tamer (and much safer). A magic circle and triangle help to establish your authority as a magician, putting you in a position to instruct demonic spirits and have them listen to you. If you leave your circle or if your circle is poorly made, nothing outrageously bad is likely to happen, but you won't have the same authority and are less likely to command the respect and obedience of the spirits you're trying to work with. In short, your magic is likely to simply not work.

A magic circle is a place of power that vests you with authority, and its accompanying triangle establishes a hierarchical relationship between you and the spirit you call. I think of it almost like a workplace: If your boss calls you into her office and speaks to you while sitting behind her desk, she has a particular kind of authority over you because of the place where you're meeting and the nature of your professional relationship. She can tell you to go do something work-related, and the onus is on you to do it. If, on the other hand, you bump into her at a bowling alley, she doesn't have that same authority; when you're off the clock and away from work, she's not in charge of you. At best, she can say something like "When you come back to work on Monday, I'll need you to…" but she doesn't have the ability to enforce that instruction until you're back in the workplace. This is the effect of the circle and triangle: They put you in the position of a boss sitting behind a desk so that your instructions to a demon actually carry weight. Otherwise, you're just like some random person at a bowling alley issuing requests that nobody has to listen to.

Different grimoires give their own instructions for the construction of a circle and triangle, often following elaborate geometric patterns and using various names of God, angels, and archangels. The setup I recommend here is on the simpler side. If you are already familiar with a different circle/triangle construction, feel free to use the one you know; likewise, you are welcome to adapt the version given here and gussy it up to suit your tastes. To construct the circle and triangle, you will need:

- A piece of chalk[28]

- A clean, flat space about ten feet long by twelve feet wide

- A nine-foot piece of rope (optional)

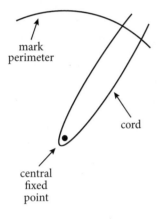

mark
perimeter

cord

central
fixed
point

Begin by drawing a circle with the chalk. Classically, the diameter of the circle is about nine feet across. Depending on how confident you are in your circle-drawing skills, you can draw it out freehand, or you can use a circular mat as a guide. Alternatively, you can use a nine-foot piece of rope to guide you. Place a fixed point (like a floor lamp) in the center of where you want the circle to be, then loop the rope around it. Take the two ends of the rope, stretch them out together until they're taut and even in length, and then mark the floor at the end of the rope with the chalk. Rotate all the way around the center until you've marked a complete circle.

When you have finished drawing the circle, you are going to draw a triangle. Different grimoires give varying instructions about where the triangle should be placed, and sometimes those instructions depend on the specific demon being worked with. For our purposes here, you can place the triangle in the cardinal direction that corresponds to the suit of the tarot card you're using for magic:

- If you're working with a demon from the suit of Pentacles, place the triangle in the north (corresponding to elemental earth and under the power of the archangel Uriel).

- For a demon from the suit of Swords, place the triangle in the east (corresponding to elemental air and the archangel Raphael).

- For a demon from the suit of Cups, draw the triangle to the west of the circle (corresponding to water and the archangel Gabriel).

- For a demon from the suit of Wands, draw the triangle in the south (for elemental fire and under the dominion of the archangel Michael).

---

28. I recommend white chalk, but you can also use colored chalk appropriate to the nature of the magical work being done and the specific tarot card you're using for that magic. See chapter 9 for some potential color correspondences.

As an alternative, you can just keep the triangle in the east as a default if you like. Once you have determined which direction you will draw your triangle in, draw an equilateral triangle (with sides about one foot in length) about six inches away from the edge of the circle. Orient the triangle so that it is pointing away from the circle.

Finally, empower the circle and triangle by writing names of power on them. There are countless ways to do this. This is the basic way I like, but you can retool it as you see fit. Around the perimeter of the circle, write the names of the four elemental archangels: Uriel in the north, Raphael in the east, Michael in the south, and Gabriel in the west. Write these names on the exterior of the circle, with the text facing inward so that you can read it while standing inside the circle.

Around the perimeter of the triangle, write the name of the thwarting angel for the demon you are trying to contact. Write the name three separate times—once on each side—around the triangle, with the text facing inward so that it can be read from within. The final result will look something like this:

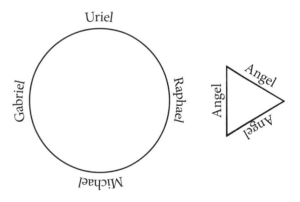

Your circle and triangle are now set up and ready to use. You can work magic from within the circle and speak to a demon with the authority of its thwarting angel. When your ritual is finished and you have dismissed the demon, you can simply mop away the markings you've drawn on the floor.

### A Ritual to Direct Demons

The following ritual uses a tarot card as a means of contacting and directing a demonic spirit, first by making contact with that demon's thwarting angel and then by speaking with the authority of that angel in order to command the demon. You will not be summoning the demon or evoking it to appear in this ritual; you'll merely be using your tarot card as a way of contacting the demon to deliver your instructions. You will need:

- Your chosen tarot card
- Appropriate incense for your chosen card and a censer to burn it in (see chapter 9)
- Copies of the sigils of the demon and thwarting angel

- A blank piece of paper
- A permanent marker
- A safety pin
- Your fire wand
- Your air blade
- Your earth pentacle
- An unopened bottle of wine or the beverage of your choice
- A cauldron or other firesafe container
- Your magic circle and triangle setup
- Matches or a lighter

Begin by constructing your circle and triangle, marking your triangle with the name of the thwarting angel corresponding to your chosen tarot card. Place all of your materials except for the cauldron inside the circle. (You may want to put them on a small table.) Light the incense and close your eyes, taking a moment to focus on the magical work you are about to do. Think about the goal you are trying to accomplish, the tarot card you've chosen for it, and the names of the associated angel and demon.

When you are ready, open your eyes and pick up your fire wand. Lift the wand and call upon the power of the decanate angel associated with your tarot card, saying:

> *Mighty and beneficent [angel], lend me your aid! Allow me to act by your*
> *wisdom and speak with your voice. I implore you to bless me with angelic*
> *grace that I may command the demon set beneath you. In your name, [angel],*
> *let my magic be done! In your name, [angel], let [demon] hearken unto me!*

Set down the wand. Pick up the blank piece of paper and pass it through the incense smoke. Then, use the permanent marker to trace the angel's sigil on the paper. When you are done, pass the newly made sigil through the incense smoke, saying:

> *By the power of this sigil, I speak with the voice of the angel [angel].*

Use the safety pin to attach the sigil to the front of your clothes, facing outward so that it could be seen by anyone looking at you.

Once you have affixed the angelic sigil to yourself, pick up your tarot card and pass it through the incense smoke. Say:

> *Let this card be purified by sacred smoke, that it*
> *may work the magic I am about to do.*

Use the permanent marker to trace the demon's sigil on the face of the card. Then, pick up your card and your earth pentacle. Step outside of the circle and place the pentacle inside of your magic triangle. Set the card on top of the pentacle, facing up so that the sigil is visible. Return to the magic circle.

Pick up your air blade. Holding the blade in front of you, turn so that you are facing toward the triangle. Say:

> *Hear me now, [demon], demon of [card]. I speak to you with*
> *the authority of the angel [angel], whom you must obey. I*
> *speak with the voice of the heavens and I shall be heard.*

Extend the blade outward and point its tip at the sigil in the triangle. Say:

> *I come to you desiring [your magical goal], which is within your*
> *power to give. In the name of [angel], I instruct you and give*
> *you your divine command. Fulfill my wish! Make it so!*

Continuing to hold the blade in your dominant hand, pick up the bottle of wine with your free hand. Say:

> *Grant me [your magical goal], and I shall reward you in turn. When*
> *your task is completed I shall pour out this libation in your name, bestow-*
> *ing joy and vitality in reward for your service. This is my promise to you.*
> *Hear me, [demon]! Obey me, [demon]! Fulfill your task, [demon]!*

Chant the demon's name, softly at first and increasing in strength. Do this until you feel that the demon has heard and acquiesced to your command. As with the angelic ritual, you may receive a physical sign, or you may just experience a subjective sense that your directions have been accepted. When you are ready, brandish your blade and say:

> *Having heard and accepted your divine command, I charge you, [demon], to*
> *depart from this place immediately and peacefully. Go forth and perform the*
> *magic that I have tasked you with. In the name of [angel], I command it!*

This portion of the ritual is now over. You may clean up your ritual space and put away your tools. Set aside the bottle of wine and the card with the demon's sigil. Hold on to these until after you have achieved the result of your magic. Then, when your magic has been successful, take the bottle outside and find a private place with exposed earth. Open the bottle and pour it out on the ground, saying:

> *[Demon], I pour this libation in your name as reward for the*
> *magic you have done. Your task is fulfilled, and I release you*
> *from my service until such time as I may call on you again.*

Return inside and burn the tarot card in your cauldron to symbolize releasing the demon from its bond.

## chapter twelve
# The Spirits of the Major Arcana

There is another kind of intercessional magic that can be done with the tarot cards. With this method, you don't simply use the cards as a tool for contacting other spirits. Rather, you treat the cards themselves as living magical entities, interfacing with them and forming a magical relationship with them. In particular, the twenty-two Major Arcana are potent spirits to whom you can appeal directly in your magical endeavors.

These were the very first spirits I worked with when I began practicing magic. I set up a shrine in my bedroom, and every morning I would light candles, recite invocations, and perform a reading for myself under the guidance of the Major Arcana. Working with the Major Arcana magically opened the door for me to explore pathworking and other meditative work with the tarot, along with subsequent explorations of angelic and demonic magic, making spells and talismans with the cards, and stacking the deck for magical readings. Treating the Major Arcana as a set of real, independent, magically efficacious spirits was the starting point of it all.

It may seem strange, then, that I have reserved the subject for the end of this book. The truth of the matter is that I think my own magical education with the tarot was somewhat backward. I learned how to do this magic entirely on my own, figuring things out by trial and error while I was living in a cramped studio apartment in France. I started by ritualizing my relationship to the Major Arcana, developing deep personal connections to the cards and then allowing them to guide me in my exploration of other magical correspondences and techniques. This was effective (here I am a decade later, writing a book about the things I learned), but it was also the hardest possible way to go about learning tarot magic. It required an incredible amount of research, experimentation, and trust in myself—allowing my own nascent intuition and magical instincts to guide my work. I didn't know what I was doing, and as a consequence a lot of what I tried fell flat altogether.

In this book, I've reverse-engineered most of that process of experimentation, starting with the magical structure of the deck and then working through practical magical techniques from the simpler to the more complex—even though that isn't the order in which I developed them. We end with the spirits of the Major Arcana because I think those spirits are easier to work with once you've already done the rest of the magic in this book. By now, you know magical tarot inside and out. You understand that magic is in tarot's bones—and you've seen various ways it can be given expression through ritual and spellcraft. You've already formed a deep, intimate relationship with the magic of tarot.

Because you've developed this magical understanding, you'll have a much easier time developing relationships with the spirits of the Major Arcana. You've already come to know these cards as magical objects; now you just have to think of them as magical persons so that you can learn how to talk to them.

Establishing a connection to the spirits of the trump cards is a long-term magical project. In angelic or demonic magic, you can more or less make a one-off petition without having established a more permanent relationship, although it's never a bad idea to take the time to get to know the spirits you're working with. The Major Arcana, however, are a different sort of spirit. The intercessional relationship you'll build with them is not one of authority, nor is it one of command; there's not a power dynamic at play between the tarot card and the tarot reader. Rather, the relationship is more like a close friendship. You get to know the cards and they get to know you in turn, and that intimacy allows you to ask them for magical help. In short, you are trying to make friends with the cards.

Some of this happens naturally over time. The more you read tarot, the better you understand the cards. When you first start out reading tarot, you have to look up the meaning of every card in a book; over time, you develop a familiarity with the cards, establishing a baseline understanding of their traditional symbolism as well as your own personal insights into their significance and themes. All of this lays the groundwork for a magical relationship, and

I'd go so far as to say that it's essential to consistently perform readings with the cards if you want to get to know them.

However, divinatory reading is where those relationships *begin*, not where they end. There's much more that can be done to cultivate a connection with the spirits animating these cards. The following are some of the ritual and magical techniques that have worked best for me.

## Building a Shrine

To build a ritual and magical relationship with a card over time, it's helpful to have a designated space where you communicate with the card's spirit. I'd recommend building a space dedicated to only one card, at least to start with; in the past, I tried having one shrine dedicated to all twenty-two major cards, and the result was that I found myself harried, overwhelmed, and unable to connect deeply with any card in particular. Choose the card you most want to work with and start there, building a one-on-one relationship. Once you have that under your belt, you can build another sacred space dedicated to a different card if you like.

Find a clean, flat surface where you can set up a shrine. A shelf, dresser, or end table works well for this. I used to use part of a bedside table, with my tarot work sharing space with other, more mundane objects (including a seashell and a souvenir replica of the Eiffel Tower), but ultimately I found this cramped and distracting. These days, I prefer to have an entire surface dedicated to this work, and I don't put anything on it that isn't relevant to the spirit relationship I'm cultivating. This is a matter of personal preference, and if you're not bothered by the presence of knick-knacks and tchotchkes then you don't have to follow my example—especially if you live in a small home and space is at a premium—but I do think it's nice to have an uninterrupted space for this kind of magical work.

The purpose of the shrine is to have a place where you can enter into ritual conversation with the spirit of your card. You fill that space with the card's presence using imagery, colors, and other key correspondences so that you can feel the card's spirit more forcefully than in everyday life. This, in turn, makes it easier for you to reach out to that spirit and engage in magical conversation with it. Your shrine can be a permanent setup, or you can set it up and take it down each time you want to do ritual work with your card. If you do have a permanent installation, make sure that you take care of it and keep it clean.

The basic components of a tarot shrine are very simple. First and foremost, since the goal of the shrine is to establish the presence of a particular card, you should have a copy of that card on your shrine. Personally, I like to have multiple copies of the card selected from a variety of decks; having the same card image from three or four different decks provides multiple artists' perspectives on that card's key themes and core personality. This allows you to forcefully bring the card's energy into your space without having to filter it through any particular artistic perspective. *

Second, since this is a tarot shrine, you should have representations of the four suits on it. The easiest way to do this is to place your four elemental tools on the shrine, but you could also lay out the four Aces from your favorite deck, or you could use more literal representations of the four elements: a bowl of water, a rock, and so on.

Beyond the card and the suits, there are two other basic components you'll need: a way to mark ritual time and a way to make offerings.

You want something to signal that you are stepping into (and subsequently out of) a liminal, magical ritual space. Your shrine is a designated meeting place for you and the spirit of your chosen card—but you need a way to signal "the meeting has begun" and "the meeting has ended." You want some kind of ritual action you can perform at the start and end of every session working with your tarot shrine in order to demarcate the boundaries between ordinary time and the magical time you spend communicating with this spirit. There are a variety of options for this, but some of my favorites include:

- A bell that you can ring at the beginning and end of your ritual sessions
- A candle that you can light when you arrive at your shrine and extinguish when you leave it
- Sticks of incense that you can burn for the duration of your ritual work (bonus points if it's an incense appropriate to your chosen card)
- A sand timer to measure out an allotted time for ritual or meditation

At various points, I've used all of these—and sometimes, I have used more than one of them concurrently. Lighting a candle, ringing a bell, and flipping over a sand timer is an incredibly effective ritual trigger and a good way to step out of ordinary time and into an appropriate place for magic. Experiment with these or other indicators to learn what you like best.

As a part of your ritual work with the spirit of the card, you'll want to make offerings of some kind. These offerings are an essential part of building reciprocity in your relationship with the spirit: You don't want to be someone who always shows up asking for favors but never offers anything in return. Remember, your goal here is to befriend the spirit attached to the card, so act the way you would if you were trying to befriend anyone else. If you're going to a dinner party at someone's house, you don't show up empty-handed; likewise, if you're going to a shrine, it's appropriate to bring a small gift.

The exact nature of your offerings is up to you. Food and drink are classic choices, and you can choose more specific foods unique to the card you're working with. For example, I like to offer pomegranates to the High Priestess, honey to the Empress, and liquor to the Devil. Other options include flowers, incense, prayers, and artwork you have composed with the card in mind. This artwork can be anything: a drawing, a poem, an interpretive dance, and so on. So long as it comes from the heart and is given by you to the spirit of the card, you're in good territory. Finally, remember that offerings can be actions rather than things. You can do trash pickup along the highway as an offering to the Chariot, volunteer at your local library in honor of the Hierophant, or learn how to spin yarn as a form of dedication to the Wheel of Fortune. Anything that sincerely expresses your wish to be close to the card is appropriate.

If you are making physical offerings at your shrine, remember to keep your space clean. Offerings should be changed out regularly so that they don't start to decay or go stale. If you're leaving food or flowers, dispose of them before they start to go bad; everything on your shrine should look fresh and appealing. If your offerings are biodegradable and safe for animals to eat, you may dispose of them in nature or put them in a compost pile; otherwise, you can throw them in the trash with an acknowledgment that they have served their purpose as offerings. Keep in mind that store-bought flowers, though biodegradable, are often treated with harmful pesticides and should not be left out in nature where they can harm animals or leach chemicals into the water supply.

Those are the fundamental building blocks for a tarot shrine: the card, the suits, a delineation of ritual time, and a way to make offerings. However, you may want to take your shrine a step further and make it more elaborate. You are free to decorate your shrine however you choose; the setup is largely a matter of personal taste and aesthetics. What looks good to you and helps you feel the presence of the spirit you're trying to contact?

If you want to embellish your shrine but aren't sure where to start, look through the various correspondences I've discussed up to this point. You can drape your surface with an appropriately colored cloth, leave herbs or crystals on your shrine, or burn specially chosen incenses. You may want to draw on astrological or elemental imagery: decorating a Judgement shrine with lots of candles, setting a scale (for Libra) on a shrine to Justice, and so on. You can also draw on particular imagery from your card, such as a crown for the Emperor or a toy dog for the Fool.

Remember, this shrine is ultimately your space and is designed to facilitate your personal relationship to a card. The most important thing is that it works for you and that it feels magical, powerful, and redolent with the presence of the tarot spirit you are getting to know.

## Working at Your Shrine

Once you have set up your shrine, it's time to use it. The ritual format for this kind of spiritual work is incredibly flexible and has a great deal of room for variation. Each step in the process can be personalized and adjusted to suit your needs and preferences. That said, the basic ritual can be broken down into seven discrete steps. Regardless of any bells and whistles you include in your magical work with a tarot spirit, your ritual interactions with them ought to look something like this:

1. Clear your mind and focus on being fully present for your magical work with the card.

2. Use the method of your choosing to formally mark the start of ritual.

3. Call the spirit's attention with a descriptive invocation.

4. Make an offering (or, if your offering is an action that must be performed elsewhere, affirm that you are going to make it).

5. Optionally, request the spirit's assistance with a magical task.

6. Spend time meditating, performing divination, or communing with the spirit in the manner of your choosing.

7. Thank the spirit for their presence, and say goodbye by formally marking the end of the ritual with the method of your choosing.

### *Clearing Your Mind*

If you've performed the spells and rituals given throughout this book, you'll have noticed that they consistently begin with an instruction to stop and center yourself before you proceed with magical work. Make sure that your attention is wholly focused on the work that you are about to do and that you check your unrelated mundane worries at the door. Try to be fully present for your magic, and don't let your mind wander away from the task at hand.

## Starting Ritual

As discussed previously, there are a variety of ways to start ritual. Choose a ritual action to signal the start of your magical work. As you perform this action, declare the opening of the ritual and the purpose of your work. For example, you might ring a bell and say:

*I am here to honor the spirit of [card].*

You can get more elaborate than that if you like, but simplicity is always effective.

## Descriptive Invocation

Once the ritual is begun, it's time to get the spirit's attention. This is easier to do at your shrine because you have already created a space that is specially dedicated to the spirit of your card, where that card's presence is strongly felt.

To invoke the presence of the card, you can use a pre-written invocation, or you can simply speak from the heart and ask the card to be with you. I like to use the following formula for just about all invocations:

1. Address the spirit directly by name or title.

2. Describe the spirit's relevant characteristics.

3. Identify yourself and your relationship to the spirit.

4. Explain what you have done for the spirit in the past.

5. Ask the spirit to join you.

Using this formula, an invocation of the Death card might sound something like this:

*I call to you, mighty Death! Scythe-wielding bringer of endings and
new beginnings, spirit of impermanence and harbinger of sacred
change. I, [name], am your humble magician. I have read the cards
in your honor, I have poured libations of milk and honey in your
name. I beseech you to join me in this space consecrated to you!*

I like this formula because of its specificity and because of the way it builds power into your relationship with the spirit before asking it to join you. However, if you prefer something on the simpler side, you could say:

*[Card], be here with me.*

Make your invocation in whatever way you choose, then wait until you feel the presence of the card before proceeding to the next step. This may feel different for each practitioner, or even from one ritual to the next. Sometimes, I'll notice a clear sign like a change in the weather or a bird landing on the windowsill. Other times, I'll simply experience a shift in my perception and a quiet feeling that I am no longer alone.

## Offering

Once the spirit of the card has joined you, make your offering. If your offering is something physical to be left on the shrine, set it out and say something to indicate its purpose. If you are offering something non-physical but are making the offering in this moment (for example, singing a song), preface the offering by saying what you are about to do. As an example, you could say:

*[Card], I thank you for joining me. I offer [item or act] in*
*your honor, because I know you find it pleasing.*

If your offering to the spirit is something that has to be done elsewhere (such as volunteering at your local soup kitchen), take this time to indicate to the spirit what you are going to do and why. For example:

*[Card], I thank you for joining me. In your honor, I vow that*
*I will [act], because I know you will find it pleasing.*

Note: If you make a promise like this to a spirit, it's important to follow through. Breaking your word will erode trust between you and the spirit and will damage your overall relationship. For this reason, make sure the promises you make are realistic. Don't bite off more than you can chew! Saying "I vow that I will volunteer at the soup kitchen this Saturday" is a much better and more feasible promise than "I vow that I will volunteer at the soup kitchen every Saturday for the rest of my life."

## Requesting Aid

You don't have to ask the spirit of a card for magical assistance every time you do ritual. As with other friendships, it's okay to just want to spend time together and not ask for anything.

Doing this deepens your relationship, shows that you're not just in it for transactional reasons, and ensures that when you *do* ask for help, it really means something. However, this is a book on magic, and it's a given that at some point you will want to draw on your magical relationship to a card in order to help you achieve some kind of change.

On those occasions when you want a spirit's help, the easiest thing to do is simply to ask. Speak aloud to the spirit and explain your situation, then say what result you're trying to achieve and the help you want. In the subsequent step of the ritual, you can wait for some indication of the spirit's response to you.

Depending on the nature and scale of the magical result you're trying to achieve, you may want to extend your request for assistance over the course of multiple rituals. Check in with the card and provide updates about your progress, the same way that you would with a friend who was helping you through a difficult problem.

### *Communing with the Spirit*

At this stage in the ritual, you spend some time with the spirit of the card. This can look like a number of different things. You can sit and meditate, particularly if you are performing a guided meditation, pathworking, or active imagination involving the card you have invoked. You can speak aloud to the card. You can paint, read a book, or perform other activities, so long as they're compatible with your ritual mindset; I would discourage something like watching television or scrolling through social media, but anything that feels like it is bringing you closer to your chosen card is fair game.

This is also an excellent time to perform divination. For several years, I performed a daily one-card tarot reading for myself (affectionately called the *daily draw* by many tarot readers), and I did the reading in the context of this sort of ritual invocation of tarot spirits. It was an effective way both to build my relationship with the Major Arcana and to deepen my reading abilities. I've never used divinatory tools other than tarot in the context of this ritual, but there's no reason that you couldn't use runes, scrying, or other tools if you wanted to blend them with your tarot work.

If you have asked the spirit for magical assistance, this is the right time to seek out a sign of the spirit's response to your request. You can look for a physical change in your environment, wait for a subjective sense of how your petition has been answered, or perform formal divination to see what the result of your request is.

*Closing Ritual*

When you have done everything you wish to do in the ritual, it's time to close things down. Perform the complement to whatever action you used to open the ritual: Extinguish your candle, ring your bell again, and so on. As you do so, thank the spirit and say goodbye:

> *[Card], I thank you for joining me. I say goodbye for*
> *now, knowing that we will meet again soon.*

With that, your ritual is complete. You may leave your shrine.

The frequency with which you do this kind of ritual work is up to you. Some people like to do ritual every day, usually first thing in the morning or before they go to bed. For these people, the regularity of ritual practice helps deepen their connection to the work they are doing. However, not everyone benefits from daily ritual; for many, it can feel like a chore and becomes exhausting rather than empowering. If you prefer to do ritual weekly, monthly, seasonally, or simply as you're moved to, that's all right. As long as you are doing your work consistently, you'll find that you're able to build a connection over time.

## Epithets of the Cards

The Major Arcana are unique in the tarot deck because they are titled cards. Rather than identifying them by rank and suit, we pick them out by individual names: the Magician, the High Priestess, and so on. These names help when you're trying to build a magical relationship with the cards' spirits. You don't have to say "Hey, you over there, with all the pentacles!" Instead, you can address the cards directly by name.

The titles we see on the card faces are not their only names, however. The Hermetic Order of the Golden Dawn had a set of descriptive epithets for each card in the Major Arcana.[29] These epithets were then picked up by Aleister Crowley and other magicians, and they have worked their way into occult tarot more broadly. Using these descriptions alongside the cards' better-known names allows you to call their spirits more directly and intimately, using names and titles that belong to them alone.

These epithets aren't just fancy descriptions; they have a real ritual use and can help you get to know the cards in new ways. You can incorporate them into the descriptive invocations you use in your ritual work with the cards. Moreover, each of these titles says something a little different about the nature of the card it describes; by choosing to use these epithets, you draw on

---

29. Mathers, *Book T*, 5–7.

different aspects of a card's energy, shifting your relationship to that card's spirit. The same way that calling someone "Katie" establishes a different connection than calling her "Katherine" does, these epithets open the door for a different kind of relationship with each card. Whether you use them or not is up to you, but I do recommend trying them on for size.

0. The Fool is *The Spirit of Aether*, expressing both their connection to elemental air and their sense of primordial formlessness.

I. The Magician is *The Magus of Power*. This name evokes the card's association with confidence, direction, and will.

II. The High Priestess is *The Priestess of the Silver Star*. The star in question is Sirius, one of the brightest stars in the sky.[30] The High Priestess guards the mysteries of the heavens themselves and the vast expanse of the starry sky.

III. The Empress is *The Daughter of the Mighty Ones*. The "mighty ones" are a choir of angels associated with the Qabalistic Sephirah of Binah—so the Empress's nurturing nature comes out of Binah's primordial form-giving power.

IV. The Emperor is *The Sun of the Morning* and *The Chief among the Mighty*. These titles show his connection to new beginnings and his sense of prowess and power.

V. The Hierophant is *The Magus of the Eternal*. He bears resemblance to the Magician— they are both miracle-workers—but his power is one of divine transcendence rather than personal will.

VI. The Lovers is *The Children of the Voice* and *The Oracles of the Mighty Gods*. These titles place an emphasis on speech and communication as central features of this card.

VII. The Chariot is *The Child of the Powers of the Waters* and *The Lord of the Triumph of Light*. These titles connect to the Zodiac sign of Cancer (the first water sign) and to the Chariot's themes of victory and achievement.

VIII. Strength is *The Daughter of the Flaming Sword*, expressing her warrior-like spirit and her willingness to fight difficult battles. The name recalls the flaming swords wielded by angels: Strength is a virtuous, holy warrior, not a cruel butcher.

IX. The Hermit is *The Magus of the Voice of Power* and *The Prophet of the Eternal*. Another magus, he connects to both the Magician and the Hierophant, uniting personal power and the eternal divine through his quest for introspective wisdom.

---

30. Eshelman, *The Mystical & Magical System of the A∴A∴*, 24.

X. Wheel of Fortune is *The Lord of the Forces of Life*. It governs all the unseen forces of change and fate that direct the course of our lives.

XI. Justice is *The Daughter of the Lords of Truth* and *The Ruler of the Balance*. These titles speak to her two chief values: truth and balance. She strives for equality and equanimity in all things.

XII. The Hanged Man is *The Spirit of the Mighty Waters*. This is a straightforward name derived from his connection to the element of water.

XIII. Death is *The Child of the Great Transformers* and *The Lord of the Gates of Death*. These names echo a refrain well-known to tarot readers: Death never represents a complete ending, but rather a transformation wherein one thing gives way to another.

XIV. Temperance is *The Daughter of the Reconcilers* and *The Bringer-Forth of Life*. This card unites disparate forces and transmutes them into something new, bringing renewal from the dialectical clash of opposites.

XV. The Devil is *The Lord of the Gates of Matter* and *The Child of the Forces of Time*. These names reinforce the card's connection to bondage and restriction—specifically, to the limitations placed on us by material circumstances.

XVI. The Tower is *The Lord of the Hosts of the Mighty*, expressing the feeling of sublime awe (and, yes, despair) that accompanies a disaster over which we have no control.

XVII. The Star is *The Daughter of the Firmament* and *The Dweller between the Waters*. These names come from her connection to the heavens and to the sign of Aquarius, the water bearer, who pours the waters of renewal onto the earth.

XVIII. The Moon is *The Ruler of Flux and Reflux* and *The Child of the Sons of the Mighty*. These names capture the moon's changing, inconstant nature, as well as a sense of its mysterious and uncontrollable power.

XIX. The Sun is *The Lord of the Fire of the World*, representing the life-giving power of the sun's light and warmth. The sun is our first source of energy and vitality, the divine spark that kindles life in the world.

XX. Judgement is *The Spirit of the Primal Fire*, a name taken from the card's elemental correspondence to fire.

XXI. Finally, the World is *The Great One of the Night of Time*, a sweeping name that captures this card's all-encompassing nature. This card represents the vastness of the universe and is almost too grand for any name to express.

I frequently use these titles in my ritual work with tarot. The astute reader will recognize some of them from the pentagram ritual provided in the previous chapter. However, I'm also in the habit of writing my own epithets based on my personal experiences with the cards. If I am trying to work with the spirit of a card and want to emphasize a particular aspect of its nature, I will write my own epithet to draw that aspect to the fore. In this way, the Sun becomes *The Joyous and Truthful One*, the Star becomes *The Lady of Healing*, and so on.

Try writing your own titles for each of the twenty-two Major Arcana, emphasizing different features of the cards than the ones highlighted here. Remember, you can adapt these at any time, and just because you use a particular epithet for a card in one context does not mean you can't write a new one for different magical work.

## Calling the Cards by Name

As you develop a deeper relationship with a particular card, you may find it awkward to keep addressing the card by a formal title. We generally address our friends and family by name, not by description; calling someone "Sarah" feels more intimate and personal than calling her "my mother's youngest sister," even if the latter is an accurate description. Working with the spirits of the Major Arcana, you may find that your magical relationship reaches a level of intimacy where it would be more appropriate to call them by name.

When this happens, you can ask the spirit to teach you an appropriate name by which they should be called. There are a number of ways to do this; probably the simplest is to make your request and then enter into active imagination where you can meet the spirit of the card, have a conversation with them, and be told their name. However, active imagination is daunting for many people, and not everyone does well with types of magic that rely heavily on visual imagination. As an alternative, you can use your tarot deck to divine a name for a given card.

In Golden Dawn Qabalah, each of the twenty-two paths on the Tree of Life—and therefore, each of the twenty-two Major Arcana—is associated with a particular letter of the Hebrew alphabet. These letters, along with the Golden Dawn's transliterations of them into the Latin alphabet, are:

0. **The Fool:** Aleph (א), *A*

I. **The Magician:** Beth (ב), *B*

II. **The High Priestess:** Gimel (ג), *G*

III. **The Empress:** Daleth (ד), *D*

**IV. The Emperor:** Heh (ה), *H*

**V. The Hierophant:** Vau (ו), *V*

**VI. The Lovers:** Zain (ז), *Z*

**VII. The Chariot:** Cheth (ח), *Ch* as in the Scottish *loch*

**VIII. Strength:** Teth (ט), *T*

**IX. The Hermit:** Yod (י), *Y*

**X. Wheel of Fortune:** Kaph (כ), *K*

**XI. Justice:** Lamed (ל), *L*

**XII. The Hanged Man:** Mem (מ), *M*

**XIII. Death:** Nun (נ), *N*

**XIV. Temperance:** Samekh (ס), *S*

**XV. The Devil:** Ayin (ע), *O*

**XVI. The Tower:** Peh (פ), *P*

**XVII. The Star:** Tzaddi (צ), *Ts*

**XVIII. The Moon:** Qoph (ק), *Q*

**XIX. The Sun:** Resh (ר), *R*

**XX. Judgement:** Shin (ש), *Sh*

**XXI. The World:** Tau (ת), *Th*

Hebrew is a complex language, and this transliteration is an oversimplification; remember that the magicians of the Golden Dawn were, by and large, not Jewish, and their knowledge of Hebrew was purely academic and quite lacking in some respects. In modern Hebrew, letters like פ and ב have multiple pronunciations, the letter ת is not pronounced as a *th*, and regional accents and dialects provide a wide range of pronunciations. Nonetheless, this is how the Golden Dawn converted between the Hebrew and Latin alphabets.

Because each card in the Major Arcana corresponds to a letter and a sound, the majors can be used to find a spirit's name.

*Naming Spread*

To divine the name of a card in the Major Arcana, perform ritual at your tarot shrine as usual. When you get to step five of the process (asking for assistance), ask for the spirit to grant a name by which you may know them. Say:

> *[Card], I know you well, but I would like to know you bet-*
> *ter. As you know me by my name, I would like to know you*
> *by yours. Please teach me a name that I may call you.*

Take your tarot deck and remove the twenty-two Major Arcana, setting aside the remaining cards. Shuffle the majors and draw three cards, laying them out in a vertical line:

```
┌───┐
│ 1 │
└───┘

┌───┐
│ 2 │
└───┘

┌───┐
│ 3 │
└───┘
```

Reading from top to bottom, these cards give the basic letters that make up the name of the card's spirit. Depending on the cards you draw, you may get the skeleton of a name composed entirely of consonants without any vowels. For example, if you draw Judgement, Wheel of Fortune, and the Lovers, your cards would correspond to *Sh-K-Z*—quite a mouthful to pronounce. This is typical of Hebrew writing, where vowels are often left off a word and are noted merely with diacritical marks (or not at all). Take the name you've been given and add vowels to it as needed in order to make something you can pronounce; for example, you might convert the name *Sh-K-Z* into *Shakaz*.

When you have received the new name, say it out loud a few times, testing how it sounds. Once you've got the feel of it, thank the spirit for giving you their name. Say:

> *Thank you, [card], for the gift of this name. I*
> *shall henceforth know you as [name].*

Proceed with the remainder of your ritual before closing. Use this name going forward in your magical work with the card.

Generally speaking, I prefer to keep these names private and do not share them with anyone else; they feel like intimate gifts that were given to me personally, and it doesn't feel right to me to spread something like that around. Other people may have their own names for the Major Arcana, but mine are for me alone. That's not to say that you can't tell someone the name you learn—but before you do, consider the circumstances under which you found the name and ask yourself (and the card) whether this is something appropriate for you to share.

As a bonus: Many (though not all) three-letter permutations in Hebrew are the roots of words with actual meanings. If you wish, you can look up the letters comprising the name you were given in order to see if the name has linguistic significance. This won't always be the case, but sometimes a spirit's name can have meanings you hadn't anticipated; my name for the Magician lines up with a Hebrew root having to do with writing and inscription, which feels deeply appropriate for my relationship with that card.

## conclusion
# The Wheel Keeps Turning

Tarot and magic are inextricably intertwined. Performing a tarot reading is a magical act that lays bare the workings of the universe and makes the unknowable future known. When viewed through a magical lens, the tarot deck becomes so much more than just a stack of images printed on card stock. It becomes a coded map of the magical universe, a symbolic expression of the dance of the elements, the planets, the signs of the Zodiac, and the whole of the interconnected cosmos.

Because of that symbolic power, the tarot deck itself can be one of your most potent and useful magical tools. Regardless of the change you are trying to create in the world—whether it's small or large, internal or external—tarot has the expressive power to help you make it a reality. The hand that deals the cards is also the hand that turns the Wheel of Fortune, and as we have seen in this book, you have the ability to stack the deck in your favor.

Both tarot reading and magic are fundamentally creative acts. They rely on the reader's (or the magician's) inspiration and intuition. The more you are able to draw connections between seemingly unrelated things, the better you become at both divination and magic; you'll find that flashes of insight open up new avenues for you, showing you the way to do things with tarot you had never imagined possible before.

There is so much to explore in the intersection of magic and tarot—and so much more than what I have discussed here. In this book, I've given you a glimpse into my own explorations of magical tarot, and I do sincerely hope that you will pick up the techniques I've set before you and apply them in your own work, both as a magical practitioner and as a tarot reader. At the same time, remember that this book is reflective of only one person's experience. I've shared how I do things and why, and I've pointed the way to how you can build on these techniques and make them your own, but there will always be things I haven't thought of and haven't done.

One of my strongest magical guides in tarot has always been the Hierophant. I'm a stodgy traditionalist; when I experiment magically, I never get too wild, and I always like to keep one eye on what has been done before me. As you've seen throughout these pages, I like using magical correspondences taken from the Golden Dawn, situating myself relative to an occult legacy that predates me and will probably continue to survive after me. I like structure and order, and I'm the sort of person who doesn't like to draw on a magical connection unless I can see its underlying rationale. This approach defines much of my magical work with tarot, as is evident in this book. The same book written by another person would doubtless not have been written in the same way.

But the Hierophant is only one card in the deck, and his is not the only way of doing magic. You may find that your magic is that of the High Priestess: intuitive, mysterious, and impossible to put into words. Or maybe you do magic with the reckless abandon of the Fool, carefree and adventurous, throwing yourself headlong into everything you do without stopping to worry about what other people before you have done. No matter what your approach is, the most important thing is that it's your own. Find who you are as a tarot reader and as a magician, and allow yourself to embrace that identity fully and unapologetically. I promise, your magical practice won't—and shouldn't—be exactly the same as my own.

Remember as well that you can and should change over time. My own magical practice is constantly evolving as I try new things. The magic in this book is a window into who I have been and who I am now, but it cannot anticipate who I've yet to become. Likewise, it is my sincerest hope that you will find new approaches to uniting tarot and magic, building on the work of this book in ways that I had never begun to dream. The nature of magic is change: As we practice magic, we transform ourselves and the world around us. More deeply, magic itself is constantly becoming something new; the force of change that drives the world must, itself, be subject to change. The Wheel of Fortune cannot ever remain still. It must always keep turning, and as it turns it is changed just as much as it changes. The magic that transforms us is also inevitably transformed by us.

As we draw to the close of this book, then, I invite you to take this magic and make it your own. Experiment and explore. Try new things, even if you're not sure they'll work. And more than anything else, do not be afraid to apply creativity and intuition in developing your own version of magical tarot. I've given you the fundamentals; now, use them to make something extraordinary and unique to you. The more you make this practice your own, the better it will work for you.

Go out into the world and turn the Wheel of Fortune for yourself.

*appendix*
# Keywords and
# Card Meanings

Over time, experienced tarot readers develop their own relationship with the deck, building nuanced and sophisticated interpretations of each card. Often, these interpretations are context-sensitive; what a card signifies in one reading might be totally different from what it means in another, depending on the question that was asked, its placement in the spread, and the other cards that were turned up.

For new readers, however, this level of nuance can be overwhelming. If you're just starting out with tarot, it's helpful to be able to refer to the established themes associated with each card. These themes can't tell you exactly what a card means in a given reading, but they can put you in the right neighborhood: If you draw a card associated with sorrow and another one associated with wealth, the meaning of the reading is going to involve both of those key themes. You still have to do the process of uniting those themes in interpretation, but you at least know where to begin doing so.

The following is a brief list of themes and keywords for each card. These are in no way definitive—each card can mean more than the things listed here—but they'll give you a decent starting point to feel out what a card is like. If you're still relatively new to tarot and trying to familiarize yourself with the cards, you can use this list (as well as similar lists given in other books) as a set of training wheels to get you going.

## The Suit of Pentacles

**Ace of Pentacles:** Investment, beginnings, seed

**Two of Pentacles:** Balance, budget, reciprocity

**Three of Pentacles:** Mastery, teamwork, creation

**Four of Pentacles:** Miserliness, security, greed

**Five of Pentacles:** Illness, poverty, hardship

**Six of Pentacles:** Charity, generosity, giving

**Seven of Pentacles:** Patience, work, endurance

**Eight of Pentacles:** Study, apprenticeship, learning

**Nine of Pentacles:** Reward, success, gain

**Ten of Pentacles:** Inheritance, legacy, wealth

**Page of Pentacles:** Practical, obedient, cautious

**Knight of Pentacles:** Persistent, reliable, patient

**Queen of Pentacles:** Caring, attentive, generous

**King of Pentacles:** Luxuriant, opulent, decadent

## The Suit of Swords

**Ace of Swords:** Clarity, logic, reason

**Two of Swords:** Decision, choice, divergence

**Three of Swords:** Sorrow, heartbreak, loss

**Four of Swords:** Respite, rest, relief

**Five of Swords:** Unfairness, cheating, discrimination

**Six of Swords:** Perspective, growth, inquisitiveness

**Seven of Swords:** Theft, dishonesty, deceit

**Eight of Swords:** Helplessness, impotence, confinement

**Nine of Swords:** Anxiety, sleeplessness, worry

**Ten of Swords:** Failure, ruin, betrayal

**Page of Swords:** Innovative, resourceful, inventive

**Knight of Swords:** Abstract, intellectual, philosophical

**Queen of Swords:** Judicious, insightful, astute

**King of Swords:** Strategic, aloof, prudent

## The Suit of Cups

**Ace of Cups:** Happiness, abundance, joy

**Two of Cups:** Romance, partnership, friendship

**Three of Cups:** Celebration, merriment, festivity

**Four of Cups:** Stagnation, pouting, sullenness

**Five of Cups:** Grief, wounds, remorse

**Six of Cups:** Childhood, nostalgia, innocence

**Seven of Cups:** Fantasy, imagination, wonder

**Eight of Cups:** Disengagement, escape, abandonment

**Nine of Cups:** Mirth, fulfillment, satisfaction

**Ten of Cups:** Community, family, kinship

**Page of Cups:** Artistic, intuitive, imaginative

**Knight of Cups:** Romantic, idealistic, dreamy

**Queen of Cups:** Sensitive, reflective, tender

**King of Cups:** Compassionate, sympathetic, attentive

## The Suit of Wands

**Ace of Wands:** Energy, passion, drive

**Two of Wands:** Plan, intention, ambition

**Three of Wands:** Development, yield, progress

**Four of Wands:** Thankfulness, gratitude, appreciation

**Five of Wands:** Competition, aggression, rivalry

**Six of Wands:** Victory, success, achievement

**Seven of Wands:** Perseverance, determination, stamina

**Eight of Wands:** Motion, speed, momentum

**Nine of Wands:** Fatigue, weariness, exhaustion

**Ten of Wands:** Burden, responsibility, duty

**Page of Wands:** Creative, impulsive, feisty

**Knight of Wands:** Adventurous, rebellious, willful

**Queen of Wands:** Charismatic, social, graceful

**King of Wands:** Confident, inspiring, decisive

## The Major Arcana

**The Fool:** Potential, naivety, beginnings

**The Magician:** Will, direction, ego

**The High Priestess:** Mystery, initiation, intuition

**The Empress:** Nurturing, growth, prosperity

**The Emperor:** Authority, leadership, control

**The Hierophant:** Tradition, orthodoxy, conservatism

**The Lovers:** Compatibility, duality, equality

**The Chariot:** Journey, discovery, impetus

**Strength:** Fortitude, gentleness, courage

**The Hermit:** Introspection, wisdom, seeking

**Wheel of Fortune:** Change, fate, luck

**Justice:** Equanimity, fairness, impartiality

**The Hanged Man:** Suffering, surrender, purification

**Death:** Change, endings, cyclicality

**Temperance:** Transmutation, becoming, synthesis

**The Devil:** Materialism, selfishness, bondage

**The Tower:** Catastrophe, disaster, collapse

**The Star:** Renewal, healing, forgiveness

**The Moon:** Dreams, illusion, concealment

**The Sun:** Truth, clarity, illumination

**Judgement:** Awakening, rebirth, metamorphosis

**The World:** Completion, culmination, finality

# Bibliography

Agrippa, Heinrich Cornelius. *Three Books of Occult Philosophy*. Vol 3. Translated by Eric Purdue. Inner Traditions, 2021.

Aristotle. *On Generation and Corruption*. Translated by H. H. Joachim. Clarendon Press, 1922. https://classics.mit.edu/Aristotle/gener_corr.2.ii.html.

Bonewits, Isaac. *Real Magic: An Introductory Treatise on the Basic Principles of Yellow Magic*. Red Wheel/Weiser, 1989.

Crowley, Aleister. *777 and Other Qabalistic Writings of Aleister Crowley: Including Gematria and Sepher Sephiroth*. Edited by Israel Regardie. Red Wheel/Weiser, 1986.

Crowley, Aleister. *Magick: Liber ABA, Book 4*. 2nd rev. ed. Weiser Books, 2000.

duBois, Page. *Out of Athens: The New Ancient Greeks*. Harvard University Press, 2010.

DuQuette, Lon Milo. *Understanding Aleister Crowley's Thoth Tarot*. New ed. Weiser Books, 2017.

Eshelman, James A. *The Mystical & Magical System of the A∴A∴: The Spiritual System of Aleister Crowley & George Cecil Jones Step-by-Step*. College of Thelema, 2000.

Frazer, James George. *The Golden Bough: A Study in Magic and Religion*. Edited by Robert Fraser. Oxford University Press, 1994.

Graves, Julia. *The Language of Plants: A Guide to the Doctrine of Signatures*. Lindisfarne Books, 2012.

Jung, C. G. *Jung on Active Imagination*. Edited by Joan Chodorow. Princeton University Press, 1997.

Kaplan, Aryeh. *Sefer Yetzirah: The Book of Creation*. Rev. ed. Weiser Books, 1997.

Leonard, Kimberlee, and Rob Watts. "The Ultimate Guide to S.M.A.R.T. Goals." *Forbes Advisor*. Updated July 9, 2024. https://www.forbes.com/advisor/business/smart-goals/.

Mathers, Macgregor, and Harriet Felkin. *Book T: The Tarot*. Benebell Wen. Accessed January 2, 2025. https://benebellwen.com/wp-content/uploads/2013/02/mathers-and-felkin -golden-dawn-book-t-the-tarot-1888.pdf.

Matt, Daniel C., trans. *The Zohar*. Pritzker ed. Vol. 2. Stanford University Press, 2003.

Peterson, Joseph H., ed. *The Lesser Key of Solomon: Detailing the Ceremonial Art of Commanding Spirits Both Good and Evil*. Weiser Books, 2001.

Regardie, Israel. *The Golden Dawn: The Original Account of the Teachings, Rites, and Ceremonies of the Hermetic Order*. 7th ed. Edited by John Michael Greer. Llewellyn Publications, 2015.

Skinner, Stephen, and David Rankine. *The Goetia of Dr. Rudd*. The Golden Hoard Press, 2010.

Wen, Benebell. *The Tao of Craft: Fu Talismans and Casting Sigils in the Eastern Esoteric Tradition*. North Atlantic Books, 2016.

## To Write to the Author

If you wish to contact the author or would like more information about this book, please write to the author in care of Llewellyn Worldwide Ltd. and we will forward your request. Both the author and publisher appreciate hearing from you and learning of your enjoyment of this book and how it has helped you. Llewellyn Worldwide Ltd. cannot guarantee that every letter written to the author can be answered, but all will be forwarded. Please write to:

Jack Chanek
℅ Llewellyn Worldwide
2143 Wooddale Drive
Woodbury, MN 55125-2989
Please enclose a self-addressed stamped envelope for reply,
or $1.00 to cover costs. If outside the USA, enclose
an international postal reply coupon.

Many of Llewellyn's authors have websites with additional information and resources. For more information, please visit our website at http://www.llewellyn.com.